WEALTH AND FREEDOM: TAIWAN'S NEW POLITICAL ECONOMY

For Bowen and Rowena

Wealth and Freedom:
Taiwan's New Political Economy

GERALD A. McBEATH
Professor of Political Science
University of Alaska Fairbanks

Ashgate

Aldershot • Brookfield USA • Singapore • Sydney

Published by
Ashgate Publishing Limited
Gower House
Croft Road
Aldershot
Hants GU11 3HR
England

Ashgate Publishing Company
Old Post Road
Brookfield
Vermont 05036
USA

HC
430.5
.M38
1998

British Library Cataloguing in Publication Data
McBeath, Gerald A.
  Wealth and freedom : Taiwan's new political economy
  1.Taiwan - Economic conditions - 1975-
  I.Title
  330.9'51249'05

Library of Congress Cataloging-in-Publication Data
McBeath, Gerald A.
  Wealth and freedom : Taiwan's new political economy / Gerald A. McBeath.
      p.   cm.
  Includes bibliographical references and index.
  ISBN 1-84014-041-0 (hardbound)
    1. Taiwan–Economic conditions–1945- 2. Taiwan–Social conditions–1945- 3. Taiwan–Politics and government–1945-
  I. Title.
  HC430.5.M38   1998
  338.95124'9–dc21   97-39118
                                                              CIP

ISBN 1 84014 041 0

Printed in Great Britain by Galliard (Printers) Ltd, Great Yarmouth

Contents

Figures and Tables

Acknowledgments

Jenifer Jey-hua Huang McBeath introduced me to Taiwan on my first trip in 1967. Then, over 30 years, she patiently challenged me to apply my training in the social sciences to an interpretation of Taiwan's political economy. She is the conscience of this scholarship. Friends and colleagues I met first while on a Fulbright-Hays lectureship in Taiwan from 1974 to 1975 assisted my research significantly over the years; also, they have been exceedingly gracious hosts. I am especially indebted to Yi Chun-po, Chu Chien-chang, Yuan Song-hsi, Hu Fu, Chen Wen-chun, Chen Yi-yan, and Liu I-chou.

During my Taiwan field work in the spring semester 1996 and in 1997, a number of scholars aided my research. I gratefully thank Chu Yun-han, Chen Ming-tong, Chu Chi-hung, Hwang Shiow-duan, Chang Ching-hsi, Shiau Chyuan-jenq, and Tsai Ing-wen. Also, I deeply appreciate the support given me by the Political Science Department of National ChengChi University, its chair John Hsieh and James Kuo-hsiung Lee. I also thank Li Wen-lang and his assistants who facilitated my work in the Legislative Yuan.

My study of Taiwan's political economy would not have been possible without a generous research grant from the Chiang Ching-kuo Foundation for International Scholarly Exchange. I thank director Li Hsing-wei and staff for their assistance. The University of Alaska Fairbanks granted me a sabbatical leave during spring semester 1997, when I collected most of the data on which this study is based.

Several scholars willingly took their time to critically review chapters of the book. I thank, in Taiwan, Chi Schive, Carl C. D. Chang, Kuo Cheng-tian, and Lin Yu-shien, and in the United States, Terrence Cole, James Robinson, Paul Hung-chao Tai, and several anonymous reviewers. Also, I thank the editors of *Taiwan on the Move*, *American Journal of Chinese Studies*, *Asian Survey*, and *The Journal of Contemporary China*, for copyright permission to use sections of published articles.

Jennifer Brice contributed immeasurably to the clarity and consistency of the manuscript by her deft copyediting work. She also assisted in production of the final copy in ways too numerous to mention.

At Ashgate, I thank Ann Newell, Sonia Hubbard, and Valerie Saunders. Finally, for special assistance, I thank Dwayne Therriault, Dixon Jones, and Judy Brainerd.

It goes without saying that remaining errors of fact and interpretation are mine alone.

A Note on Chinese Names

I use the Wade-Giles system of romanization when referring to places and people in Taiwan. For place names in mainland China after the establishment of the People's Republic of China in 1949, and for Chinese officials, I use the *pinyin* system of romanization. I introduce Chinese who do not use initials or Western first names by their surnames.

1 Introduction

When Chinese Nationalists retreated from the mainland to Taiwan in 1949-50, they governed a people barely recovered from the Japanese occupation and Pacific War. Wartime damage to factories, plants, and buildings had not been completely repaired; housing was scarce for the flood of mainland Chinese immigrants; food was barely sufficient to feed a population that within a year had increased by over 20 percent. Per capita gross domestic product (GDP) was about US $110, which placed Taiwan among the poor, or "underdeveloped", countries emerging from the Second World War.

In 1997, nearly a half-century after it became the headquarters of the Republic of China, Taiwan has entered the select list of wealthy nations. New office buildings and skyscrapers reconfigure the urban landscape, and few buildings date to the 1940s. Most people can own their own homes, and housing is abundant at affordable prices. Few think twice about eating out at expensive restaurants. Per capita GDP is about US $13,000. Taiwan is the world's fourteenth largest trading nation, has the third largest foreign reserves, and is the sixth largest outbound investor. The International Monetary Fund reviewed Taiwan's economic indicators in 1997 and placed it for the first time among the world's "developed" nations. This transition from poverty to affluence in less than 50 years constitutes an "economic miracle", and its explanation is the first theme of this book.

For its first 40 years on Taiwan, the Nationalist government ruled under martial law. Public demonstrations of any kind were banned, as were strikes, peaceful marches, and rallies. Although free elections were conducted at the local level, no party could form in opposition to the ruling Kuomintang (KMT or Chinese Nationalist Party). Newspapers and electronic media were censored. Vocal opposition to the regime was hazardous, and dissidents routinely were arrested and imprisoned during the KMT's "White Terror".

Now, in 1997, Taiwan's government has been operating without the crutch of martial law for ten years. Demonstrations, rallies, marches and strikes, while not daily events, happen freely and usually peacefully. Since 1986, political parties have organized. The Democratic Progressive Party (DPP) and New Party (NP) together control nearly half of the seats in the

Legislative Yuan and can stall and sometimes defeat government proposals.Taiwan has a free press and alternatives to government broadcasting stations. Critics of the regime do not face arrest. This transition from authoritarianism to democracy in little more than a decade constitutes a "political miracle", and its explanation is the second theme of this book. Wealth and freedom have been goals of statesmen throughout the 20th century, and they have been achieved more nearly in Taiwan than in any other Chinese state system in world history. Their achievement, however, has come at the cost of increases in pollution, in social disorder, and in "black and gold politics" (influence of organized crime and the super-rich in politics) to name three negative externalities of rapid economic development and political liberalization. We will consider these negative correlates along with the positive consequences of Taiwan's economic and political development, but our main objective is to examine the conjunction of wealth and freedom. Specifically, we seek to understand the impact that economic systems, forces, and changes have had on Taiwan's political system and, conversely, the impact that changes in the state and democratization have had on economic fortunes. Before turning to the plan of the book, however, we need to introduce Taiwan: its land and environment, people and culture, institutions, and geopolitical status in the late 1990s.

Land and Environment

Taiwan's geography, climate, and resources distinguish it from all of its East Asian neighbors.

Geography

The island of Taiwan is the largest body of land between Japan and the Philippines. It lies on the edge of the Asian continental shelf in the western Pacific. Resembling the shape of a tobacco leaf, Taiwan is located between 21°53'50" and 25°18'20" north latitude and between 120°01'00" and 121°59'15" east longitude. It crosses the Tropic of Cancer in a position comparable to Cuba. The island is about 240 miles long from north to south and 98 miles broad at its widest point. No part of Taiwan is more than 50 miles from the sea. (See Figure 1)

   With a total area of 13,884 square miles, Taiwan would be the second smallest province of China (after Hainan island). It is about the size of the American states of Connecticut and New Hampshire, a little larger than the Netherlands, and a bit smaller than Switzerland. Politically, 77 surrounding islands, 13 of them abutting the Chinese mainland and 64 comprising the Penghu group in the Taiwan Strait, form part of Taiwan.

Figure 1. Map of Taiwan

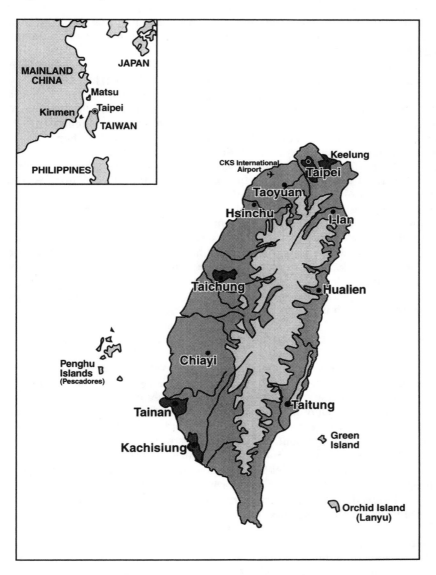

Source: Government Information Office, ROC, 1997.

The strait itself separates Taiwan from the Chinese mainland by 100 miles of turbulent waters. Taiwan lies some 700 miles south of Japan and 200 miles north of Luzon, the northernmost island in the Philippines. Taiwan is equidistant from Hong Kong and Japan and sits astride strategic shipping lanes in East Asia.

Mountains form the central backbone of Taiwan, stretching from northeast to southwest. About 32 percent of the land area is steep mountains of more than 3,280 feet in elevation; hills and terraces between 328 and 3,280 feet above sea level comprise 31 percent of the land area; and alluvial plains under 328 feet in elevation make up the remaining 37 percent.[1] Most of Taiwan's 21.4 million people live on the plains, giving Taiwan a population density of 590 persons per square kilometer, the second highest (after Bangladesh) in the world.

Taiwan has 151 rivers and streams, most of which originate in the central mountain range and flow either east or west. Rivers are short and swift, lending the island a radical drainage pattern as they become torrential during heavy rainstorms and disgorge silt and mud as they descend from the mountains.

The vegetation zones of Taiwan range from tropical to alpine, and natural flora resemble those of the Chinese mainland. Once, the island was heavily forested; today, stands of acacia cover many areas, and bamboo groves grow in central and southern regions. Soils range in fertility because of leaching through centuries of irrigation and heavy rainfall.[2]

Climate

Taiwan is hot, steamy, and windy much of the year because of its position relative to the ocean and the Asian mainland, ocean currents, and the pattern of its mountains. Northern Taiwan has subtropical weather, and the south is tropical. During the winter, from October to March, monsoon winds from the continent hit the northeastern part of the island, bringing steady rain; central and southern areas, lying in a rain shadow area, have sunnier and drier winters than those in the north. During the summer, from May to September, the southwest monsoons control Taiwan's climate; they bring rain to the south, leaving the north relatively dry.[3]

Tropical cyclones or typhoons rage across Taiwan three to five times a year, usually from July through September. The storms carry heavy rainfall, a major source of water for Taiwan. Their violent winds often severely damage crops and buildings.

Taiwan's rainfall is abundant throughout the year, but it is not evenly distributed. The driest part of the island is the southwest coast, which averages 40-60 inches annually and has experienced mild droughts in recent years. The eastern coast and mountainous areas have absorbed about 148 inches of rainfall. Average rainfall is approximately 98 inches annually, and the relative humidity is 80 percent.

Summers in Taiwan are long and hot, while winters tend to be very short and mild. The annual mean temperature is higher than 70° F. There is little temperature difference from east to west, but as one travels from north to south, with each degree of latitude, the mean temperature increases 1.5° F. Winter temperatures average in the mid-60s, while summer temperatures hover above the low 80s.

Natural Resources

Taiwan has a varied endowment of resources but is richest in those considered renewable, particularly agriculture and fisheries.

Renewable resources Fertile lowland alluvial soils have supported a rich agricultural industry in Taiwan for centuries, but the types and quantities of crops produced are changing rapidly. The historical staple has been rice, both double- and triple-cropped, in which Taiwan is self-sufficient. Other crops include betel nuts, sugar cane, corn, mangoes, peanuts, grapes, watermelons, tea, bananas, and pears. Of increased importance to Taiwan's agricultural industry are horticultural products, such as flowers, exotic fruits and vegetables, and chemical-free organic products.

Livestock production now comprises about one-third of Taiwan's total agricultural production. Taiwan is self-sufficient in production of pork, chickens, eggs, and milk, even exporting pork to Japan.

Fish is Taiwan's second most important renewable resource. Once, fishing was a small-scale coastal industry, but in recent years over-fishing has propelled Taiwan's fishermen to engage in deep-sea commercial fishing, which now produces the lion's share of Taiwan's catches. Also, aquaculture's role in the fishing industry has expanded recently.

The wood products industry is less important in Taiwan now than in the years immediately following World War II, when nearly 3 percent of the population earned a living by logging, lumbering, or processing wood products. Forests cover about half of Taiwan's terrain, but most are located in less-accessible mountainous areas. Also, growing environmental consciousness has led to the withdrawal of forested lands into preserves and parks.

A final renewable resource is Taiwan's beautiful scenery and attractive cultural fare, which drew 2.3 million tourists to the island in 1995.

Non-renewable resources Taiwan is poorly endowed with valuable rocks and minerals. The chief minerals produced on the island in the post-war period have been gold and sulphur; other mineral resources of importance include copper, salt, dolomite, and nickel. Marble has been mined near Hualien to support production of vases and other artifacts; Taiwan's jade is considered of low quality, although it is used for some jewelry production.

Taiwan is particularly deficient in natural energy resources. Coal deposits occur in the northern parts of the island. Taiwan's coal was sufficient to make it attractive as a coaling station in the nineteenth century; in 1996, however, coal reserves amounted to only 170 million tons, and coal comprised only 34 percent of gross power generation.[4]

Small amounts of oil and natural gas have been found in onshore and offshore areas, but almost all of Taiwan's petroleum supplies are imported (70 percent from the Middle East and the remainder from Indonesia, the Congo, and Australia). Global energy crises have prompted Taiwan to reduce its use of petroleum in energy consumption from 51 percent in 1979 to 14 percent in 1995.[5]

Hydroelectric resources supplied much of Taiwan's power needs during the Japanese colonial and early post-war period. However, total hydropower reserves consist of only 5,048 megawatts, of which 1,592 megawatts have been developed along several major rivers. Hydropower accounts for only 7 percent of gross power generation.[6]

Three nuclear power plants produce nearly 29 percent of Taiwan's total electrical output, and this resource had become much more important by the 1980s. However, growing environmental awareness and vigorous protests against construction of a fourth nuclear power plant have brought into question the expansion of energy generation from this source.

Taiwan has not been uniformly blessed with the bounties of nature; moreover, as its industrial economy matures, it has become more and more dependent on the importation of energy resources from abroad.

The Peopling of Taiwan

Five historical processes describe the development of Taiwan's modern population and its ethnic divisions: aboriginal settlement, foreign interest and brief occupations of Taiwan, successive waves of immigration from mainland China, Japanese colonialism, and Taiwan's retrocession to the Republic of China upon the Japanese defeat in World War II.

Aboriginal Settlement

Archaeologists date Taiwan's pre-history to 15,000 years ago, with its settlement by aborigines who came either from Southeast Asia and the islands of the central and south Pacific or from southern China. Their origin is reflected in aboriginal languages used today that belong to the Malayo-Polynesian family of agglutinative languages.

Although there are nine different aboriginal peoples in Taiwan, they once shared several characteristics: lack of shrines or sanctuaries within tribal settlements; lack of written languages; bark cloth making; iron smithing to make knives and other implements; slash-and-burn cultivation; growing of millet and tuber crops, such as taro and sweet potato; treatment of disease by trained female shamans; hunting of boar, deer, and other wild animals with bow and arrow; and head-hunting (except among the Yami).[7] Today, Taiwan's aborigines include both plains and mountain residents; they numbered just under 370,000, or about 1.7 percent of the population, in 1995.

Early European Pressures

The first Europeans to reach Taiwan were Portuguese navigators. In 1590, they arrived off the coast of Taiwan and coined the name "Ilha Formosa" (beautiful island) in homage to the majestic green mountains rising out of the deep blue waters of the Pacific. The Portuguese departed soon after establishing a settlement in the north. Formosa remained as the name that introduced Taiwan to the western world.

The Dutch proved to be more intrepid colonizers than the Portuguese. In 1622, the Dutch East India Company, then the world's largest trading company, established a military base in the Pescadores. The Chinese repelled the Dutch from the Pescadores, who then established a base called Fort Zeelandia and the town of Anping on the southwestern coast of Taiwan. By 1630, this had become a thriving trading center with Dutch merchants, missionaries, sailors, soldiers, and officials. Chinese immigrants already living in Taiwan fell under Dutch control and taxation.

Briefly, the Spaniards competed with the Dutch for influence over Taiwan. In 1626, the Spaniards sent a fleet from Manila to the northern part of Taiwan, establishing a fort first in the area now known as Keelung and, by 1629, in the area of Tamsui (adjacent to modern Taipei), where they established Fort San Domingo. Repeated Dutch attempts to dislodge the Spaniards from the north failed until a native rebellion in the Philippines drew off three-fourths of the Spanish troops, leaving the remainder at the mercy of Dutch forces.

From 1642 until 1662, the Dutch exercised effective control over Taiwan.[8] They moved the capital of the colony from Fort Zeelandia to Fort Providentia, site of the modern city of Tainan, and maintained there a garrison of more than 2,000 soldiers and some 600 officials. Dutch rule was indirect. The Dutch government's chartered agent was the Dutch East India Company, which appointed the colonial governor, who had full powers of taxation and control over both aborigines and the rising population of immigrant Chinese.

The primary function of the colony was as a transshipment center for goods between Holland, Batavia (the primary center of Dutch power in Asia), China, and Japan.[9] Taiwan's settled agriculture developed apace, and nearly 300 Chinese villages came under Dutch jurisdiction. Dutch missionaries launched the first systematic effort to convert aborigines to Christianity. A series of Chinese revolts against the Dutch did not succeed until Cheng Cheng-kung ended Dutch control in 1662.

Chinese Immigration and Political Integration

Chinese immigration to Taiwan began in the 12th century, but it was the peace and stability of Dutch rule that lured thousands of Chinese to the island. Two forces propelled the Chinese across the strait. First, the Manchurian invasion that overthrew the Ming dynasty in north China in 1644 destabilized the south, where Ming loyalists continued to oppose the Manchus. Second, Japanese pirates took advantage of the power vacuum to raid coastal towns. As a result, thousands of residents of coastal Fukien and Kwangtung provinces—a total of 100,000 during the years 1626-1644—immigrated to Taiwan.[10]

As Manchu troops consolidated control in south China, Ming loyalists joined the refugee flood to Taiwan. In 1661, one resistance fighter, Cheng Cheng-kung (also known as Koxinga), established a base with his troops in Quemoy island. By 1662, he had expelled the Dutch from Taiwan and turned Tainan into a rebel Chinese capital, developing fortifications to support an attack on the mainland. Chinese officials reacted to Cheng's plans by forcing residents within 10 miles of the coast to move inland, which increased the flight of refugees to Taiwan.

During the rule of Cheng Cheng-kung (who died in 1662) and his son Cheng Ching, agricultural development accelerated and sugar refining and salt production advanced.[11] Chinese laws, customs, and traditions were transplanted, and Taiwan's first Confucian temple was built. However, military forces were insufficient to resist a large naval invasion. Within a year of Cheng Ching's death in 1682, the Cheng family forces suffered defeat, and Taiwan was absorbed into Ch'ing Dynasty rule as part of Fukien province. Continued underground resistance to Ch'ing rule led Manchu officials to bemoan Taiwan's instability: a place with "a riot every three years, an uprising every five".[12]

Over the next two centuries, migration from China's two closest coastal provinces (Fukien and Kwangtung) to Taiwan continued, notwithstanding repeated Ch'ing bans on immigration. The population expanded northward, and successful rice cultivation made Taiwan a net exporter of rice by the early 19th century. Development of the cash crop camphor precipitated conflicts between aborigines and Chinese, pushing the former deeper into the mountains. Although the Ch'ing court sent administrators to Taiwan, it neglected the island's development and defense until the Opium Wars and ensuing defeats opened China's ports to imperialistic powers. By the mid 1850s, British, American, and Prussian ships had trespassed in Taiwan's waters, followed over the next three decades by Japanese and French.

The new foreign interest in Taiwan prompted the Ch'ing court to reform its administration of the island. The ban on immigration was lifted, and efforts began to develop Taiwan's infrastructure—construction of fortifications along the coast, development of telegraph lines, organization of local militias, and surveys of energy resource potential. Finally, in 1885, the Ch'ing dynasty made Taiwan its 22nd province, and its first governor, Liu Ming-chuan, launched a campaign to modernize Taiwan's defenses, reform its tax system, and educate its populace. However, these reforms were as short-lived as Taiwan's provincial status.[13] Under the terms of the Treaty of Shimonoseki in 1895, Taiwan was ceded to Japan. In response, Ch'ing officials stationed in Taiwan declared the formation of the Democratic Taiwan Nation on May 25, 1895, a resistance that was peremptorily and violently suppressed by the Japanese.[14]

Japanese Colonialism

Upon Taiwan's transfer to Japanese sovereignty, immigration from the Chinese mainland ceased, and the island underwent a 50-year period of development isolated from Chinese influences. Moreover, Japan ruled Taiwan directly, unlike the Dutch whose only purpose had been to enrich themselves through trade. Japan sought to use Taiwan as an agricultural colony to supply its population with food, as a market for Japanese industrial products, and as living space for its crowded populace.

During the first two decades of colonial rule, the Japanese suppressed Taiwanese resistance and established an efficient administrative apparatus for managing the population. They surveyed the population and land, standardized measurements and the monetary system, established monopolies for trading and manufacturing goods, and developed a modern transportation and communication infrastructure (which included the first north-south railway).

During the second two decades of colonial rule, the Japanese both modernized and intensified Taiwan's agriculture. They introduced new seed and crop varieties (including round-grain Japanese rice) and improved the irrigation system, which nearly doubled the amount of arable land.[15] This enabled Japan to import about 60 percent of its rice, and 90 percent of its sugar from Taiwan. Banana and pineapple production increased greatly under Japanese rule.

During the final decade of colonial rule, the Japanese developed Taiwan into an area of heavy industry. Hundreds of small factories produced chemicals, metals, aluminum, and refined oil—all in support of Japan's southward expansion and war effort. To cultivate loyalty among Taiwan's residents, the Japanese introduced assimilationist reforms, including naturalizing Taiwan's residents as Japanese, as well as having them adopt Japanese names, wear Japanese-style clothing, observe Japanese religious rites, and eat Japanese food.[16]

Japanese economic and political changes transformed Taiwan's economy and society. By the end of Japanese rule, Taiwan was among the most advanced populations in East Asia. Despite numerous minor resistance efforts, it was largely loyal to Japan until the surrender of Japan at the end of World War II.

Retrocession

Japanese forces in Taiwan surrendered on October 25, 1945, and most of the colonial officials, soldiers, and residents were repatriated to Japan soon after. The initial occupying Nationalist army was a ragtag affair whose incompetence led to the February 28 incident (discussed in Chapter 2). Events on the Chinese mainland, however, determined the post-war course of Taiwan's development.

The fortunes of Nationalist armies worsened decisively in 1949, and the communist party established the People's Republic of China (PRC) on October 1. Nationalist forces retreated to Kwangtung and Amoy, and then, in December, the government of the Republic of China moved to Taiwan. Preceding the move, the Taiwan Garrison Command proclaimed the Emergency Decree (martial law) throughout Taiwan province.

The Nationalist retreat increased the population of Taiwan by over 20 percent, from 6.2 million to 7.39 million in 1949. Of greater significance, it placed in ruling positions those who had neither been born in Taiwan nor were familiar with its historical development, economy, and society.

Taiwan's Population Today

By 1997, Taiwan's population numbered 21.4 million.[17] A tiny part of the population, 370,000 or 1.7 percent, was composed of aboriginal residents— those who were in Taiwan from the beginning of its civilization. Almost all of the remainder were Han Chinese, who shared memories of China's long historical development and engaged in the varied routines of the Confucian cultural system. It has been the division of the Han Chinese population into speech groups, however, that has provided much of the dynamism and tension of Taiwan's polity in the postwar period. Minority-majority relations in modern Taiwan are configured almost entirely in terms of these speech group differences.

Ancestors of two groups of Han Chinese migrated to Taiwan before the end of the 19th century from Fukien and Kwangtung provinces. Collectively, they are called Taiwanese, but their region of origin and native speech group have great bearing on their social and political behavior. The larger group, originating from southern Fukien province, call themselves *Ben-sheng* or *Ben-ti jen* (local province people or natives). They speak a variant of the Amoy (*Min-nan* or southern Fukien) language, which has a greater number of tones and different inflections than Mandarin, the national language of mainland China and Taiwan. These Taiwanese comprised 72 percent of the population and in 1997 were the clear majority.

Most of the second group of Taiwanese hails from Kwangtung province, but the ancestors of some came from southern Fukien, too. They call themselves *Ke-chia jen* or Hakka, which literally means "guests", for their ancestors migrated to the south from north China over many centuries. A sometimes persecuted minority in mainland China, the Hakka have their own speech, which, like Amoy Chinese, is unintelligible to Mandarin speakers. Most recently, the Hakka comprised 12 percent of Taiwan's population, and their residential pattern was concentrated, making them electorally significant. In note of this, President Lee Teng-hui reshuffled the cabinet in May 1997 to admit two Hakkas, a means of fortifying their support for the end-year elections of county magistrates.

The final group of Han Chinese is also the most recent in Taiwan residence. These are the Nationalist officials, soldiers, and residents who left the mainland at its fall to communist forces in 1949-50, and their progeny. Collectively they are called *wai-sheng jen*, or those from "outside (Taiwan) province", and we refer to them as mainlanders. In fact, they represent most of the other Chinese provinces, but former residents of Chekiang and Kiangsu provinces are a raw plurality. At their arrival in Taiwan, they assumed most of the elite positions in government, education, the military, and socio-cultural groups, despite their status as a numerical minority. The onset of democratization in the late 1980s began dislodging them from positions of control, but their national influence still surpasses their percentage of the population (in 1997 about 14 percent).

Institutions

Taiwan is a highly organized nation, and it is within groups and institutions that we understand economic and political interactions. We consider briefly the institutions of society and culture, the economy, and the polity.

Society and Culture

Traditional Chinese society and culture were based on ancient and unique thought systems and folk practices described under the rubric of Confucianism. Although Confucian culture was bolstered by elements of legalism, and later by both Buddhist and Taoist emendations, its core is an ethic, a humanistic and rational view of the world based on relationships and roles. The chief aspects pertain to the idealized relationships found within the family and clan,[18] particularly those of respect for ancestors (including obedience to heads of family and clan), loyalty, and benevolence toward one's inferiors.

The nuclear family and the extended family or clan are the center of life. Other loyalty patterns are based on family relationships. For example, the bonds of region (expressed in the preferential regard for those from one's own county (*Tung-hsiang*) or province *(Tung-sheng),* resemble those toward one's clan. Similarly, the bonds of friendship are based on relations between sibs in a family, which are usually hierarchically arranged in order of age, with complementary duties of respect, obedience, loyalty, and benevolence. Thus, relationships with classmates or office/work mates are also fictive family ties. This Confucian family-based tradition still dominates in Taiwan, notwithstanding changes in family structure consequent to industrialization and modernization.

A majority of Taiwan's people are religious believers, and more than 16,000 temples and churches dot the island. The largest single group of adherents are Buddhists, who number about one-quarter of the population. Buddhism, with its emphasis on achieving enlightenment through self-denial and meditation, potentially competes with Confucian family values, but the variety of sects in modern Taiwan, and the tendency for them to accommodate other religions, alleviates this tension. Probably the second largest number of adherents follow Taoism, both a philosophy and religion, which enlists another 20 percent of the population. Smaller numbers are believers in the I-Kuan Tao cult (a mixture of Taoism, Buddhism, Christianity, Islam, Judaism, and Hinduism), Christianity, Islam, and Judaism. The religious sense of most Taiwan residents, however, is not exclusively restricted to one sectarian tradition; far more prevalent is a syncretism and amalgamation of different traditions.

Taiwan's various folk religions, with their broad pantheon of gods and goddesses, resonate to some extent with most of Taiwan's residents.[19] Neighborhoods in Taiwan have temples to the most popular folk deity, *Tu-di Kung* (Earth God). Temple festivals called *pai-pai* frequently unite neighborhoods and provide a supra-family form of social organization.

Economic Institutions

Approximately 80 percent of Taiwan's labor force works for firms that are small- and medium-size enterprises (SMEs). Over 95 percent of Taiwan's 930,000 registered companies are SMEs, and they account for half of Taiwan's aggregate export value.

The organization of these enterprises is based on the model of the family firm, with members of one family (and in some cases an extended family or clan) providing the capital. The amount of paid-in capital does not exceed an equivalent of US \$2.2 million. Such SMEs typically hire fewer than 200 regular workers, usually an average of 40-50.

One reason that labor organizations are relatively weak in Taiwan is because of the small size of firms and the personal relationship between the boss and workers, who may be relatives, neighbors, or friends. The importance of the SME as a business ideal is seen in the reluctance of workers to remain within larger corporations once they have saved enough to start their own business or gain access to capital from others.

Taiwan has large economic organizations called *Tsai-tuan* or *Chi-yeh Ji-tuan* (conglomerates or business groups), and these tend to be collections of unrelated business enterprises managed by those with kinship ties. The other large-scale business organizations in Taiwan are state-owned enterprises (SOEs) and multinational corporations. They operate at the commanding heights of the economy, but they are closely connected to the small- and medium-size enterprises.

Political Institutions

The outlines of Taiwan's political institutions resemble those of the western rational-legal state system. The institutions are comprehensive and universalistic: each resident falls within several government jurisdictions and, in theory, the reach of the state applies equally to each citizen. Political institutions are also ordered in descending levels of geographic comprehensiveness, from the nation through the province and county to the township or municipality.

Political parties form a second set of institutions. Oldest and largest is the Kuomintang (KMT) or Chinese Nationalist Party, with 2.1 million members in 1996, or 10 percent of the population. An additional 80 political parties exist also, the largest being the Democratic Progressive Party (DPP) and New Party (NP).

Political institutions are the only organizations without a clear basis in the family system of Taiwan. Nevertheless, as we shall see, they are strongly influenced by *Kuan-hsi* (personal relationships) and local-level factions, based on familistic relationships.

Geopolitical Challenges

At the time of this writing in 1997, Taiwan remained one of only two nations divided by revolutionary movements growing out of the Second World War (the second is Korea). When the government of the Republic of China retreated to Taiwan in 1949-50, it continued to claim legitimacy as the political authority for all Chinese on the mainland as well as those on Taiwan and the offshore islands. (In 1991, the government "realistically acknowledged the fact that Taiwan is currently separated from the Chinese mainland and that the ROC government and the Chinese communists must coexist peacefully".)[20]

After a period of uncertainty from late 1949 through mid-1950, when Taiwan's fate seemed sealed as communist Chinese prepared to launch an invasion, Taiwan benefited from the onset of the Cold War. The United States opposed the invasion of South Korea and China's enlargement of that conflict and redrew its defense perimeter to include first Taiwan and then, in 1956-58, the offshore islands. War in Vietnam, with the United States and the PRC on opposite sides, created another incentive for America to support Taiwan internationally.

Until 1971, Taiwan maintained diplomatic relations with most of the non-communist states and membership in the United Nations (including the permanent Chinese seat on the Security Council). Radical developments on the mainland, such as the Great Leap Forward and Cultural Revolution, as well as China's revolutionary rhetoric in foreign affairs, garnered support for Taiwan's international position. However, America's rapprochement with China in the 1970s led to the loss of Taiwan's UN seat and, in 1979, her derecognition by the United States and the cancellation of the mutual security treaty that had guaranteed Taiwan's defense.

Thereupon, the number of nations conducting diplomatic relations with Taiwan declined precipitously. In 1997, only 29 states recognized Taiwan formally, and these were all small and weak countries in Africa, central America, and the South Pacific. Taiwan's attempt to rejoin the United Nations foundered four times upon opposition from the PRC, and its campaign to join the World Trade Organization (WTO) hinges on China's prior entry.

Although Taiwan maintains substantive relations, mostly economic ties, with 140 nations and has joined international organizations (such as the Asia-Pacific Economic Cooperation or APEC) under the rubric Chinese-Taipei or Taiwan, it is buffeted by new international challenges. Most serious is the newly economically powerful China, which on July 1, 1997, exercised territorial control over Hong Kong for the first time in 155 years and will assume control over Macau in 1999.

Taiwan's international position became more precarious partly because of its democratization. Under authoritarian rule, separatist fighters in Taiwan who sought independence for the island could be arrested and deterred. The chartering of the Democratic Progressive Party in 1986, with announced goals of seeking independence for Taiwan, increased Taiwan's risk exposure. The consolidation in power of Lee Teng-hui, a native Taiwanese, and his decision to make "Taiwan the priority" in the Republic of China greatly increased the anxiety of mainland Chinese leaders.

President Lee's efforts to elevate Taiwan's international status, and particularly his visit as the head of state to the United States in 1995 (although explained as a private visit to his alma mater, Cornell University), provoked nationalistic mainland authorities to initiate military exercises near Taiwan's offshore islands in July and August 1995. The first freely contested presidential elections in Taiwan provoked broader military exercises in March 1996. Unofficial cross-strait negotiations to destabilize tensions and increase contacts and communications abruptly halted.

Cross-strait relations are not the primary focus of this study, but both their domestic and international ramifications influence development and change in Taiwan's political economy. The largest political issue in Taiwan of the late 1990s (and some say the only political issue) is *Tung-tu*, unification with China versus independence for Taiwan. Although an overwhelming majority of Taiwan's citizens support the continuation of the status quo, meaning *de facto* independence, a growing minority supports the creation of a Republic of Taiwan, which would chart an independent course in foreign affairs.

Plan of the Book

The argument of the book unfolds in seven substantive chapters. Chapter 2 describes the kind of state system Taiwan had from 1945 to the onset of democratization in 1986. It assesses integration after the war and proceeds through the stages of economic development, from agricultural modernization and import substitution industrialization to the strategy of export promotion, which propelled Taiwan's drive to wealth. Throughout, the state's role in relation to market forces is compared and contrasted. As a means of keeping the discussion comparative, the narrative in chapter 2 begins with analysis of the different approaches that have been taken to explaining the development of Taiwan (and other newly industrializing countries).

Chapter 3 evaluates the "organizational weapon" that set policy for economic development while maintaining political stability. It begins by considering the nature of Kuomintang power in Taiwan and the way in which opposition to it developed—and was tolerated—by the regime. The chapter analyzes how the party changed in response to democratization and then investigates inter-party competition in campaigns and elections of the 1990s. We also ask whether transformation of the party-state is complete, constituting an authoritarian withdrawal from politics, a topic of relevance to democratization movements in other parts of the world.

Then we turn, in chapter 4, to examination of changes in the Chinese state system in Taiwan. The chapter reviews major organs of government—the presidency, Executive Yuan, and legislature—as well as ancillary branches. During 1997, the National Assembly considered a unique set of proposals to reform the Chinese constitution. These reform attempts illustrated the strengths and shortcomings of the traditional state system under democratic conditions. The outcomes will shape the future of democratic government in Taiwan.

Chapter 5 asks whether Taiwan is in transition toward a plural society, as found in many western states. It considers changes in agricultural interests and labor, and in the different strata within business and commerce. By examining the conditions of access of these economic interests to the state, the chapter reviews their degree of autonomy.

In chapter 6, discussion turns to policy areas in which state systems customarily affect economic growth and change: monetary and fiscal policy-making and regulatory policy. The chapter points out who the major decision-makers are and the extent to which decisional processes have been influenced by democratization. The chapter concludes with a large, recent case of bureaucratic policy-making highly relevant to the structure of Taiwan's political economy: privatization of state-owned enterprises.

Chapter 7 integrates the elements of Taiwan's domestic political economy in a focused analysis of Taiwan's internationalization campaigns, particularly the attempt to enter the World Trade Organization (WTO). Discussion proceeds through economic sectors, and both political and economic obstacles are reviewed. The chapter also considers briefly a second internationalization strategy—establishing Taiwan as an Asia-Pacific Regional Operations Center. Both American and Chinese roles and reactions to these globalization plans are examined.

In chapter 8, we consider Taiwan's political economy in comparative perspective. Taiwan's primary Asian competitors are Japan, China, Korea, Hong Kong, and Singapore. The chapter compares the countries with respect to their economic structures, business associations, business-government relations, and industrial policies.

The book concludes, in chapter 9, with a summary and review of the dimensions of Taiwan's wealth and freedom. Both the constraints of these conditions and the opportunities they present are analyzed. Also, we attempt to explain the particular conjunction of wealth and freedom in

Taiwan's development, which may be instructive in the review of other changing nations.

Notes

[1] Government Information Office, *The Republic of China Yearbook 1997*, (Taipei: 1997), 3.
[2] Chiao-min Hsieh, *Taiwan—ilha Formosa: A Geography in Perspective* (Washington, DC: Butterworths, 1964), 89-100.
[3] Hsieh, 1964, 44.
[4] *Republic of China Yearbook 1997*, 164, 166.
[5] *Republic of China Yearbook 1997*, 166.
[6] *Republic of China Yearbook 1997*, 164, 166.
[7] See I-yuan Li, *Society and Culture of Taiwan's Aboriginal Peoples* (Taipei: Linking Publishing Co., 1982); also see *Republic of China Yearbook 1997*, 20.
[8] John K. Fairbank, Edwin O. Reischauer, Albert M. Craig, *East Asia: The Modern Transformation* (Boston: Houghton Mifflin Co., 1965), 81.
[9] See George M. Beckman, 'Brief Episodes—Dutch and Spanish Rule', in Paul K.T. Sih, ed., *Taiwan in Modern Times* (Jamaica, NY: St. John's University Press, 1973).
[10] *Republic of China Yearbook 1997*, 61.
[11] See George Phillips, 'The Life of Cheng Cheng-kung', *The China Review*, 13, nos. 2 and 3, 1985.
[12] *Republic of China Yearbook 1997*, 62.
[13] James W. Davidson, *The Island of Formosa: Past and Present* (New York: Oxford University Press, 1988), 3.
[14] See Harry J. Lamley, 'The 1895 Taiwan War of Resistance: Local Chinese Efforts against a Foreign Power', in Leonard H. D. Gordon, *Taiwan: Studies in Chinese Local History* (New York: Columbia University Press, 1970), 23-65.
[15] Samuel P. S. Ho, *Economic Development of Taiwan, 1860-1970* (New Haven: Yale University Press, 1978), 28-30.
[16] *Republic of China Yearbook 1997*, 64-65.
[17] *Republic of China Yearbook 1997*, 16.
[18] Maurice Freedman, *Lineage Organization in Southeastern China* (London: The Athlone Press, 1958), 81.
[19] David K. Jordan, 'Changes in Postwar Taiwan and Their Impact on the Popular Practice of Religion', in Steven Harrell and Chun-chieh Huang, *Cultural Change in Postwar Taiwan* (Boulder, CO: Westview Press, 1994), 140-42.
[20] *Republic of China Yearbook 1997*, 135.

2 The Client and Corporate State of Taiwan: 1945-1986

Introduction: Political Economic Approaches to Taiwan's Post-War Development

Scholars use a variety of approaches to explain state-society relations in Taiwan. Some focus on the dynamism of autonomous economic forces as the agents of Taiwan's industrialization. Others point to the role of the state both in developing economic foundations and creating an environment for political change. Still others combine characteristics from both the capitalist and corporatist approaches, in what can be termed a pluralistic interpretation.

These three are the approaches most frequently employed to understand Taiwan's political economy. Each takes a different slant on the nature of the state (its strength and autonomy), the amount of strategic intervention by the state in the economic system, the nature of social forces (and, particularly, the strength and autonomy of business organizations), and the amount of influence the latter exercise in national policy-making.

In addition, a fourth approach explains Taiwan's development as dependent on forces in the world system and, in particular, on global power relationships. A fifth interpretation explains Taiwan's development in terms of a nexus of cultural factors, primarily by means of Confucianism. The fourth and fifth approaches are used less frequently, because they seem to analyze Taiwan's development experience less well in the context of East Asian states. We consider each of the five approaches before we describe the state's role in economic development of Taiwan from 1945 through 1986.

18

Capitalist Development

A large literature on Taiwan's economic miracle portrays the vigor of private entrepreneurs operating in a relatively open social system.[1] Advocates of this approach do not ignore the state. Indeed, they justify the use of strong governmental action to eliminate import substitution policies, which by the 1950s constituted a brake on economic growth. In general terms, however, their view is of Taiwan as a *laissez-faire* state that did not saddle the economy with inefficient regulations and state agencies, and which stimulated the economy through its low tax, high interest rate, and infrastructure development policies.

Perhaps the best illustration of this perspective is Ian Little's attribution of Taiwan's spectacular economic success to market conditions that approximated economists' hypothesized "perfect market"—many small autonomous firms with few barriers to entry.[2] Robert Wade calls this version of the capitalist development approach the "free market theory", which he distinguishes from a "simulated free market theory" that assigns greater leadership responsibility to the state.[3] Whether real or simulated, the approach posits the market as the engine of Taiwan's growth and development. The small size of the market impelled manufacturing firms to compete aggressively in the international market, and Taiwan's competitiveness globally is recognized as the product of its capitalist success.

Corporatist State

The second approach, certainly the most popular interpretation of Taiwan's development in the scholarly literature, emphasizes characteristics of the state. Proponents picture the state as strong enough to formulate economic policy without becoming captive to rent-seeking groups.[4] During the primary industrialization drive from the 1950s through the 1980s, the authoritarian party-state was organizationally strong. The KMT itself was financially autonomous, which limited predatory tendencies of the national elite. Moreover, as Chalmers Johnson notes, social control functions of the dominant party were sharply distinguished from the governing functions of the economic bureaucracy, which he calls a key feature of the "developmental state".[5]

This approach is nested in studies of political economy, for it describes the state as actively involved in the market, able to influence the use of both public and private resources in accordance with a vision of how the industrial structure of the country should be evolving.[6] The state used bountiful economic aid from the United States in the 1950s through the late 1960s to subsidize the growth of those manufacturers critical to the industrialization of Taiwan—fertilizers, plastics, and textiles.[7] State-owned enterprises (SOEs), a larger and more permanent part of Taiwan's economy than South Korea's or Japan's, fed materials to downstream industries and absorbed the shocks of global price changes in raw materials such as oil.

Like the European corporatist states, the KMT in Taiwan used a distributive coalition, an authoritarian corporatist framework for interest representation. However, the state remained autonomous and independent from penetration of business. The state chartered or created interest groups and gave them monopolies in the representation of occupational interests but monitored them carefully to discourage conflicting demands.[8] Alice Amsden argues that "the balance of power between the state and both labor and capital was weighted far more to the state's advantage" than in European or other Asian corporatist states.[9]

The corporatist perspective does not ignore the development of new social forces but denies them autonomy. Although some industries may have led the state on occasion, overall, proponents of the strong state thesis argue, the government led the market and some industries at least some of the time. Thomas Gold summarizes the role of the state by remarking that it "controlled the way Taiwan incorporated into the world system in a way few other countries have".[10]

Pluralist Society

The third approach has become popular only since the onset of democratization in Taiwan, but sociologists (especially Gary Hamilton) did spade work in the early 1980s to establish the thesis. In most respects, advocates of pluralism consider both characteristics of the state and those of the market, and they pay particular attention to changes in Taiwan's society over time.

The first difference between the capitalist and corporatist approaches, on one hand, and the pluralist approach, on the other, is that the latter examines the actual behavior of economic groups and organizations and tries to explain the structure of the economy. For example, Hamilton and C. S. Kao regard economic relationships as networks generated by personal ties based on reciprocal trust, loyalty, and predictability.[11] The interpersonal relationships (or *Kuan-hsi*) that glue together Chinese social organizations stood independently from government, especially during the formative period of Taiwan's industrialization when rulers were predominantly mainlanders and business people Taiwanese.

This leads to the second difference, the role that interest groups play in the operation of the state. The pluralist approach pictures interest groups as voluntary associations, free to organize and gain influence over state policy equivalent to their political resources. Even those who have taken the corporatist perspective acknowledge evolution in the role of Taiwan's interest groups. For example, in the mid 1980s, Harmon Zeigler noted a shift from state corporatism toward social corporatism.[12] Based on his four months of Taiwan research in 1983 (supplemented by two months in 1988), Robert Wade observed that the balance between state and interest groups was shifting toward greater equality.[13]

A third difference pertains to the scope and effect of state intervention in the economy. Hamilton acknowledges that at the start of Taiwan's industrialization, the state controlled many upstream, largely import-substitution industries, most of which required large economies of scale, and on which small- and medium-size enterprises (SMEs) in the export sector depended. This "public interest" economic sphere, however, was "organizationally decoupled from the rest of the economy".[14] The public sector responded to market demand generated by the private economy; the public sector was demand-driven. SMEs were the engine of growth, as they dominated the export manufacturing sector. The state played a limited role in investment (SMEs borrowed from the curb market), and it could not implement upgrading or progressive change in the business sector. For this reason, notes Hamilton, Taiwan failed to develop large trading companies, special banks to assist export industries, and an automobile export industry that could compete with South Korea's or Japan's.

World Systems and the Client State

The fourth approach explains the development of nations through their dependent linkages to broader forces and powers of the world system. An early version of dependency theory attempted to explain Latin America's slow development in the 1950s and 1960s through US imperialistic policies; later versions acknowledged that some development had occurred, but it was distorted toward serving needs of national elites instead of masses and still dependent on external forces. The dependency literature has not been found useful in explaining Taiwan's development.[15]

The broader world systems theory developed by Immanuel Wallerstein is an important corrective to dependency theory. It provides a way of looking at the relationships between global economic and political powers, such as Japan in the 1930s and early 1940s and the United States in most of the 20th century, and semi-peripheral nations such as Taiwan. Rivalries between core states (and multinational corporations) cause them to seek out peripheral states and firms, which are provided opportunities to develop as "associated dependent" allies.[16]

This focus on worldwide processes functions as an important alternative to the preceding three approaches, and may help explain interactions between Taiwan and global actors such as Japan and the United States, and their role in Taiwan's economic and political development. The "client state" concept, which expresses the reliance of peripheral or semi-peripheral states on global powers, may be useful in explaining Taiwan's relationship to the United States from 1950 to 1968.

Neo-Confucianism

The fifth approach is primarily cultural. It suggests that the rapid development of Taiwan cannot be explained through situational factors alone. Institutional practices and underlying attitudes are essential to develop the high levels of coordination and teamwork, knowledge, and management skills integral to the industrialization process.

Ezra Vogel's popular interpretation selects four clusters of traditional Confucian attitudes and institutions, which are common to Japan and the four rapidly industrializing East Asian societies: Taiwan, South Korea, Hong Kong, and Singapore. First is the meritocratic selection of bureaucratic elites, who have broad social responsibilities, including the nurturing of private enterprises. Second is the use of examinations as gatekeepers to higher levels of schooling and preferred places in the work force. Studying for examinations breeds discipline, which translates into motivated behavior in the work place.

The third cluster of Confucian attitudes centers on the importance of the group over the individual. The type of groups to which one is loyal has changed, remarks Vogel, but the willingness to sacrifice present wants for future gains and to limit personal consumption for the sake of the group leads to production efficiency. Finally, the desire to cultivate the self creates a high drive for achievement, comparable to the idealized Protestant work ethic.[17]

Scholars differ in their selection of Confucian attitudes and institutions that play a positive role in the industrialization process.[18] A difficulty in the use of this approach, however, is that it fails to facilitate comparative analysis within the East Asian region.

The five approaches offer a rich diversity in interpretations of Taiwan's development. Several of the differences between them can be traced to the disciplinary lenses used to observe Taiwan's political economy; these lenses reflect the different units of analysis and methodologies that economists, political scientists, sociologists, and anthropologists employ when conducting research into Chinese societies. The time periods during which research was done also differed. For example, many of the political economic studies of Taiwan were conducted in the 1970s and early 1980s, before the onset of broad-scale economic liberalization and democratization.

In the sections that follow, we apply the variables of strength and autonomy to the state, market, and social organizations in Taiwan. The sections are arranged chronologically, from adjustments after retrocession in 1945 up to the launching of democratization in 1986.

Post-War Integration

Situation upon Retrocession

Japanese troops surrendered to the Allied command in Taiwan on October 25, 1945. The Cairo Declaration of the Allied powers in World War II provided for the transfer of Taiwan from Japan to the sovereignty of the Republic of China at the conclusion of hostilities. The first group of Chinese troops sent to exercise control over Taiwan were poorly trained and undisciplined offshoots of the main fighting elements of the Nationalist army, which remained on the mainland to fight the growing communist revolution. A professor, among the few Japanese permitted to remain in Taiwan after the Chinese takeover, had these recollections on the military transition:

> We all went down to greet the Chinese troops carrying Nationalist flags, and the Formosans really were sincere in welcoming the new government. But the mainland troops were so poor and shabby that the Formosans were disillusioned even before experiencing the graft and corruption that led to the 1947 revolt. They'd been used to smartly-dressed and disciplined Japanese soldiers who were clean, neat, and well-behaved. Now these KMT troops were filthy, illiterate, and treated the Formosans as an occupied people.[19]

President Chiang Kai-shek appointed an executive team to assume control over the administration of Taiwan (then in a limbo between military and civilian rule) and selected as its head Chen Yi, the former governor of Fukien province. Chen worked with the Taiwan Garrison Command to secure an orderly transfer of power.

Chen personally was a clean official, but he brought into subordinate positions a host of opportunists and carpetbaggers who polluted the administrative core of the transitional government. Moreover, occupying mainlanders were biased against the local population, viewing them as collaborators who had prospered under Japanese rule while the mainlanders had resisted Japanese invaders during the eight-year Sino-Japanese War.

The predacious behavior of early Nationalist officials antagonized large numbers of Taiwanese. Bureaucratic corruption was rife, with payoffs to most KMT officials expected, expensive permits required for virtually every transaction, and mountains of time-consuming and expensive government red tape. The Nationalist government also seized all Japanese assets, which became state property. Commissioners in Chen Yi's administration monopolized tea, sugar, and tobacco/alcohol production as well as the supervision of foreign trade.

Smuggling was rampant after the Nationalists took control. Corruption was widespread, ranging from burglary of homes and stores to looting of warehouses and factories. Profiteers diverted local goods and Japanese supplies to the mainland black market. According to George Kerr:

> Conscript peasants from China stole or commandeered bicycles but, unable to ride, carried them on their backs . . . . by January 1946, members of the American Army's Formosa Advisory Group were predicting serious uprisings against Chen Yi.[20]

The February 28, 1947, Incident

On the evening of February 27, 1947, police and agents of the Tobacco and Wine Monopoly Bureau (which controlled the production and sales of matches, alcohol, camphor, and tobacco) visited a crowded park to interdict unlicensed sales of cigarettes. They apprehended a widow in her late 40s, confiscated her cigarettes and cash, and knocked her down when she objected. When those nearby came to her defense, police fired into the crowd, killing at least one person.[21] This catalyst incited a group of Taipei residents to surround police headquarters, demanding the arrest of the police who had done the shooting.

The next day, a much larger crowd of several thousand marched on the headquarters of Chen Yi and the offices of the Tobacco and Wine Monopoly Bureau with demands for punishment of the murderer, compensation for affected families, relaxation of monopoly controls, and apologies.[22] Chen Yi's guard fired on protesters, killing several, which brought about a general uprising against Chinese officials that spread to every city on the island. In response, Chen Yi declared martial law and ordered military units into cities to suppress rioters. He claimed involvement of communists and Japanese sympathizers in the disturbances.

During the following week, reformist protest flowered throughout Taiwan. Taiwanese elites organized the February 28 (in Chinese, *erh erh ba*, for the 28th day of the second month) Incident Management Committee and proposed democratic local elections, appointment of more Taiwanese to high government positions, government guarantees for human life and property, protection of the freedom of speech, publication, and assembly, and elimination of government monopolies. Chen Yi temporized, agreeing to negotiate with the ad hoc committee. Meanwhile, however, the KMT command identified the Taiwanese activists, and Chen Yi called for reinforcements from the Chinese mainland. On March 8, several thousand troops from the 21st Division in Shanghai arrived in the port of Keelung north of Taipei.

Chen Yi disbanded the ad hoc committee and directed that all those who had participated in the uprising be arrested. Troops sought a long list of suspects, including landowners, doctors, lawyers, editors, teachers, professors, and entrepreneurs. Some were beaten and killed on the spot; others were taken away, never to be seen again. Estimates of the total number of Taiwanese killed in 1947 range from 10,000 to 20,000, if prisoners presumed dead and those who disappeared are included.[23]

The Aftermath

The central government's response to the February 28 Incident was muted and cosmetic. Chiang Kai-shek transferred Chen Yi to a field command position in the mainland civil war. (Only when Chen attempted to join the communists was he arrested; opponents of the KMT saw poetic justice in his return to Taipei in 1950 and execution for treason.) Replacing Chen was Wei Tao-ming, a former Chinese ambassador to the United States. The central government elevated the island's status from a military district to a province of China, as it had been briefly before Japanese colonial occupation in 1895. The regime relaxed martial law and censorship, converted a few government monopolies to private ownership, and replaced several mainlander officials with loyal Taiwanese.[24]

However, security police continued to check for subversive influences, and the atmosphere was considerably less than free. The central government, at that time wholly involved in the civil war, neglected Taiwan until January 1949, when communist armies crossed the Yangtse River and launched their southern campaign to unify China. Chiang Kai-shek then replaced Wei with an old friend, General Chen Cheng. By early 1949, a force of about 300,000 Nationalist troops was stationed in Taiwan. In May, Chen and the Garrison Command proclaimed martial law throughout Taiwan province.

The final routing of the KMT from mainland China began in December, and over the next several months more than a million Nationalist soldiers, officials, supporters and dependents crossed the strait to Taiwan. American observers reported then that "(t)he island is badly and inefficiently run at a time when the best possible efforts are needed unless developments on the mainland are simply to be transferred to Formosa".[25]

For more than 30 years, information about the February 28 Incident was officially suppressed; however, resistance circles kept the event alive. At the end of martial law in 1987, leaders of opposition to the KMT brought it into their campaigns. The government conducted an investigation, and by 1992 several reports had been published on the incident. In 1995, President Lee Teng-hui formally apologized to the families of victims, and the Taipei city mayor, Chen Shui-bian, named the "2-28 Peace Park" to commemorate the incident. The Legislative Yuan enacted legislation to compensate relatives of victims in that year. Finally, just before the 50th anniversary in 1997, the Legislative Yuan declared February 28 a national holiday.

Taiwan's first five years under Nationalist rule were highly inauspicious. KMT rulers achieved political integration, but only through military means. While military strength remained a regime priority, it was economic development that provided the opportunity to gain popular support, a subject to which we now turn.

Agricultural Modernization

Taiwan's Post-War Economic Situation

Allied bombing in addition to neglect during the war left much of Taiwan's economy in shambles in 1945. War-related damage to industrial sites, other buildings, and infrastructure reduced Taiwan's capital stock. Rural areas were in disarray, without electricity and functional water systems. After the war, Japanese managers, technicians, administrators, and laborers returned to Japan, which disrupted growth because their skills could not be replaced immediately.[26] The level of production in 1945-46 declined to one-half the peak attained during the colonial period; agricultural production fell to the level of 1920.[27]

Probably the most damaging economic indicator in the immediate post-war period was inflation. The Taipei wholesale price index rose 260 percent in 1946, 360 percent in 1947, 520 percent in 1948, and 3,500 percent in 1949.[28] This especially damaged public confidence in the new government, given the Nationalist government's inability to control rampant inflation on the Chinese mainland.

Offsetting these liabilities were a number of economic assets. Despite wartime damage, the basic infrastructure was more developed than that in most parts of mainland China. Taiwan's agricultural economy was the second most advanced in Asia (after Japan's). The economic institutions fostered by the Japanese, such as farmers' associations and credit cooperatives, remained largely in place. Importantly, the population was orderly and hard-working.

The Nationalists' precipitous departure from the mainland also brought some advantages to Taiwan. Accompanying the flood of refugees were many talented managers, officials, and entrepreneurs who could succeed to the positions left by repatriating Japanese. The outbreak of the Korean War in June 1950 was the most fortuitous event for Taiwan's economic and political development. This change in the East Asian power balance brought the United States to the defense of Taiwan by patrolling the Taiwan Strait and providing billions in military aid and assistance.[29]   Of equal importance, the United States gave economic aid critical to Taiwan's economic recovery and long-term economic growth.

Land Reform

During the Japanese colonial period, Taiwan's agriculture focused on three crops: rice, sweet potatoes, and sugar cane. Sugar cane production served the Japanese market, which absorbed more than 90 percent of Taiwan's output. The termination of the protected colonial relationship devastated the sugar industry, and resources were allocated to other crops such as corn, wheat, vegetables, and fruits.

Traditional methods of production revived agricultural production to its pre-war peak by 1952, but growth opportunities were limited. Most of the land that could be farmed economically was already under cultivation. The large agricultural labor force (about 1.8 million in 1952) was already underemployed. Improvements in agricultural productivity resulted from four changes in the early 1950s.[30] First, crop areas expanded through the development of new cropping patterns and inter-cropping. Second, the average number of days worked by agricultural laborers increased. Third, mechanization advanced, and power tillers quickly replaced draft animals in clearing and preparing land. Finally, farmers began to use high-grade imported commercial feeds, intensively applied fertilizers and insecticides, and used new seed varieties. Samuel P. S. Ho estimates that about 90 percent of Taiwan's agricultural growth (most of which occurred in the 1950s and 1960s) is attributable to these types of farming modernization, identified by inputs as "6 percent to crop area, 15 percent to labor, 59 percent to working capital, and 10 percent to fixed capital".[31]

A major change in agricultural structure created incentives producing vigorous growth in output (greater than 5 percent annually) during the 1950s and most of the 1960s. That change was land reform, carried out from 1949 to 1953. The three stages of the land reform movement were 1) compulsory reduction of land rents, 2) sales of public lands to actual tillers, and 3) compulsory sales of private lands to tillers.

The problem of unequal distribution of land at retrocession was not one of large landed estates, for most of Taiwan's agricultural holdings were small in size. Instead, the problem was that most farm laborers were sharecroppers who did not own the land they tilled. Rents paid by tenants ranged from 40 to 60 percent of output. Shortly after the Nationalist government moved to Taiwan, it decreed that agricultural rents would be reduced to 37.5 percent of the standard yield of the primary crops, which had been the target figure used in land reform campaigns on the Chinese mainland.[32]

The second stage of the land reform process occurred in 1951, when the government began to sell public lands to tenant farmers. At the conclusion of World War II, 176,000 hectares of land owned by Japanese citizens was transferred to the government, and this formed the bulk of public lands; about one-half was sold to tenants,[33] and most of the rest was reserved for use by the Taiwan Sugar Corporation, a state-owned enterprise (SOE). Those who had been cultivating public lands had first priority to purchase them, and other tenant farmers had the second chance. Sales terms were generous: lands were valued at 2.5 times the yield of the main crop and could be paid for over a 10-year period.

The third and most important stage of the land reform process occurred in 1953, the land-to-the-tiller program. It took from landlords all land in excess of 2.9 hectares (unless they worked a greater area with normal seasonal help) and sold these lands at the same price described above to tenants.   Taiwan's landlords were easy targets of the Nationalist government as they had no political clout. Developing the land-to-the-tillers program allowed the KMT to neutralize potential opposition to the regime (for landlords were elites and power brokers in rural communities) and distribute land widely to land-poor farmers. The government gave bonds in kind (rice for paddy land and sweet potatoes for dry land) and shares of four SOEs—Taiwan Cement, Taiwan Pulp and Paper, Taiwan Agriculture and Forest, and Taiwan Industry and Mining Corporations—to landowners in exchange for their land.[34] These bonds and stocks were hedges against inflation, which made the compulsory sales process somewhat easier for the landlords to stomach.

Sales of public and private lands created about 215,000 hectares of owner-cultivated land; it affected one-fourth of the total cultivated area in Taiwan. Nearly three-fourths of Taiwan's tenant and part-tenant farm households were able to purchase some land in the land reform process.[35] Sharecropping was virtually eliminated, and this directly affected agricultural productivity. Additionally, land reform increased the incomes of small holders and reduced the holdings and incomes of landlords, thereby cutting down on inequality in the distribution of rural income. This policy had a significant impact by shifting the power base from mainlanders to Taiwanese in later years, as land values skyrocketed during industrialization.

The US Role in Agricultural Modernization

In addition to significant amounts of aid in direct grants and loans for agricultural development, the United States also strongly influenced Taiwan's agricultural policy formation and implementation. The primary vehicle was the Sino-American Joint Commission on Rural Reconstruction (JCRR), established by the 1948 China Aid Act[36] and authorized to conduct a coordinated program for rural reconstruction in China.

The JCRR operated only briefly in mainland China; Taiwan was the major site of its operations, and its period of maximum influence was in the 1950s and 1960s. The structure of the JCRR was bi-national. Of its five commissioners, two were appointed by the US president, and three were selected by the president of the Republic of China. The staff, numbering around 250 in the early 1960s, was mostly Chinese.

The predecessor of the contemporary Council of Agriculture, the Agricultural Planning and Coordination Committee of the Ministry of Economic Affairs was linked to the JCRR through one of its Chinese commissioners. The JCRR specialists held senior positions in the state's highest agricultural policy making body. Thus, the design of agricultural change, and a sizable part of the structure of implementation, were open to American influence.

This link to the United States, which during the 1950s and 1960s funneled billions in developmental aid to Taiwan, as well as the competence of the staff, made the JCRR the primary voice in Taiwan's agricultural policy-making and planning. It gave wholehearted support to the land reform program. The JCRR's technical staff spearheaded the introduction of improved farm machinery and tools. They encouraged the adoption of pesticides and insecticides, and they supported new agricultural product lines, such as artificially cultivated mushrooms.[37] The JCRR also stimulated the expansion of farm credit in support of agricultural modernization.[38]

The Impact of Agricultural Modernization on Taiwan's Political Economy

Policies of the government, strongly assisted by the United States, successfully increased Taiwan's agricultural productivity after the Second World War. Not only did agricultural growth make Taiwan self-sufficient in foods, but agricultural and processed food products constituted the lion's share of Taiwan's exports, earning badly needed foreign exchange. Agricultural modernization had two other effects, improving both the state's control of the rural population and increasing state revenues.

In the early 1950s, the government revived farmers' organizations, credit cooperatives, and other rural community groups, forming a new national Farmers' Association organized on three administrative levels. The township-level associations were sites for agricultural extension work and were primary organizations for mobilizing rural savings and providing rural credits. As we shall see in chapter 5, domination of the farmers' associations by the KMT ensured party-state control of farmers' political behavior.

The government also extracted revenue from farmers through two methods of collecting rice, which contributed significantly both to government solvency and to the development of industrialization in Taiwan. The first method was the land tax. After World War II, the government required that landowners pay a quantity of paddy rice based on the land taxes they had paid to the colonial government. Those cultivating paddy fields also were required to sell paddy rice to the government at an official purchase price, which remained consistently 25-30 percent below the wholesale market price of paddy.[39] The difference between the official purchase price and the wholesale price constituted a tax on farmers.

The second method used by the government to collect rice was through bartering fertilizer for rice at stipulated ratios that were considerably above market prices. The government held a monopoly in the production, importation, and distribution of chemical fertilizers. Until the early 1970s, the barter ratio that the government set between rice and fertilizer always favored fertilizer.[40] (Taiwanese farmers paid 50 percent more for the most popular fertilizer, ammonium sulphate, than did Japanese farmers.) Using this means, the government was able to subsidize the initially very expensive domestic manufacture of chemical fertilizer through high, controlled prices. The difference between the inexpensive foreign fertilizers imported by the government and the official price charged farmers constituted another tax on farmers.

Adopting these two methods, the government collected one-quarter of Taiwan's annual rice production. Because farmers consumed about half the rice they produced, this meant that during the 1950s and 1960s the government controlled half of the rice leaving the agricultural sector. The majority of the rice collected by the government was rationed to the armed forces or distributed to military dependents and civilian employees of the government, thereby reducing government cash outlays. The remainder of the rice was sold on the open market to stabilize rice prices or exported through another government monopoly.

Together, these policies allowed the government to extract a relatively large share of the agricultural surplus. It used the surplus to reduce government outlays and to invest in industrial development. In this way, agriculture contributed to Taiwan's economic growth.

Import Substitution Industrialization (ISI), the 1950s

At the end of World War II, except for the sugar industry, manufacturing stood at a rudimentary level of development. By the early 1970s, however, Taiwan was an industrializing economy, with manufacturing producing 31 percent of Taiwan's GDP and accounting for over 90 percent of her exports. This section discusses the way in which the government policy of import substitution affected industrial growth and the important role US aid played in maintaining economic stability. The following section considers a change in state policy emphasizing exports.

Industrial Growth Policy

An early economic policy of the Nationalist government was to rehabilitate industries damaged during the war, and this spurred some economic growth. The major policy of the 1950s, however, was import substitution, whereby the state promoted new industries to manufacture products customarily supplied as imports from abroad. From 1949 to 1954, this import substitution policy brought about an increase in manufacturing production of 22 percent a year.

After the early 1950s' spurt in industrial growth attributable to import substitution, manufacturing production slowed to 11 percent from 1955 to 1962. Import substitution continued to be of importance into the 1960s, however (and secondary import substitution was an important economic policy in the 1970s). Sectors benefiting from ISI later were rubber products, leather and leather products, petroleum and coal products, and metal products.

Policy Instruments

Three policy instruments promoted import substitution: import controls, tariffs, and multiple exchange rates. The most effective constraint on imports was the system of import controls. Imports were classified in four categories: prohibited, suspended, controlled, and permissible. A small number of import categories, about 5 percent, were prohibited because they were regarded as luxury goods or dangerous. About 40 percent of imports were either suspended or controlled, meaning that they could be brought in only by government agencies under special circumstances. The bulk of imports, about 55 percent, were in the permissible category, including capital goods, essential consumer goods, and raw materials. Controls tightened in the late 1950s as many goods were shifted from the permissible to the controlled or suspended categories (especially imported goods that competed with new domestic manufactures).

In the immediate post-war period, the government also raised the nominal rate of taxation on imports from 20 percent to 45 percent.[41] The government used the tariff rate system in a discriminatory fashion to give greater protection to non-durable consumer goods than to capital goods used in industrial production.

During the 1950s, the government also kept the value of the New Taiwan dollar (NT$) artificially high. This reduced the effective cost of imports and also reduced the competitiveness of Taiwan's exports. Too, the state maintained a system of multiple exchange rates. Exchange rates for exports were lower than for imports, and within imports, rates were lower for raw materials and capital goods than for non-durable consumer products.

Policy Results

The 1950s were years of strict protectionism in Taiwan. The policy instruments effectively sealed off new manufacturers from foreign competition. They also conserved foreign exchange for imports of raw materials and capital goods. Table 1 shows the impact of the policy in terms of its encouragement of industrialization.

Table 1. Industrial Structure, Selected Years (Percentage of Total)

	Real GDP at factor cost			*Real GDP*	
	1952	1960	1967	1967	1973
Total	100.0	100.0	100.0	100.0	100.0
Agriculture, forestry, hunting,and fishery	35.3	28.9	25.3	21.3	11.4
Mining	1.9	2.4	1.7	1.8	1.0
Manufacturing	9.8	17.2	21.4	27.6	43.5
Construction	3.7	3.3	3.8	4.0	3.2
Utilities	0.9	1.7	2.1	2.2	3.0
Transportation and communication	3.0	4.4	6.1	5.7	6.7
Trade	14.9	13.8	16.9	14.4	13.1
Housing services	6.3	6.1	6.7	5.9	5.1
Government services	14.9	13.9	10.2	9.6	6.5
Other services	9.3	8.2	5.8	7.5	6.4

Source: Adapted from Samuel P. S. Ho, *Economic Development of Taiwan, 1860-1970* (New Haven: Yale University Press, 1978), 129.

The benchmark years of 1952, 1960, 1967, and 1973 represent a trend in which manufacturing played an increasingly important role in Taiwan's economy. Less than 10 percent of GDP originated in manufacturing shortly after the retrocession; by 1967, however, it had become 28 percent of GDP. Correspondingly, the share of agriculture in Taiwan's GDP declined. It accounted for 35 percent of real GDP in 1952; by 1967, it had declined to 21 percent, by 1973 to little over 10 percent.

Import substitution benefited the cotton textiles sector first. When the small domestic market was saturated with processed cotton goods, import substitution shifted to other textiles, such as synthetic yarn, and other sectors, such as bicycles and flour. In such technologically simple industries, the effects of import substitution showed within four years; for more complex sectors, such as chemical fertilizers and electrical products, it took a decade to lower imports.[42]

Politically, ISI strengthened government control. SOEs dominated the economy, mainland entrepreneurs expanded their enterprises, and the party-state used import controls selectively to benefit loyal Taiwanese firms.

Other results of the import substitution policy were less favorable. The overvalued NT dollar damaged Taiwan's developing export industry. Although the import substitution policy reduced the importation of consumer goods, it increased the demand for importation of intermediate and capital goods, changing the structure without reducing the total demand for imports.[43] In fact, the share of imports rose, widening the deficit of goods and services, and aggravating the balance of payments problem. American aid financed most of these deficits.

Impact of US Aid on Taiwan's Economic and Security Policy-Making

From 1950 to 1968, American aid exerted a major force in Taiwan's economic development. (Table 2 shows the trends and elements of American aid.) America gave Taiwan a total of $4.2 billion in economic and military assistance from 1949 to 1967, of which 59 percent was military aid. Per capita, Taiwan maintained one of the world's largest armies in the 1950s and 1960s, numbering nearly 600,000 soldiers. The military absorbed about 12 percent of GDP and about 65 percent of government current expenditures at all levels.[44] Without US aid, these military expenditures would have bankrupted the state.

Per capita, Taiwan received US $425 for each civilian during 1950-67. A greater portion of economic aid arrived in the 1950s than in the 1960s, and over the period of US economic support, loans were more frequent than grants. Nevertheless, there is no discounting the roles that US aid played in economic stabilization, reducing foreign exchange constraints, and increasing capital formation.

Economic stabilization When America resumed aid to Taiwan in late 1950, the economy hovered on collapse, and inflation was very high. US military assistance reduced the government's need to shift domestic resources from economic to military uses. Economic aid was invaluable in stabilizing the economy by supplying cereals, fibers, daily essentials, fertilizers, and raw materials.   US aid continued to help stabilize the economy when its foundation became more secure.   When bad weather cut agricultural productivity and raised prices, US aid limited price swings.   When military expenditures increased in 1954 and 1958 to counter attacks by communist forces on Quemoy, US aid again controlled inflationary tendencies.[45]

Table 2. United States Economic and Military Assistance to Taiwan (US fiscal years, millions of US dollars)

	1949-52	1953-57	1958-62	1963-67	Total 1949-67
I. Total economic	467.8	529.5	502.3	268.9	1,768.5
Loans	-----	60.0	161.0	168.0	389.0
Grants	467.8	469.5	341.3	101.0	1,379.5
A. AID and earlier agencies	467.4	501.9	383.3	16.6	1,369.2
Loans	-----	60.0	139.3	15.0	214.4
Grants	467.4	441.9	244.0	1.6	1,154.8
B. Food for Freed'm	0.4	27.6	119.0	188.8	335.9
C. Export-Import Bank	-----	-----	-----	63.5	63.5
II. Military assistance program	48.0	1,178.9	720.4	436.9	2,384.2
Credit assistance	-----	-----	-----	0.9	0.9
Grants	48.0	1,178.9	720.4	436.0	2,383.3
III. Total economic & military	515.8	1,708.4	1,222.7	705.8	4,152.7
Loans	-----	60.0	161.0	168.9	389.9
Grants	515.8	1,648.4	1,061.7	536.9	3,762.8
IV. Assistance received per capita (US$)	66.7	188.3	113.4	56.4	424.8
Economic	60.5	58.4	46.6	21.5	187.0
Military	6.2	130.0	66.8	34.9	237.9

Source: Samuel P. S. Ho, *Economic Development of Taiwan, 1860-1970* (New Haven: Yale University Press, 1978), 110.

Reducing foreign exchange constraints In the 1950s, Taiwan encountered a foreign exchange gap, and US aid supported a higher rate of economic growth and a better utilization of other factors in the economy.[46]   From 1951 to the end of economic aid in 1965, US economic aid financed nearly 80 percent of Taiwan's import surplus.[47] (Although US aid authorizations were curtailed in 1965, aid in the pipeline lasted until 1968.) In the especially critical years between 1951 and 1956, US aid financed nearly 100 percent of the import surplus. Also, American aid provided about 40 percent of the gross domestic capital formation in the 1950s.[48]

Until the mid-1960s, comments Neil Jacoby, domestic revenues in Taiwan paid for less than 75 percent of the expenditures of the central and provincial government; US aid financed most of the deficits.[49] This gave the United States leverage over Taiwan's economic and security policy-making in three areas: creating an environment for private sector growth, liberalizing economic policy, and curbing military spending.

Private-sector growth Taiwan's government was not antagonistic to a large state-owned sector. In fact, the last and least well-defined of Sun Yat-sen's Three People's Principles—*Min-sheng* or the people's livelihood—committed the state to a strongly interventionist economic role. For the government to guarantee popular welfare required a wealthy state and necessitated government ownership of vital economic sectors. However, the government could not allocate many domestic resources to economic development and depended on US aid to finance development projects.

The American Agency for International Development (AID) had a strong commitment to the development of private enterprise, and it used its influence to improve the private sector climate in Taiwan. AID's influence was largest in financing government projects with large external spread effects. Samuel P. S. Ho's seasoned judgment is that "(w)ithout AID's influence and active intervention, the private sector would not have become Taiwan's foremost source of economic growth".[50]

AID provided little direct aid to private enterprises; only about one-third of its funds went to mixed public-private enterprises, and of this, only one in five dollars went to purely private businesses. However, most US aid and capital assistance were funneled to infrastructure and human resource projects in which there were substantial external economies.[51] Thus, aid to public enterprises helped increase the productivity of private industrial development.

Economic liberalization The American AID officers also pressured Taiwan officials to liberalize economic controls. Several times AID used economic aid as both a carrot and a stick: it promised to increase the level of assistance if favorable government actions resulted and threatened to reduce aid if the government failed to respond. An example of this tactic was AID's successful effort in 1959-60 to induce the government to adopt the 19-Point Program of Economic and Financial Reform.[52]

Military spending   AID also attempted to wield its resources to limit Taiwan's military expenditures.   This attempt partly conflicted with American defense policy, which sought a militarily strong Taiwan that could defend itself, with limited foreign assistance, against the communist threat. Nonetheless, excessive growth in military spending had serious inflationary impacts, and AID repeatedly urged the government to exercise fiscal restraint.   AID protested to Taiwan leaders' seemingly deaf ears,   because the Nationalist government continued to enlarge the military budget.   In this case, scholars lack a counterfactual that would establish the leverage that AID had. An argument can be made, however, that the military budget would have increased even more rapidly in the absence of American pressure.

Taiwan depended heavily on American economic and military assistance during the period from 1950 through the late 1960s, and this dependence reduced its autonomy in policy-making.   Clearly, during this period, Taiwan resembled a client state more than a capitalist or corporate one.

Export Promotion in the 1960s

From the late 1950s through the early 1960s, Taiwan's policy-makers shifted focus from an inward-looking, import substitution policy to an outward-looking, export promotion policy. The causes of this shift demand attention, as do the means and effects of its achievement.

Critical Factors in Redirecting Policy toward Export Promotion

The state had fallen into the policy of import substitution without much conscious investigation. By the mid-1950s, however, economic growth was slowing, and the small domestic market was becoming saturated with the products of ISI. Policy makers debated revisions to the industrialization strategy that would expand growth without compromising price stability or defense needs. The role of economic technocrats such as T. C. Liu, S. C. Tsiang, and K. T. Li was particularly important in launching this economic reform.[53]

A second pressure was external. AID officials pointed critically to the blanket of government regulations and controls that made Taiwan's economy inefficient and slowed economic development. Many of the regulations had been short-term controls to deal with war and inflation. They included the multiple exchange rate system, hidden subsidies, controls on imports and foreign exchange, and rationing and price controls over some goods and services.[54] AID urged the government to relax economic controls and improve the climate for private investment.

Some policy-makers looked specifically at Taiwan's performance in international trade as predictive of future opportunities. Even in the dismal days of the early 1950s, Taiwan's ratio of foreign trade to GDP was large, about 23 percent. (By the early 1970s, this ratio had grown to more than 80 percent.) With limited resources and a small domestic market, Taiwan could not hope to compete with larger, resource-rich nations. However, Taiwan's population was literate, disciplined, and hard working, suggesting that a labor-intensive industrialization strategy directed toward export promotion would spur economic growth. Because effective wage rates were lower than those of most trading nations, Taiwan had a strong comparative advantage.

Liberalization Measures

In 1959, the regime began removing controls. By the early 1960s, it had coined a new slogan, "Developing agriculture by virtue of industry, and fostering industry by virtue of foreign trade". Essentially, the strategy called for Taiwan energetically to promote its exports to the world market.

Over a five-year period, the government liberalized controls and also developed new programs to stimulate exports. The reforms included gradual devaluation of the NT dollar. Too, the multiple exchange rate system was dismantled, and officials developed a simpler system to allocate foreign exchange for permissible imports. The cumbersome lists of controlled and suspended import commodities were partially decontrolled and pared.[55] Effectively, the government reduced its use of import quotas to reduce non-durable consumer goods and relied primarily on tariffs to restrict imports.

The government also developed a series of export promotion measures. These included investment incentives, tax reductions and rebates of customs duties paid on raw material imports used in manufacturing, special loans to exporters at low preferential rates, and improved availability of loans to private enterprises.[56] Too, the government supported the formation of export cartels and selectively restricted investments in over-expanded industries.

It was during this period that the government established export processing zones (EPZs) to streamline administrative procedures and attract foreign investors. Kaohsiung was the site of the first EPZ, established in 1966, and by the mid-1970s, zones were set up in Nantze and Taichung. Although, in the late 1990s, EPZs play a relatively small role in Taiwan's trade promotion, in the late 1960s and 1970s they were major forces in the economy.[57]

Impacts on Export Performance

Table 3 presents information on the change in export performance over the 20-year period from 1956 to 1976:

Table 3. Sources of Growth of Output Expansion

	Output Expansion Due to Domestic Expansion (percent)	Output Expansion Due to Export Expansion (percent)	Output Expansion Due to Import Substitution (percent)	Output Expansion Due to Technology Change (percent)
1956-61	61.6	22.5	7.7	8.2
1961-66	63.2	35.0	0.5	1.3
1966-71	51.4	45.9	5.7	-3.0
1971-76	34.7	67.7	-2.4	0.0

Source: Shirley W. Y. Kuo, Gustav Ranis, and John C. H. Fei, *The Taiwan Success Story: Rapid Growth with Improved Distribution in the Republic of China, 1952-1979* (Boulder, CO: Westview Press, 1981), 110.

Table 3 clearly shows that exports were the primary factor contributing to Taiwan's rapid growth in the 1960s and 1970s. In the late 1950s, export expansion was a secondary factor in growth, comprising 22.5 percent. By the late 1960s, export expansion had increased to 45.9 percent, and by the mid-1970s, it had become the primary source of output growth, comprising 67.7 percent. In contrast, after the 1950s, import substitution became a secondary or tertiary factor.

The value of exports changed in an equally noteworthy way. Although exports of agricultural products and processed foods increased in the 1960s, new industrial exports grew far more rapidly. During this decade, growth in industrial exports increased by an average of 36 percent a year (compared to an average of 24 percent for agricultural products and 16 percent for processed food products).[58]

Export opportunities were critical to the success of Taiwan's industrialization and, in particular, to its labor-intensive strategy. (Taiwan's exports could compete internationally because they had a higher labor content at a lower cost of labor than those of its competitors.) Exports increased the markets for Taiwan's goods, which created more opportunities for production, which in turn increased the demand for labor. Exports also earned foreign exchange crucial to import the equipment and materials needed for further production.

The success of the export promotion strategy also significantly improved Taiwan's balance of payments. Trade deficits declined steadily, and by the early 1970s, Taiwan was producing healthy trade surpluses. Promotion of exports also brought an influx of foreign investments, which increased gross capital formation. Fixed capital stock in the manufacturing sector increased more than threefold from 1952 to 1966.[59]

Changes in Economic Structure

Export-oriented industrialization affected the structure of the economy in three major ways: 1) it changed the roles of different economic sectors; 2) it altered the opportunity structure for large and small enterprises; and 3) it transformed the inputs of labor and capital.

The development of export-oriented industrialization in the 1960s accelerated the economic transition of early, middle, and late industries. The traditionally most important manufacturing industries, such as food processing, beverages, tobacco, wood and leather products, declined as a share of value-added originating in manufacturing.[60] Textiles, once the leading non-food industry during the period of import substitution until sluggish growth reduced their position in manufacturing value-added, rebounded under the export promotion strategy. By the end of the 1960s, textiles had become Taiwan's most important manufacturing industry.

Increasingly, however, it was middle and late industries, the newest to be developed, that contributed most to export growth. They accounted for 38 percent of the total increase in manufacturing value-added in the late 1950s, and for 62 percent of the increase during the 1960s.[61] Particularly impressive among the middle industries were chemicals, nonmetallic mineral products, and petroleum and coal products. Several of the late industries were strongly export oriented, such as metal products and machinery.

During the period of ISI, state-owned enterprises played a large role in industrial development. As a share of gross capital formation in the early and mid-1950s, they nearly equaled the share of the private sector. SMEs operated at the margins of the state-led industrial structure.

SOEs in the 1960s and early 1970s had a considerably lower share of gross capital formation.[62] Their role changed with the new export promotion strategy, as they provided valuable inputs to downstream industries, most of which were small in scale. Multinational corporations formed a new part of the large business sector, as did large and growing domestic corporations.

The most significant change in economic structure, however, concerned SMEs, which became the core of many export industries. Because they were flexible and could quickly respond to market changes, SMEs became highly successful, and the numbers of profitable firms increased several fold during the 1960s. Observers coined the term "guerrilla capitalism" to reflect the firms' aggressive and audacious entrepreneurship.[63] SME operators were of broader significance, however, forming the kernel of the new middle class in Taiwan. Not yet a counter elite to the KMT leadership, they nevertheless were a developing force in support of broader liberalization.

Export promotion also changed the scope and influence of labor and capital inputs. As manufacturing assumed a larger and larger share of national production, employment in manufacturing industries increased at the rate of about 6 percent a year. And, in fact, the fastest growing industries with the largest export shares were also the most labor intensive. The entry of women workers fed much of the expansion in manufacturing labor force participation. Another significant change was the reduction in the percentage of unpaid family workers, from 22 to 7 percent of the total labor force in manufacturing.[64] This signifies a reduction in the influence of very small-scale enterprises, which usually did not employ anyone outside of the family.

Until the lifting of martial law in 1987, Taiwan's workers could not strike, and this orderly, disciplined, and compulsorily docile work force was a major element in the industrialization push. The work force also improved qualitatively during the export promotion strategy. Simultaneously, the government increased the number of years of compulsory schooling from six to nine, effective in 1968.

Investments in industry also increased greatly. From 1952 to 1966, the fixed capital stock in the manufacturing sector grew more than threefold. Investment tended to flow toward newer industries, such as petroleum, metals and metal products. Along with increased investment came technological change.

An important source of increase in capital was direct foreign investment (DFI), which has grown dramatically since 1960. The largest investors were from the United States, Japan and Europe or were overseas Chinese. This DFI was an efficient conduit for technology transfer, and it played a special role in the export sector.[65]

The export promotion strategy began with liberalization of controls and incentives for industries to export. Taiwan had a comparative advantage in following a labor-intensive path of growth. The trade orientation and policy changes in concert achieved the remarkable spurt in industrial growth, which brought wide attention to Taiwan's "economic miracle".

Adjustments of the 1970s and Early 1980s

Taiwan's aggressive entry into the world market occurred at a time of worldwide growth and expansion by industrial economies. Also, global trade was expanding at unprecedented rates, energized by the Kennedy Round of negotiations, which achieved large reductions in tariff rates. Moreover, just as Taiwan was vigorously promoting export industries, mature industrial states such as the United States and Japan were seeking opportunities to out source production to take advantage of cheaper factors of production abroad.

Taiwan entered the 1970s with one of the world's most stable (albeit authoritarian) governments. Its real growth rate was in the double digits at the start of the decade, and per capita GDP was moving quickly toward US $ 1,000. Then Taiwan encountered both economic and political shocks and underwent a major political transition as Chiang Kai-shek died and was succeeded by his son, Chiang Ching-kuo.

In response to these changes, the state adapted and adjusted. Taiwan adopted flexible and pragmatic relations with most of her trading partners, and under Chiang Ching-kuo's leadership, the state tolerated more dissent. Leaders also revised economic strategies to accommodate global economic changes. We consider both stimuli and state responses as they bear directly on Taiwan's new political economy.

Oil Shocks

Two exogenous shocks in the 1970s tested the resilience of Taiwan's policy-makers. In 1973 and 1974, the Organization of Petroleum Exporting Countries (OPEC) quadrupled the price of oil, which had instant and negative repercussions. Because imports then were a third of GDP, import price increases reverberated throughout the economy. For 1974, GDP growth dropped below 1 percent (from 10 percent during the 1960s and early 1970s), and inflation reached 40 percent. The trade deficit in 1974 exceeded US $1 billion.[66]

The state responded radically but effectively. The Central Bank of China raised interest rates sharply, and the government raised prices of oil and electricity by 80 percent. These quick responses moderated the rise in prices. To stimulate economic activity, the government pumped money into public construction projects and reduced both income tax rates and customs duties. For the second half of the decade, growth rates returned to 10 percent.

The second oil price increases of 1979 and 1980 were milder in Taiwan than the first shocks. Inflation rose less sharply, and growth rates did not fall so steeply; the government responded by gradually raising interest rates, oil and electricity prices. Taiwan's extreme dependence on imported fossil fuels did prompt two policy revisions: planning to bring nuclear power plants on line accelerated, and economic policy-makers refocused industrial policy to emphasize less energy-intensive projects (discussed below).

Political Shocks

The Republic of China's international status rested on the diplomatic and political support of the United States and Japan, also Taiwan's major trading partners. This support allowed the Republic of China to hold membership in the United Nations and a permanent seat on the UN Security Council. In addition to US and Japanese diplomatic recognition, in 1970 Taiwan was recognized by 66 nations, while only 53 recognized the PRC (two countries recognized both, and 14 recognized neither).[67]

The American rapprochement with mainland China removed the primary prop to Taiwan's international status, and during the 1970s, Taiwan's diplomatic status plummeted. After 20 years of supporting Taiwan's retention of UN membership, the United States in 1971 declined to protest the seating of the PRC. Facing a certain vote by the UN General Assembly to seat the PRC and expel the ROC, Taiwan withdrew from the United Nations in late 1971. The next year, President Nixon traveled to China and signed the Shanghai Communiqué, in which the United States acknowledged that "there is but one China and that Taiwan is a part of China".

Following the American decision to normalize its relations with China, at the expense of diplomatic support for Taiwan, the Japanese government derecognized Taiwan in late 1972. There then ensued a series of diplomatic setbacks, the most serious of which was President Carter's announcement in 1978 that the United States would recognize the PRC (which came in 1979, followed by the cancellation of the US-ROC Mutual Defense Treaty in 1980).

Taiwan responded to these political shocks by shoring up support where it could and making flexible arrangements that would protect its security and trading interests. Supporters of Taiwan in the US Congress passed the Taiwan Relations Act (TRA) in 1979, which directed the president to "inform the Congress promptly of any threat to the security or the social or economic system of the people on Taiwan", pledged the United States to "make available to Taiwan such defense articles and defense services in such quantity as may be necessary to enable Taiwan to maintain a sufficient self-defense capability", and expressed its expectation "that the future of Taiwan will be determined by peaceful means".[68] Conflicting with the Shanghai Communiqué respecting weapons sales and the use of force in reunification, the TRA nevertheless gave a modicum of security to Taiwan.

The TRA also delineated a new modality for quasi-diplomatic relations, based on the Japanese model. The United States established the American Institute of Taiwan, a private, nonprofit corporation staffed by officials formally separated from the US Foreign Service or other federal government employment. Taiwan, in turn, established the Coordination Council for North American Affairs (renamed the Taipei Economic and Cultural Representative Office in the 1990s). These offices continued most of the work done by previous embassies.

In 1970, Taiwan established the China External Trade Development Council (CETRA) to replace commercial attachés and official trade missions. CETRA is a private organization funded by mandatory dues from exporters, which occupies handsome office buildings in Taipei and more than 40 overseas offices. Modeled on JETRO, the Japanese trade promotion agency, CETRA sponsors exhibits of Taiwan's products in Taiwan and abroad, organizes trade missions, and provides services to business firms. Through flexible organizations such as CETRA, Taiwan has been able to maintain a presence in many countries in which it does business.

Although some apprehensive residents sent their capital out of the country or emigrated because of Taiwan's loss of diplomatic status, a patchwork of government measures permitted Taiwan to retain its most vital linkages with other nations. As we shall see in chapter 3, political shocks to Taiwan also made the regime more responsive to dissent.

Political Transition

In 1949, Chiang Kai-shek arrived in Taiwan with impressive leadership credentials tarnished by the loss of the mainland to the communists. From his leadership of the Northern Expedition in 1926-27, through the war of resistance against Japan, Chiang was the most powerful figure in China: *Tsung-ts'ai* or KMT party leader, commander-in-chief of the armed forces, and elected president.

Taiwan offered few obstacles to Chiang's rule from 1949 until his death in 1975. In the simpler and more unified environment, Chiang could use with success the pattern of rule that had failed in the mainland: consolidation in his hands of broad powers to appoint, transfer, and dismiss officials, and a check and balance system in the assignment of officials that prevented any from becoming a potent rival.[69] He was an obvious master of the subtle art of political maneuvering.

Chiang commanded the party, army, security agencies, and government, and he brooked no opposition to his rule. Loyalty was the chief requirement in his use of people, but he did appoint capable officials such as Chen Cheng, long-term vice president and premier who orchestrated the land reform campaign, and he selected outstanding economic officials who developed Taiwan's early economic growth strategies.

The leadership style Chiang followed was traditional and Confucian. His austere habits and lifestyle created an image of virtuous authority. He was neither a warm nor popular leader but communicated well his concern for the people's welfare and the paternalistic obligations of the state. This earned him the respect of Taiwan's population, most of whom genuinely mourned his passing in 1975.

Chiang Ching-kuo, the only son of Chiang Kai-shek, succeeded his father in power after a very smooth transition. He had been groomed for national leadership over the previous decades, and upon assuming the premiership in 1972, had a thick portfolio of experience. This included stints in the KMT high command, supervision of intelligence and security activities, and direction of the Vocational Assistance Commission for Retired Servicemen and the China Youth Corps. In the 1960s, Chiang served as defense minister and vice premier of the Executive Yuan. Throughout, he was loyal to his father and careful to avoid alienating the KMT's fanatically anticommunist old guard, who remained somewhat suspicious of Chiang because as a youth he had spent 12 years in the Soviet Union and had a Russian wife.

Chiang Ching-kuo's leadership style differed radically from his father's. As premier and later as president, he regularly went out among the people—to schools, factories, hospitals, offices, and fields. Dressed casually and often wearing a golf cap, Chiang easily projected concern for people's problems and their welfare.

As an executive, Chiang centralized power in his hands then established clean authority lines to subordinates. He paid particular attention to the rectitude of government officials and campaigned actively for honest and efficient government. As premier, he banned bureaucrats from dance halls, bars, and expensive restaurants. He quickly discharged corrupt officials, including those in high positions (such as the Garrison Command). When the former personal secretary of his father was found guilty of taking bribes, Chiang declined to interfere in the punishment.[70] Chiang's use of people and personal integrity earned him respect and trust.

Upon consolidating his power, Chiang launched a major program of political reform. He appointed a large number of Taiwanese to government and party positions, including Hsieh Tung-min as governor of Taiwan province and Lee Teng-hui as minister without portfolio. He paid more attention to youth and brought officials still in their 30s and early 40s into leading positions. Chiang also appointed technocrats with demonstrated ability to cabinet positions.

Although the regime continued to censor publications, monitor political activity, and conduct surveillance and arrests of dissidents, it became more tolerant of political opposition. After his father's death, Chiang Ching-kuo reduced sentences of political prisoners and released 200. He was particularly sensitive to charges of Taiwan's human rights violations, which caused him to offer to cooperate with any international commission interested in investigating Taiwan's human rights record.

A watershed event in Taiwan's political development, the Kaohsiung Incident of 1979, showed the changing nature of authoritarian rule. The incident was preceded by formation of an electoral opposition to the KMT in 1977 called the *Tang-wai*, which won more than a quarter of the seats in provincial assembly elections. In 1979, the *Tang-wai* held a series of public rallies and used as their rallying point the political journal *Formosa*. Journal offices established through the island became meeting places for *Tang-wai* activists. On December 10, the Kaohsiung office of *Formosa* organized a rally to promote human rights. The rally turned into a bloody riot as participants confronted police, and several police officers and bystanders were injured.[71]

Police arrested dozens of participants, and the regime brought eight defendants to trial on sedition charges in a military court the next March. The tribunal sentenced the defendants, some of whom had been forced to sign confessions, to prison terms from 12 years to life. Among those drawing life sentences was Shih Ming-de, the mastermind of the rally. The government's severe handling of the incident, during a time when the regime was reeling from the American change in diplomatic recognition, brought on a storm of foreign protest. Some observers believe that foreign pressure, which led to the reduction in Shih's sentence, encouraged the regime to tolerate dissent. (In 1996, Shih was a legislator and president of the DPP.) In any event, the Kaohsiung Incident represented the last episode of summary arrests and convictions of organized opponents to the KMT regime.

Structural Adjustments

Socio-political and economic changes in Taiwan as well as changes in the global environment were the background for four adjustments to growth strategy. The government expanded SOEs to provide basic steel, chemical, and petrochemical products needed by industry. It engaged in major infrastructure improvements. The government assisted the upgrading of industries, helping them become more technology-intensive, and it introduced economic liberalization and internationalization as new economic development principles.

The oil shocks stimulated the strengthening of Taiwan's public sector.   Chinese Petroleum Corporation and China Petrochemical Development Corporation both expanded during this period. Construction of a shipyard began in 1973, and three years later, China Shipbuilding Corporation was inaugurated as a wholly owned state enterprise.   Re-entry of state capital in this secondary import substitution stage was economically justifiable because the high capital intensity and long gestation of investment might have deterred private entrepreneurship.[72]   During the 1970s, the government successfully promoted merger and consolidation of SOEs, such as the consolidation of China Phosphate, Taiwan Alkali, and Caprolactam with the China Petrochemical Development Corporation.[73] In fact, SOEs as a share in gross fixed capital formation reached their high point in 1975, at 40.3 percent.

The second structural change was the improvement of infrastructure. Rapid industrialization and foreign trade growth had clogged harbors, highways, airports, and railways. Power generation was insufficient. In response, a series of public construction activities were planned, including a north-south freeway from Keelung to Kaohsiung, a new international airport at Taoyuan, expansion of the Suao harbor, construction of a new port at Taichung, electrification of the east coast railway, and construction of additional nuclear power plants.   Chiang Ching-kuo combined these projects into an integrated public construction program named the Ten Major Development Projects. The initial projected cost of the construction program was US $6 billion but spending far exceeded that amount. The projects created jobs and pumped money into the economy; altogether they had a strongly countercyclical economic effect in the mid-1970s. The success of this strategy for improvement of infrastructure was such that leaders in the 1990s remembered it.

Taiwan's successful export promotion strategy had led to rising wages and social prosperity, which began to price Taiwan out of the low-cost labor niche in the global division of labor.[74] As a result, the third structural adjustment was a shift in industrial policy emphasizing technology-intensive sectors that used less energy and were non-polluting. Machine tools, computers, semiconductors, telecommunications, robotics, and biotechnology became areas of emphasis. Industrial technology was not an entirely new area of emphasis, as the government had sponsored research and development since the 1950s. Given the large number of small and medium enterprises that could not afford to make technology investments, the government's role was critical. In the 1970s and 1980s government support for R&D capacity in new growth areas intensified. It established the Industrial Technology Research Institute in 1973 and the Hsinchu Science-based Industry Park in 1980.[75] Too, during this period, the government systematically tried to repatriate science graduates who had gone abroad for further training.

The fourth adjustment became policy in the eighth four-year plan introduced in 1982. The government announced that economic liberalization and internationalization would be "new guiding principles" for Taiwan's economic development. However, global economic recession of the early 1980s delayed implementation until mid-decade.[76] American pressures on Taiwan to liberalize also were an important factor in this adjustment, which continues through the 1990s.

Together, the four adjustments increased the government's intervention in the economy, causing some observers to label the changes the emergence of a "new-developmental state" in Taiwan.

Conclusions

In 1997, Taiwan was the world's 14th largest trading state and a mature industrial economy. This chapter has identified the causes of change in economic structure and output, from the Nationalist government's retreat to Taiwan in 1949-50 up to the onset of democratization in 1986. We now review the five periods covered in terms of the political economic approaches with which the chapter began.

The integration of Taiwan into the Nationalist Chinese system of rule from 1945 to 1949 awakened opposition of the Taiwanese population, expressed in the February 28, 1947, Incident. The KMT regime's brutal suppression of this uprising effectively curbed dissent. Imposition of martial law in 1947, and consistent monitoring by intelligence and security agencies, prevented the formation of autonomous groups. The period of integration was directed by the KMT party-state.

The state also initiated and guided agricultural modernization in the 1950s. The government's land reform program was a clear attempt to reverse its failures to improve equality of land distribution while on the mainland. In Taiwan, opponents of land reform, the landlord establishment, were also potential opponents of KMT power. Land reform succeeded economically, giving incentives to the new owner-cultivators to increase agricultural production. It also succeeded politically, by removing the landed base of traditional local elites and creating a new class of cultivators whose increasing prosperity reminded them of their debt to the KMT. Agricultural modernization was primarily directed by the state; over time, it promised to increase the autonomy of farmers, but this was not obvious until the 1980s. Too, the government depended on the United States for the successful implementation of agricultural modernization.

Although the state fell into the policy of import substitution industrialization in the 1950s, it directed implementation. State-owned enterprises were both agents and beneficiaries of ISI. The extensive pattern of controls during this period enhanced state power and seriously inhibited the private sector. In fact, the ISI period was one of the most intensely regulated eras in modern Taiwan history. The ISI strategy did not serve American economic interests in that US non-durable consumer goods exported to Taiwan declined; nevertheless, ISI launched Taiwan's industrialization, which was in the political and international interests of the United States. American economic and military aid to Taiwan played a critical role in economic stability and industrial development during this period, and the term "client state" is appropriate.

The period of export-oriented industrialization, which launched a decade of double-digit growth, seems to be explained through market forces. Small and medium enterprises aggressively expanded abroad, finding niches in the global marketplace because of labor-intensive production, and they fueled most of the surge of growth. Taiwan's linkage to the United States remained an important element, too, for American advisors urged Taiwan to liberalize, and the United States provided a very large market for Taiwan's goods. However, the state's influence over the process of export-led industrialization was unmistakable. Central policy- makers decided to liberalize by removing exchange and import controls. Government agencies created opportunities for the private sector and stimulated growth in export sectors. The term "developmental state" is indeed appropriate for this stage in Taiwan's modern history.

The adjustments of the 1970s and early 1980s in response to oil shocks, political shocks, and leadership succession showed the strong hand of the state again. State-owned enterprises were perhaps as vital to the economy in the mid-1970s as they had been in the early 1950s. Government spending on infrastructure projects and government support of industrial upgrading facilitated business expansion.

Throughout Taiwan's post-war history up to the mid-1980s, it was the state that led the way. The state depended on the United States, especially during most of the 1950s and 1960s. And the state faced increasingly autonomous forces in the private sector by the 1970s. But no force or institution could compromise the autonomy of the state, directed by the KMT, for most of the post-war era. We turn in chapter 3 to an examination of how the party-state began to change.

Notes

[1] See, for example, W. Galenson, ed., *Economic Growth and Structural Change in Taiwan: The Postwar Experience of the Republic of China* (Ithaca, NY: Cornell University Press, 1979).

[2] I. Little, 'An Economic Reconnaissance', in W. Galenson, ed., *Economic Growth and Structural Change in Taiwan: The Postwar Experience of the Republic of China* (Ithaca, NY: Cornell University Press, 1979), 489.
[3] Robert Wade, *Governing the Market: Economic Theory and the Role of Government in East Asian Industrialization* (Princeton, NJ: Princeton University Press, 1990), 22-23.
[4] See, among others, Andrew MacIntyre, ed., *Business and Government in Industrializing East Asia* (Ithaca, NY: Cornell University Press, 1994); Frederic C. Deyo, ed., *The Political Economy of the New Asian Industrialism* (Ithaca, NY: Cornell University Press, 1987); and Gary Gereffi and Donald L. Wyman, *Manufacturing Miracles: Paths of Industrialization in Latin America and East Asia* (Princeton, NJ: Princeton University Press, 1990).
[5] Chalmers Johnson, 'Political Institutions and Economic Performance: The Government-Business Relationship in Japan, South Korea, and Taiwan', in Frederic C. Deyo, ed., *The Political Economy of the New Asian Industrialism* (Ithaca, NY: Cornell University Press, 1987), 138.
[6] Wade, 1990, 292.
[7] Yun-han Chu, 'The Realignment of Business-Government Relations and Regime Transition in Taiwan', in Andrew MacIntyre, *Business and Government in Industrializing Asia* (Ithaca, NY: Cornell University Press, 1994), 152.
[8] Wade, 1990, 27.
[9] A.H. Amsden, 'The State and Taiwan's Economic Development', in P. B. Evans, D. Rueschemeyer, and T. Skocpol, eds., *Bringing the State Back In* (Cambridge: Cambridge University Press, 1985), 98.
[10] Thomas B. Gold, *State and Society in the Taiwan Miracle* (Armonk, NY: M. E. Sharpe, Inc., 1986), 126.
[11] G. G. Hamilton and C. S. Kao, *The Institutional Foundation of Chinese Business: The Family Firm in Taiwan* (Davis: University of California, Institute of Governmental Affairs, 1987), 98.
[12] Harmon Zeigler, *Pluralism, Corporatism, and Confucianism: Political Association and Conflict Regulation in the United States, Europe, and Taiwan* (Philadelphia: Temple University Press, 1988), 213.
[13] Wade, 1990, 290, 295.
[14] Gary G. Hamilton, 'Organization and Market Processes in Taiwan's Capitalist Economy', in Marco Orru, Nicole Woolsey Biggart, and Gary C. Hamilton, *The Economic Organization of East Asian Capitalism* (Thousand Oaks, CA: Sage Publications, 1997), 290. Also, see Karl J. Fields, *Enterprise and the State in Korea and Taiwan* (Ithaca, NY: Cornell University Press, 1995), who makes similar observations about the state's role in Taiwan's economic development.
[15] Edwin A. Winckler and Susan Greenhalgh, eds., *Contending Approaches to the Political Economy of Taiwan* (Armonk, NY: M. E. Sharpe, Inc., 1988), 7; see also Richard E. Barrett and Martin K. Whyte, 'Dependency Theory and Taiwan: Analysis of a Deviant Case', *American Journal of Sociology*, vol. 87, no. 5 (March 1982), 1064-89.
[16] Winckler and Greenhalgh, 1988, 9.

[17] Ezra F. Vogel, *The Four Little Dragons: The Spread of Industrialization in East Asia* (Cambridge, MA: Harvard University Press, 1991), 92-101.

[18] For example, see Gilbert Rozman, ed., *The East Asian Region: Confucian Heritage and Its Modern Adaptation* (Princeton, NJ: Princeton University Press, 1991), 3-42.

[19] Quoted in Douglas Mendel, *The Politics of Formosan Nationalism* (Berkeley, CA: University of California Press, 1970), 27.

[20] George H. Kerr, *Formosa Betrayed* (Boston: Houghton Mifflin, 1965), 136.

[21] Mendel, 1970, 31.

[22] Mendel, 1970, 32.

[23] Kerr, 1965, 310.

[24] Mendel, 1970, 37.

[25] *United States Relations with China* (the White Paper) (Washington, DC: Department of State Publications 3573, 1949), 309-10.

[26] The Japanese colonial administration had limited the number of places in schools for the native population, and it had restricted the number of professions available to Taiwanese.

[27] Samuel P. S. Ho, *Economic Development of Taiwan, 1860-1970* (New Haven: Yale University Press, 1978), 104.

[28] Ho, 1978, 104.

[29] See Jon W. Huebner, 'The Abortive Liberation of Taiwan', *China Quarterly* 110 (June 1987), 274.

[30] See Ho, 1978, 150-55.

[31] Ho, 1978, 155.

[32] Ho, 1978, 180.

[33] Ho, 1978, 161.

[34] Hung-chao Tai, *Land Reform and Politics: A Comparative Analysis* (Berkeley, CA: University of California Press, 1974), 202.

[35] Ho, 1978, 164.

[36] Public Law 471, 80th Congress.

[37] Ho, 1978, 178.

[38] See John D. Montgomery, Rufus B. Hughs, and Raymond H. Davis, *Rural Improvement and Political Development—The JCRR Model* (Washington, DC: AID, 1964).

[39] Ho, 1978, 180.

[40] Ho, 1978, 181.

[41] Yu-chi Tao, *The Tariff System of the Republic of China* (Taipei: 1969), 175-78.

[42] Ho, 1978, 189 and Ken Ching-yuan Lin, *Industrialization in Taiwan, 1946-1972* (New York: Praeger, 1973).

[43] Ho, 1978, 193-94.

[44] Ho, 1978, 108.

[45] Ho, 1978, 113-14.

[46] Neil H. Jacoby, *U.S. Aid to Taiwan: A Study of Foreign Aid, Self-Help and Development* (New York: Praeger, 1966), 124.

[47] Ho, 1978, 115.

[48] Ibid.

[49] Jacoby, 1966, 51.

[50] Ho, 1978, 117.

[51] Ibid.

[52] Jacoby, 1965, 134-35.

[53] Samuel P. S. Ho, 'Economics, Economic Bureaucracy, and Taiwan's Economic Development', *Pacific Affairs*, vol. 60, no. 2 (Summer 1987), 243.

[54] Ho, 1978, 119.

[55] Mo-huan Hsing, John H. Poser, and Gerardo P. Sicat, *Taiwan and the Philippines: Industrialization and Trade Policies* (London: Oxford University Press, 1970), 242-43.

[56] Shirley W. Y. Kuo, Gustav Ranis, and John C. H. Fei, *The Taiwan Success Story: Rapid Growth with Improved Distribution in the Republic of China, 1952-1979* (Boulder, CO: Westview Press, 1981), 74-81.

[57] Personal interview with Tin-bai Pan, Director General, Export Processing Zone Administration, MEA, Kaohsiung, April 19, 1996; see also, MEA, *Comprehensive Functions of the Export Processing Zone Administration* (Taipei: MOEA, 1995).

[58] Ho, 1978, 199-200.

[59] Ho, 1978, 215.

[60] Ho, 1978, 201.

[61] Ho, 1978, 203.

[62] See Ramon H. Myers, 'The Economic Transformation of the Republic of China on Taiwan', *China Quarterly* 99 (September 1984), 515, and Chi Schive, 'Industrial Policies in a Maturing Taiwan Economy', *Journal of Industry Studies*, vol. 2, no. 1 (August 1995), 8-11.

[63] Danny K. K. Lam and Ian Lee, 'Guerrilla Capitalism and the Limits of Statist Theory', in Cal Clark and Steven Chan, eds., *The Evolving Pacific Basin in the Global Political Economy: Domestic and International Linkages* (Boulder, CO: Westview Press, 1992), 109.

[64] Ho, 1978, 211.

[65] Chi Schive, *The Foreign Factor: The Multinational Corporation's Contribution to the Economic Modernization of the Republic of China* (Stanford, CA: Hoover Institution Press, 1990), 102.

[66] Wade, 1990, 96.

[67] Ralph N. Clough, *Island China* (Cambridge, MA: Harvard University Press, 1978), 154.

[68] Dennis VanVranken Hickey, *United States-Taiwan Security Ties: From Cold War to Beyond Containment* (Westport, CT: Praeger, 1994), 30-31.

[69] Clough, 1978, 48.

[70] Clough, 1978, 63.

[71] Hung-mao Tien, *The Great Transition: Political and Social Change in the Republic of China* (Stanford, CA: Hoover Institution Press, 1989), 96-97.

[72] Tun-jen Cheng, 'Political Regimes and Development Strategies', in Gary Gereffi and Donald Wyman, eds., *Manufacturing Miracles: Paths of Industrialization in Latin America and East Asia* (Princeton, NJ: Princeton University Press, 1990), 170; also see Schive, 1995, 11-17, and Council for Economic Planning and Development, *Economic Development, Taiwan, Republic of China*, 1996.

[73] Fields, 1995, 71.

[74] Cal Clark, 'Successful Structural Adjustment and Evolving State-Society Relations in Taiwan', *American Journal of Chinese Studies*, Vol. 2, No. 2 (October 1994), 189.
[75] Wade, 1990, 98.
[76] CEPD, 1996, 32.

3 Transformation of the Party-State in Taiwan

Introduction

Taiwan's *Kuomintang* (KMT) is the oldest political party in East Asia, with the longest continuous pattern of rule in the world.[1] When party leaders retreated from mainland China to Taiwan in 1949-50 after losing the Chinese civil war, few thought the party would survive the reverberations of that conflict. No one could have predicted that the KMT would lead the state through a phenomenal economic growth miracle, with per capita GDP increasing from US $224 in 1950 to over $13,000 in 1997.

The political changes initiated by the KMT, or made by it in response to changing social forces, are equally remarkable. In 1924, the party's organizational structure became Leninist, and for its first 37 years on Taiwan, it adhered roughly to this model. No other party challenged the dominance of the KMT, whose strictly centralized command system extended to all sectors of society. The party monopolized ideological life, producing a unified vision of national construction, and individuals were largely dependent on authorities through a comprehensive system of punishments and rewards. The primary differences between the KMT in Taiwan and the Chinese Communist Party (CCP) on mainland China during this period were the KMT's lack of a Marxist ideology, its pro-capitalist domestic policies, and its pro-Western foreign policy. It was also a "soft" authoritarian state that restricted freedom under temporary provisions, until full constitutional democracy could be instituted.[2]

However, in 1986, at the direction of party chair and president Chiang Ching-kuo, the KMT inaugurated Taiwan's democratic transition.[3] Before Chiang's death in January 1988, party leadership acquiesced to the establishment of the first formal opposition to KMT rule, the Democratic Progressive Party (DPP). It began crafting national security statutes to replace martial law (lifted in 1987) and to accommodate political competition. In 1988, the KMT party congress agreed to "realize constitutional democracy" and make the three parliament bodies fully representative and capable of performing their functions.[4] President Lee called representatives of all parties (by then more than 40) to a National Affairs Conference in 1990 to focus and advance reform. This led to competitive elections for all seats of the Legislative Yuan and National Assembly, to mayoral posts in Kaohsiung and Taipei, to the provincial governorship and the national presidency. Wu Yu-shan calls these reforms the "marketization of the KMT", for the party now faced competition for votes in Taiwan's new political market.[5] In the 1995 Legislative Yuan elections, the KMT emerged with only a razor-thin majority (initially, four seats in the 164-member chamber, later reduced to two) but won only 46 percent of the aggregate vote. In March 1996, Taiwan held the first democratic presidential election of any Chinese state; incumbent president Lee Teng-hui won a clear victory in the four-candidate race but admitted that to govern effectively he would need the cooperation of opposition parties.

This chapter analyzes the transformation of the party-state in Taiwan as the KMT's Leninist authoritarian rule has been challenged by competitive opposition parties in a context of democratic elections. The dominance of Leninist authoritarian parties is based on their ability to capture forces of change within the party, to prohibit opposition from developing interests, to control organs of state power, to resist factionalizing tendencies within the party, and to avoid electoral contests that they cannot win. We analyze changes along these five variables in six sections. First, we review the structure of KMT power—the operation of the Leninist model within the party, the network of social controls, and KMT enterprises. Second, we chronicle the rise of opposition to KMT power, from its roots in the *Tang-wai*, to the formation of the DPP, and finally to the creation of the New Party (NP). Third, we examine intra-party dynamics as the KMT has indigenized, liberalized, and weathered factional splits and realignment. Fourth, we examine the changing patterns of electoral competition between the KMT and new opposition parties. Fifth, we ask what prevents the demise of the party-state in Taiwan. The chapter concludes with a brief discussion of the theoretical implications of the KMT's role in Taiwan's democratic transition.

The Structure of KMT Power

The organizational form of a Leninist party was adopted by Sun Yat-sen, on the advice of Comintern agents, in 1924. Sun's objective was to create an effective power behind the state that would implement the Three People's Principles and restore China as a great state. In Taiwan, the Leninist aspects of the party underwent changes. The party established a network of social controls and gradually built party businesses that gave it an independent financial base.

The Leninist Model in Taiwan

Leninist systems emphasize rule by political elites who are adjudged to know best the needs of the nation and how to achieve its revolutionary transformation. The central operating principle of Leninist systems is democratic centralism: the movement of ideas, discussion, and debate upward from the grassroots (the party cell), through stages of territorial congresses, to the pinnacle of party power; and then the flow of power downward, from the leader (or, ideally, the collective leadership) to the local levels.

When the KMT retreated to Taiwan after the loss of the mainland, Chiang Kai-shek attributed the party's defeat to its weak organization, among other factors.[6] He called for a party reorganization commission, whose recommendations led to a tightening of party organization. The basic pattern of organization, adopted in 1951, remains in place in 1997.

The structure of the KMT is complex. Vertically, the party parallels each level of government from the national to the provincial and county (or municipal) down to the township or urban district. At every level are found a cluster of three institutions—a congress or other representative body, a decision-making center, and the party's administrative machine.[7]

At the national level, the representative body is the party congress. The congress meets once every four years. (The 15th party congress met in August 1997.) It discusses the party's situation, takes action on proposed party policies, and elects members of the central committee. This committee has become quite large, with 210 members; it selects the party chairman and the 31 members of the central standing committee. Both Chiang Kai-shek and Chiang Ching-kuo hand-picked the members of the central standing committee. A rules change at the 14th party congress in 1993 allowed the party chair to select no more than 15 members of the central standing committee.

The central standing committee, headed usually by the party chairman, has been the action center of the party and state. Its Wednesday morning meetings are the primary decision-making forum in Taiwan. Although the central standing committee in theory operates through collective leadership, during the party's history on Taiwan, the party chair has had decisive influence.

Day-to-day affairs of the party are managed by a secretary-general and three deputies. Career staff run various party departments and commissions.   At lower levels, party organizations have their own secretariats and administrative staffs.

Social Controls

For its first four decades on Taiwan, the KMT tightly controlled social groups and interests that might challenge its dominance, in what Tien Hung-mao calls "corporatism with pluralist characteristics".[8]   The regime organized farmers and laborers, the two largest occupational groups, and controlled their elections and activities.[9]   Business and educational interests were also subject to supervision and monitoring.   In addition, the party organized participation through mass organizations such as the Youth Corps and Women's Association. The martial law statutes of the regime specified exactly the exterior limits of participation.[10]   Until the 1980s, no demonstrations or protests were permitted.

The network of controls involved both party and government agencies. The KMT's social affairs department directed all party activities in social groups, including farmers', labor, and business associations, with national, provincial, and city/county offices.   Party cells operated in all social groups at all levels. Their role was to monitor carefully the elections of social groups and associations, ensuring that KMT members became directors and chairmen. Organizational bureaucrats, who usually were party members and often retired military, conducted the day-to-day operations of the associations.

In the government, relevant councils or ministries supervised groups. Thus, both the Council of Agriculture and the Council of Labor Affairs have offices responsible for farmers' and labor associations, respectively, at the national level; there are comparable offices at the provincial and city/county government levels too. The seventh division of the Industrial Development Bureau in the Ministry of Economic Affairs guides the industrial associations, but each of the other divisions also works with them. Integrating government supervisory functions is the Ministry of Interior, which has a social affairs office; it implements the law on organizations at the national level.[11]   A provincial-level office observes associations centralized at that level, and each county or major city has a department of social affairs to supervise the very large number of organizations at the lowest level. These linkages guarantee nearly complete state autonomy from social forces and a high party-state capability to penetrate the society.

Each occupational category has had its own representative organization.   Farmers' associations *(Nung-hui)* have been more than membership organizations. They have enrolled about 85 percent of farm households and have 1.5 million members. They play economic roles in agricultural modernization and rural development; they are a very important source of credit (through rural credit cooperatives found in most small communities). They are social organizations in Taiwan's countryside; and historically they have been available for mobilizing rural voters electorally (often through vote buying).

Labor has been organized into unions, but under martial law these organizations had no autonomous ability to call strikes or engage in aggressive organizational activity. Labor laws allowed only one union within each plant or geographic area, and the KMT encouraged its members to found unions and seize leadership positions within them. The Chinese Federation of Labor has been dominated by the KMT since its inception.

Industrial and commercial associations and chambers of commerce are organized vertically, with national, provincial, and city/local units. Industrial and commercial associations also are organized by sector, to a fine degree of specialization. In textile manufacturing alone there are nearly two dozen associations. The law on organizations requires that if five or more companies operate in a sector, they must register with the government as an association and elect a chairman, directors, and supervisors.[12] Initially, monitoring of both policy and personnel extended to the individual trade associations. Trade associations and chambers of commerce also play quasi-official roles, particularly in the issuing of certificates of origin for export purposes, export quota administration, quality control, and technology diffusion.

KMT Finances

The KMT is a wealthy party; in the opinion of some observers, it is the richest party in the world. Party finances have come from three sources: government subsidies, membership dues, and KMT enterprises. Probably the most important early source of party finance was direct subsidies by the government. This source is no longer available as opposition parties scrutinize the budget for any indication of support for the ruling party. Members of the party pay dues, and these have been assessed at 1 percent of monthly income (the amount collected often falls short). Also, the party increasingly has solicited donations from wealthy businesspersons who are party members.[13]

The third and most controversial source of party finance is KMT enterprises. Only one KMT-owned company followed the party on its retreat to Taiwan in 1949-50. Over the next 40 years, however, with direct support of the state, the party established a large number of enterprises. In 1997, there were nearly 150 KMT enterprises. Some were quite small, but others were large trading companies, investment houses, and manufacturing firms. The total amount of party assets in December 1995, was US \$3 billion, and profits during 1996 were about \$300 million.[14]

The KMT's revenue base is large, but so are its obligations. The party operates more than 300 community service centers throughout Taiwan, and its employees number 7,000.[15] In 1997, about 85 percent of its budget of \$80 million went to personnel expenditures.[16]

Opposition to KMT Power

From the February 28, 1947, Incident to 1977, there was little organized opposition to KMT rule in Taiwan. In addition to the KMT, two small parties operated—the Young China Party and the Democratic Socialist Party. Both were established in mainland China before the rise of communist power. Neither enrolled more than 10,000 members, and both remained small and generally inactive. They were rubber stamps for the KMT, even allegedly receiving subsidies from it.[17]

The laws on political organizations did not allow the organization of new parties, thus opponents of the regime were forced to use other vehicles of protest. One was the *Free China Journal*, which began publishing in 1949 and was organized by Lei Chen as a reformist call for constitutional democracy. In the 1950s, several Taiwanese entered elections as independents; in 1958, they formed the Association for the Study of China's Local Self-Government to reform electoral politics.[18] Two years later, they combined with Lei Chen in forming the China Democratic Party. Lei's arrest on a sedition charge in 1960 eliminated this threat to KMT monopoly.

During the 1960s, little overt opposition to the regime surfaced. Then, in 1964, political science professor Peng Ming-min was arrested along with two of his students for distributing anti-KMT materials. (Peng spent the next 20 years in exile abroad, returning to become the DPP's presidential candidate in 1996.)

Tang-wai Roots

Until 1986, no party organized formally in opposition to KMT dominance of Taiwan's political system. The Taiwan Independence Movement operated surreptitiously but, under martial law, saw little purpose in attempting to organize openly (leaders who did were arrested during the KMT's White Terror).

Criticism of KMT dominance increased at the ascension to power of Chiang Ching-kuo and in response to Taiwan's increased diplomatic isolation as the United States prepared to recognize mainland China. In 1977, independent candidates campaigned for office for the first time, voicing opposition to the KMT's dominance of Taiwan and its goal of reunification with China. Significantly, the KMT tolerated the independent candidates. Edwin Winckler notes that the nationalist regime "responded by co-opting the least partisan, arresting the most committed, and learning to live with the rest".[19] These candidates called themselves *Tang-wai* (outside the party or non-party opposition). The regime prohibited this movement from organizing as a party, but in 1978 its leaders began coordinating campaigns of non-KMT candidates. In the course of elections in the 1980s, the *Tang-wai* candidates (most of them Taiwanese) received an average 30 percent of the vote at the local and provincial level.[20] This illustrated a softening in the KMT's treatment of dissent, while it increased gradually the penetration of the state by changing social forces.

Formation of the DPP

Throughout the 1980s, a number of elites, including some from the KMT, sought vehicles to liberalize the political system, while mobilization of youth, intellectuals, and interest groups focused on the KMT's stranglehold on political power. On September 28, 1986, *Tang-wai* leaders decided to formalize their opposition in a new political party, the Democratic Progressive Party (DPP). Its establishment contravened the laws on political organizations, but the regime did not arrest party leaders. Within one year, this opposition party's status was legitimized by changes to the statutes. By 1997, the DPP had approximately 84,000 members.

Organizationally, the DPP mirrors the structure of the KMT. Its national congress elects 31 members to the central executive committee and 11 members to the central advisory committee. The central executive committee in turn elects the 11 members of the central standing committee, which is the party's nerve center. The national congress also directly elects the party chairman, an office held by Hsu Hsin-liang in 1997. The DPP emphasizes full democracy of its processes in contrast to the democratic centralism of the KMT. Its primary system involves two stages: a closed primary for party members and an open primary for all eligible voters.

The party's platform includes a call for self-determination for Taiwan's residents concerning the island's future. Other policy stands include a campaign to re-enter the United Nations, downsizing the armed forces, and opposition to communism. Reflecting the social democratic orientations of some of its leaders, the DPP has sought an expansion of social welfare services and campaigned for greater support for SMEs in the economy.

The DPP has been the major opposition party to the KMT since its foundation; it also has steadily improved its standing in elections, nearing 40 percent in 1992 races. However, the party is split into four factions which reflect ideological and philosophical differences on the independence of Taiwan, and continued expansion of democratization, among other factors. The New Tide *(Hsin-chao-liu)* faction has fervently clamored for Taiwan independence as the ultimate solution to the island's problems, advocating that no compromise or negotiation with the government should be sought. The Formosa *(Mei-li-tao)* faction is considerably more moderate and pragmatic and has favored working within the political process (a larger portion of its members are professional politicians).[21]

In the early 1990s, two further factions split off from the New Tide and Formosa factions: the Justice Alliance (*Cheng-yi Lien-hsien)* and the Taiwan Welfare State Alliance *(Taiwan Fu-li-kuo Lien-hsien).* Both splinter groups objected to the way factional conflict within the party interfered with a united front against the KMT.

Finally, in December 1996, dissidents within the DPP and some independent supporters formed the *Chien-kuo-tang,* selecting the English name of Taiwan Independence Party (TAIP). They objected to the slow pace of action in declaring Taiwan's independence but took only two DPP legislators from within the Legislative Yuan fold.

Formation of the New Party (NP)

In August 1993, a group of radical, primarily mainlander members of the KMT bolted from the ruling party to form the *Hsin-tang* (New Party). NP members were younger than the KMT elites, and generational differences helped cause the split. More important, however, were differences in ideology and power.

NP members saw themselves blocked within the KMT power structure as Taiwanese came to hold a majority of party seats and positions. They also strongly opposed what they saw as the KMT's softening on the Taiwan independence stance of the opposition. They believed that movement toward unification with China was progressing too slowly. In 1997, NP claimed a membership of nearly 72,000.

The NP differs from the KMT and DPP organizationally and stresses leadership in the party of those holding public office. Heading the party is the National Campaign and Development Committee. The committee convener (in 1997, this was Yok Mu-ming) serves as party leader.

The NP's platform contains a laundry list of items—from attacks on money politics and corruption, to opposition to environmental deterioration and nuclear power plant construction, to a plea for further modernization and rationalization of Taiwan's economy and social system, including a five-day work week.

Internal KMT Changes in Response to Democratization

The structure of the KMT of 1997 resembled strongly dominant party traditions. Its chairman was president; its large, 2.1 million membership, or 10 percent of the population, was represented through party congresses that select party leaders. While the outer shell of the party seemed little altered, significant changes had taken place in party composition, party processes, and factional alignment.

Party Composition

At the retrocession of Taiwan to the Republic of China in 1945, the Chinese Nationalist Party was exclusivist and narrow in its representation of interests and groups. Lacking many Taiwanese, women, youth, peasant, or labor members, the KMT could not broadly appeal to the population. Government institutions from mainland China similarly underrepresented the Taiwanese.

Table 4. Composition of the KMT Central Committee, 1952-1993

Election Year	Date Date	Congress	Taiwanese %	Military %	Legislature %	Total No.
1952	10/19	7th	3.1	31.3	15.6	32
1957	10/23	8th	6.0	22.0	30.0	50
1963	11/22	9th	5.4	21.6	18.9	74
1969	4/8	10th	6.1	16.2	16.2	99
1976	11/17	11th	14.6	16.2	11.5	130
1981	4/3	12th	19.3	10.0	20.0	150
1988	7/12	13th	34.4	11.7	20.6	180
1993	8/17	14th	53.3	3.8	31.9	210

Source: Adapted from Michael Ying-mao Kau, "The Power Structure in Taiwan's Political Economy," *Asian Survey*, vol. XXXVI, no. 3 (March 1996), 291.

Party chairman and president Chiang Kai-shek made few attempts to increase party representativeness. On his death in 1975, the party increased recruitment of native Taiwanese and seated them as chairs of local party organizations.[22] To reinforce changes in economic policy and direction, the party also recruited from the growing body of younger technocrats, entrepreneurs, and university-educated leaders, and made concessions to women.[23] It also replaced parochial factional leaders with progressive candidates. By Chiang Ching-kuo's death in 1988, party composition had changed dramatically, as noted in Table 4, and these changes are continuing.

The crowning symbolic change was the selection of Lee Teng-hui as vice president; he assumed the presidency and party chairmanship on Chiang's death. Lee, a native-born Taiwanese, increased the indigenization of the KMT, so that by 1997, over 70 percent of party members and a majority of the members of the central standing committee were Taiwanese. Mainlanders held a larger percentage of party and governmental (including military) positions than their numbers (14 percent of the population) warranted. More significant, however, was majority control of leading party and governmental positions exercised by Taiwanese elites.

Liberalizing Party Processes

Softening the democratic centralist aspects of KMT party processes gave party members a larger role in party governance. The first reform expanded participation in the selection of the party's central committee. At the 13th party congress in 1988, for the first time in party history, the party chair put his list of central committee candidates to an open vote of delegates and allowed delegates to propose alternative candidates from the floor. Although delegates approved 81 percent of party chair Lee Teng-hui's list, the final rankings varied from those proposed. This damaged the prestige of some older, traditional members of the party elite.[24]

The second reform began at the central committee meeting of February 1990, when opponents of the majority faction called for a secret ballot in voting on the party's nominees for president and vice president.[25] (The historical practice was for party members to rise in acclamation, which reduced any appearance of dissent.) At the 14th party congress in 1993, delegates could use secret ballots to vote on who should chair the party.[26]

The third reform concerns use of primaries for selection of party candidates, but this reform was more apparent than real. In 1986, KMT organizational affairs director Kuan Chung introduced primaries, which gave rank-and-file members access to the party recruitment process. His objective was to maintain the power of the old ruling clique in succession to Chiang Ching-kuo. The rate of participation in primaries by mainlanders, particularly retired military, was very high (some say nearly 90 percent), while Taiwanese participation was low, thus enabling party leaders to control primary outcomes. When James Soong was party secretary-general, he took advantage of primaries to fortify support for Lee Teng-hui in the 1992 elections. Currently, the nomination system is flexible, allowing primaries when no candidate enjoys overriding party support.[27]

The first two of these reforms reduced the influence of party leaders over important aspects of recruitment and policy formation. Also, they popularized and modernized the party, and to a certain extent rejuvenated it. Flexible use of primaries, however, gave only the appearance of liberalizing nomination processes.

Factionalism, Pluralism, and Realignment

Leninist parties oppose challenges to their power from other parties and customarily treat factionalism as heretical to party ideology. While on mainland China, the KMT cooperated with other parties reluctantly and relentlessly sought to expunge factional conflict. Like other Leninist parties, however, the KMT could not extirpate factional divisions.

The KMT's revolutionary ideology has waned as the party pursues electoral fortunes, and the nature of factional conflict has changed. Intra-party factionalism initially was rigorously suppressed; however, after the death of Chiang Kai-shek, policy differences appeared more frequently in party councils and were tolerated in fact (but still opposed in principle). At the start, these concerned differences over speed and direction of economic development and reaction to diplomatic reversals. Soon, those with divergent policy positions competed for influence over policy-making in the central committee. Recent policy conflict concerns Taiwan's international position, the national identity issue, and attitude toward reunification with mainland China, including moderation of the "three no" policy (no negotiation, no compromise, and no contact). Quality of life issues, such as environmental protection have appeared too. The change in the value of political resources in Taiwan's new political market is partly responsible for altering the distribution of views. Now, legislators, businessmen, campaign managers, and media specialists have greater clout in party debates.[28] The overall pattern is one of increased pluralism in party decision-making.

By 1990, primary policy differences coincided with the division between mainlanders and ethnic Taiwanese in the central party leadership. They surfaced in the *mainstream* faction (the Taiwanese majority led by Lee Teng-hui, who advocated the policy direction of *Taiwan You-hsien,* "Taiwan as the Priority") and the *non-mainstream* faction, including mostly mainlander officials who did not want the party to lose its reunification goal.[29] The majority faction accommodated the *non-mainstream* leaders with positions including the selection of retired general Hao Po-ts'un as premier in 1990.[30] This compromise proved fragile, however, and Hao left the government at the request of President Lee. This action precipitated the departure of most of the *non-mainstream* faction and its formation of the New Party in 1993, which was the most significant party realignment of the 1990s.

The departure of the *non-mainstream* faction had serious repercussions for KMT electoral success in the 1995 Legislative Yuan elections and also in the 1996 National Assembly elections: the party fell short of a majority of the aggregate vote in both contests. Yet the party was able to retain its majority of seats in both parliaments. Moreover, Lee Teng-hui won a comfortable 54 percent of the presidential vote in 1996. He faced not only DPP candidate Peng Ming-min but also two former members of the KMT central standing committee—Chen Li-an (mainlander and son of Chen Cheng), and Lin Yang-kang (Taiwanese, former provincial governor and Judicial Yuan president) whose running mate was former premier Hao Po-ts'un.

Contemporary Campaigns and Elections

Three changes in law, constitution, and judicial interpretations have made elections the primary means through which Taiwan selects leaders. Until 1992, most of the 287 seats in the Legislative Yuan were held by elderly representatives, first elected on the Chinese mainland in 1947-48. Representatives from Taiwan joined the Legislative Yuan in supplementary elections beginning in 1969, but by 1989 they comprised no more than 35 percent of the seats. Elections for all seats were held in 1992, and it was then that the Council of Grand Justices ruled that the newly elected legislature could represent the Republic of China on Taiwan only: senior representatives of mainland provinces (the popular reference was "old thieves") were involuntarily retired.

A second change made the executives of Taiwan province and Taipei and Kaohsiung cities into elective positions. The first election of provincial governor and city mayors was held in 1994. The third change concerned the nation's highest office, the presidency. The president had been elected indirectly for a term of six years, by the National Assembly (and it, too, had been composed largely of elderly representatives, elected on the Chinese mainland). In 1994, representatives of the second National Assembly, all elected locally, amended the constitution to provide for direct election of the president and vice president; the amendment also limited their terms to four years.

Electoral Rules

Taiwan's voting eligibility rules encourage participation. The minimum voting age is 20, and there are no restrictions based on gender, ethnicity, property or educational qualifications. Moreover, the state automatically registers voters and publicizes upcoming elections with information identifying each candidate. Also, elections are held on Saturday, and this becomes a holiday for most people. Through these means, voting turnout in the late 1980s and 1990s has averaged 70 percent of eligible voters.

The design of electoral districts in Taiwan is complex. Elections for executives—president, provincial governor, mayor, county and township magistrates—are based on a single-seat constituency, plurality election (comparable to the Anglo-American system). Each voter casts only one vote, and the candidate receiving the most votes is elected. This system tends to favor the larger parties.

However, elections for representatives—members of the Legislative Yuan, National Assembly, city, county, and township councils—use the single non-transferable vote (SNTV) system (comparable to that used previously in Japan). Constituencies are larger, and several representatives normally are elected from each. Elections commissions form constituencies based on population distribution, geography, access to transportation, and existing administrative districts.[31] Each voter casts only one vote, and the leading candidates are elected.

In addition, a number of seats in the Legislative Yuan and National Assembly are reserved for at-large and overseas Chinese representatives. The seats are allocated using the proportional representation method. Each party submits two lists of candidates, one for at-large seats and the other for overseas Chinese representatives. After voters cast their ballots, the votes gained by candidates are aggregated by party affiliation; at-large and overseas Chinese representatives are then distributed proportionally among parties attaining 5 percent or more of valid votes nationwide.[32]

Andrew Nathan notes that the electoral system works to the KMT's advantage.[33] However, a counter argument is equally credible: the electoral system favors the party that can mobilize voters most effectively within districts, and whose support is island-wide. Increasingly, the DPP has benefited from the electoral system, and the KMT would benefit most from a single-member constituency, plurality election system such as that used in Britain and the United States.

Campaigns

After we review characteristics of Taiwan's election campaigns, we consider the role of local factions, campaign costs, and party strategies.

Characteristics Taiwan's election campaigns are short, personal, noisy, and frenetic. The period of official campaigning is limited to around 10 days. Because several candidates, often as many as 18, are campaigning in the same district for just four or five seats, candidates focus on establishing name recognition. They hang huge campaign banners from buildings, hold rallies in public parks, and parade through the streets in sound trucks blaring their names and begging for votes.

Before 1991, candidates could not broadcast campaign ads on television. Then, time was allocated to political parties in a formula that favored the KMT.[34] For those running for office as a representative or local executive, TV is an inefficient medium. The three major networks broadcast one program series nationally and do not create regional markets for political advertising. As a result, candidates use radio advertising and spend most campaign dollars on printed advertising: mail-out flyers, posters, newsletters, and bulletins.

Role of factions Local factions have been a critical element in Taiwan's elections since the 1950s, when electoral districts were enlarged to county and city limits. They replaced landlords, the traditional local elites, who lost their power base during land reform. The factions were interpersonal, clientelistic networks, based primarily on *Kuan-hsi*, relationships of lineage or marriage, or geographic or academic ties.[35] Most factions then were incorporated into the KMT, and the absence of party competition fostered their growth (to a total of more than 100). Usually, there were at least two local factions, and the local party committee could alternate elected offices between factions or divide top posts among factions. This gave the party control at the local level and stabilized factional relationships.[36]

Local factions exchanged resources for votes. They obtained resources from parties and candidates and then distributed them to members of their networks. The KMT provided its local factional leaders with four economic resources:

> 1) monopolistic economic activities in local areas with special permits from the government, as in banking, bus companies, credit unions, etc.; 2) special loans and credits with especially favorable terms from state-owned commercial banks; 3) local government public contracts; and 4) land speculation in connection with urban planning and zoning for construction projects, or tacit permission to operate illegal businesses such as gambling houses and dance halls.[37]

Factional leaders used these resources to mobilize voter turnout and support. Invariably, this involved buying votes. Joseph Bosco distinguishes two kinds of vote buying. The first used money as a gift, much like the soap, pens, and cigarettes candidates and parties give to voters. The amount of money was small, usually from the equivalent of US $7 to $12, and handed to voters in loose bills along with a flyer or campaign ad. This money was designed to firm up support. The second kind used money as a bribe for the vote in areas where the candidate lacked support; it usually cost more money (US $19-23).[38]   Neither kind of vote buying was legal, but more often than not it went unreported; if reported, it was rarely investigated.

Some scholars report a decline in factional strength from 1954 to 1989, while others argue that its influence has stayed constant over time. It is clear, however, that candidates affiliated with local factions were more likely to be nominated, and that KMT candidates with connections to local factions were more likely to be elected.[39]   Also clear is the recent transformation of factions in three respects: opposition parties have penetrated them; their reach now extends nationally; and conglomerates have developed relationships with factional leaders.

Over the last decade, DPP party branches increasingly have worked with local factions, which increases tensions at the local level as local factions interface with party rivalries.   Until 1988, factions were not allowed to cross county lines, but over the last decade they have taken root at the national level, too.   Of equal importance, conglomerates, once influential only at the national level, have reached into local areas, serving as patrons to factional clients.[40]

Campaign costs and corruption   The amount of money spent in campaigns recently has been staggering. Joseph Bosco reports that the two factions in a 1990 township executive race spent US $370,000. Candidates for country assembly representative spent US $148-185,000 in 1990.[41] In a series on the 1991 National Assembly elections, the *Independence Weekly Post* reported that the amount of money candidates needed to distribute in handouts was from US $1.2 to $2 million. Most of more than 100 reports of vote buying investigated by the newspaper were in the range of US $12 to $20 million. The paper called the election a victory for *chin-nyou* (gold cows, or moneyed interests).[42]

In the 1992 election, vote buying was commonplace, with prices for votes ranging from US $17.50 to $74.[43]   In fact, reports of vote buying, gift-giving, lavish free banquets, and free trip offers have been widespread for all the 1990s elections. As campaign costs increase, only candidates able to raise huge sums are competitive.   Two-thirds of the KMT nominees in recent elections have been connected to major enterprise groups or local factions, and DPP nominees have similarly relied on external sources of funding, some of them illegal. As Tien Hung-mao notes, "Democratization and the decline of the KMT's institutional effectiveness have led to a new coalition of power elites, larger enterprise groups, and local factions . . . Money has translated blatantly into political power".[44]

Corruption, once a problem of local-level factional competition, became a factor in national-level elections in the 1990s.   The 1995 legislative elections were expensive, with candidates spending from US $360,000 to $2 million. Flagrant cases of vote buying in this election became a focus of attention in Taiwan's democratization. For example, in 1996 the Tainan district court convicted a record 981 people in a vote buying scandal surrounding KMT legislative candidate Wang Tao-fu. Wang and his campaign staff distributed bribes of more than US $19 each to nearly 900 voters, disguising them as payments for campaign services. Wang lost the race, the court stripped him of his civil rights for eight years, and he was sentenced to 4.5 years in jail.[45] The case was one outcome of Justice Minister Ma Ying-jeou's three-year campaign against electoral corruption. Ma lost his cabinet post earlier in June 1996 because his investigations were endangering KMT members.

Taiwan's money politics took an international twist in probes of illegal donations to the US Democratic party during the 1996 presidential elections. The Hong Kong weekly newspaper *Yazhou Zhoukan* charged KMT business management committee chair Liu Tai-ying with offering a US $15 million donation to Bill Clinton's re-election campaign. Liu angrily denied the charge and sued for libel (he lost), complaining that mainland Chinese authorities fabricated the charge to reduce the heat from accusations that China had made illegal donations to the Clinton campaign. *Newsweek* alleged that James Wood, director of the American Institute in Taiwan, a long-time Clinton friend, had urged Taiwan's businessmen to "reward" the Clinton administration for its pro-Taiwan policies. Charges even reached into religious circles, implicating Suma Ching Hai, the head of a Buddhist sect in Taiwan. None of these allegations had been verified by mid 1997, but six staff members of the US Senate's Governmental Affairs Committee traveled to Taiwan to investigate them.[46]

Strategic actions During the nomination process, party strategists attempt to ensure that the optimum number of candidates appears on the ballot. During elections, party branches compare their lists of candidates with those of other parties and make allocation decisions to avoid wasting votes. For example, they may divide a district into zones of equal size and ask candidates to campaign only in their zone.[47] KMT organization resources have been far superior to those of the opposition parties, but the capability of the party to mobilize voters is now waning. The KMT also pays attention to nurturing candidates likely to improve party electoral fortunes and strives to preserve its voter bases.[48] For nearly a decade, the KMT has conducted elaborate polls of party members to ascertain which candidates would run well in what areas. Too, the KMT sends "paratroopers" (well-qualified candidates without local ties) to win highly competitive races. The effect of these strategic decisions is to increase competition in all parts of the country and to improve the representativeness of assemblies and councils.

Its transformation into a political machine that can win competitive elections has cooled the ideological (and revolutionary) fervor of the KMT. The DPP was far more likely to use ideological appeals in election campaigns up to the mid 1990s; recently, its ideological ardor has begun to fade, as it sees the need to absorb all strands in order to become the majority party. Increasingly, both KMT and DPP resemble Japan's LDP, a "department store" with everything inside. The KMT's restraints on successful candidates have loosened, a development related to the recent increase of corruption in politics.[49]

The nature of the electoral system also affects party discipline. In multiple-candidate races, candidates from the same party compete with one another, and the party has to remain neutral. As a result, candidates rely on their own connections and their candidate support groups. Under these circumstances, elections become very personalized, and party affiliations are less important. Elections also become more expensive because candidates can improve their fortunes with relatively few votes changing sides. John Hsieh observes in this regard that "candidates running under the SNTV system have little incentive to remain loyal to party discipline after election."[50] A recently re-elected KMT legislator remarked:

> The bad influence of the KMT cancels out the good. There are as many people who dislike the KMT as like the party, so it doesn't help to have the party's endorsement. The KMT can't control us. I relied on myself to get elected, not on them.[51]

Party Recognition and Salience

Some early studies of Taiwan's elections indicated that parties were less important in influencing voters' choices than candidates' positions or personalities.[52] More recent research, however, suggests the finding was an artifact of the methodology, which solicited socially desired answers, such as, "one should vote on the basis of candidates' policy positions".

The emergence of new parties and political competition gradually has increased voters' recognition of differences between the major political parties. For example, studying the 1992 Legislative Yuan elections, Liu I-chou shows that KMT supporters differed significantly from DPP supporters. Party-related differences were the most important predictor of voting behavior for respondents who voted for the KMT or the DPP.[53]

Surveys conducted by Chu Yun-han over the 1980s indicate a moderate degree of partisan affiliation of voters. He found that about one-half of a sample of voters had a positive attachment with either the KMT or the Tang-wai/DPP.[54]

Party identification has salience in the era of competitive party politics. Taiwan's voters still pay close attention to characteristics of the candidate: sincerity, probity, effectiveness, and, increasingly, service to the constituency. Voters take issues into consideration, too.

Issues in Campaigns and Elections

A canard about Taiwan's politics is that there's only one election issue, and that is *Tung-du* (unification versus independence). The formation of the DPP and competitive party politics reduced the prominence of democracy versus authoritarianism as an issue, seeming to leave only *Tung-du*. It has been the primary political issue over the decade of democratization, but others have emerged.[55]

At the DPP's party congress in 1991, the New Tide faction threatened to withdraw from the party if the Taiwan independence clause was not added to the party charter, and the Formosa faction acquiesced. This placed the issue of unification v. independence on the national agenda. The issue is paramount primarily because it so clearly divides the three parties. It highlights Taiwan's major ethnic cleavage between mainlanders and Taiwanese. While the issue consolidated DPP elites, it intensified the schism between *mainstream* and *non-mainstream* factions of the KMT, resulting in the formation of the New Party in 1993. That splintering of the KMT removed from its electoral base many mainlanders and the "iron votes" of the military and civil service employees.

Research by Cheng Tun-jen and Hsu Yung-ming on the 1991 and 1992 post-election surveys indicates that although party elites developed and framed the unification/independence issue, most voters had a clear and strong position on it. Moreover, they were more cognizant of this than of any other issue.[56]

Three other issues of the 1990s may increase their profiles in the eyes of Taiwan's voters: economic inequality, corruption, and environmental deterioration. Economic justice issues also show signs of becoming increasingly important.

At the onset of democratization, economic equity was not a significant political concern. The success of Taiwan's export promotion strategy had left the society relatively free from conflict over the distribution of wealth. Several developments of the late 1980s and 1990s (to which we turn again in chapter 5) have heightened consciousness about growing disparities in wealth.

Economic restructuring in recent years has increased the concentration of ownership in business, making conglomerates (and also KMT enterprises) larger figures in the economy. Correspondingly, small businesses have faced increased difficulty in becoming established. Related to this trend are data on increasing social inequality resulting from a sharp escalation in land and stock prices that benefited asset owners but brought higher costs of living to those on fixed incomes. The government's budget, accounting, and statistics office reported that the income ratio between the highest 20 percent of household incomes and the lowest 20 percent, which was only 4.10 in 1980 (among the world's lowest) had risen to a ratio of 5.2 by 1992.[57] The National Wealth Survey, conducted by the same office in 1991, pointed out that asset values owned by the richest 20 percent of households were worth 17 times those of the poorest 20 percent. Moreover, the wealthiest 20 percent of families owned 54 percent of Taiwan's total wealth; the wealthiest 3 percent owned 27 percent of the total land.[58] These data put into question the government's heralded success in achieving "growth with equity".

In 1990s elections, the DPP has focused on equity issues. In the 1992 Legislative Yuan elections, DPP introduced a "welfare state" platform, calling for broad improvements in Taiwan's social welfare programs, such as universal health insurance, retirement income for the elderly, and subsidized housing programs.

The increase in corporate wealth, occurring at the time of increased political freedom, has made money politics and corruption an issue as well. Chu Yun-han and Lin Tse-min attribute this to factional conflict within the KMT:

> (T)he power struggle forced competing blocs within the party to co-opt new allies, and the mainstream faction reached out to the business community and local factions because it suffered from a weaker power base within the party-state. As a result, the corruption that had long tainted elections for local officials seeped into elections for national representative bodies. This institutionalized vote buying, the relentless pursuit of pork, economic prerogatives, and outright bribery . . . (T)he party gradually transformed itself from a coalition of a mainlander state elite and collateral native politicians to one of socioeconomically conservative state elites, local factions, and big business.[59]

A review of the backgrounds of members of the KMT's central standing committee, divided between conglomerate executives, factional leaders, senior bureaucrats, and a few legislators, confirms this analysis.

Both the DPP and NP have attacked corruption of the KMT and money politics, forcing the government to undertake even more campaigns to cleanse the system of gangsters, influence peddling, collusive deals, and other shady arrangements. These issues figured in the 1992 and 1995 legislative elections and were discussed in the 1996 presidential election as well.

Finally, environmental issues, particularly compliance with Taiwan's new Environmental Protection Agency policies but also objections to plant construction and exorbitant levels of pollution (such as mountains of garbage in the streets of Chungli) have provoked responses from opposition campaigners.

New Patterns in Electoral Competition

Since 1988, the DPP has competed in national, provincial, and local elections; at every level, the party has succeeded in winning an average of 30 percent of votes. The New Party gained nearly 15 percent of the vote in its first campaign for Legislative Yuan seats. The legislative elections are probably the best indicator of changes over the last 15 years in party fortunes, displayed in Table 5.

Table 5. Party Vote in Legislative Yuan Elections

	1980	1983	1986	1989	1992	1995
KMT	73.64%	71.86%	69.06%	60.6%	60.5%	46.3%
TW/DPP	8.28%	16.68%	22.22%	28.2%	31.9%	33.5%
Others	18.09%	10.46%	8.72%	11.2%	7.6%	20.2%

Source: 1980-1989 elections, Yun-han Chu, *Crafting Democracy in Taiwan* (Taipei: Institute for National Policy Research, 1992), 55; for 1992 election, Shao-chuan Leng and Cheng-yi Lin, "Political Change on Taiwan: Transition to Democracy?" *China Quarterly 136* (December 1993), 832; for 1995 election, author's compilation.

The DPP campaigned strongly for direct election of the president, and this party earns the most credit for pushing the perimeters of political liberty in Taiwan. Leng Shao-chuan and Lin Cheng-yi observe that the DPP does not yet compete on an equal footing with the KMT because of discriminatory aspects of electoral rules.[60] Continued KMT control over the three major television networks and party wealth limit opposition competitiveness.[61] Nevertheless, the entrance of the DPP and NP cracked the hegemony of the KMT in electoral politics. This represents the most significant new pattern of politics in Taiwan—multi-party competition.

Throughout this section, we have referred to other new aspects of campaigns and elections. Structural changes in the economy, pushing mostly Taiwanese business leaders of conglomerates into positions of increasing economic ownership and control, have intersected with structural changes in the polity—particularly the indigenization of the KMT elite. Changing norms of electoral competition, requiring vast new resources, have opened the doors to penetration of the state by economic interests, a subject to which we turn in chapter 5.

While large economic organizations now play an active role in Taiwan's campaigns and elections, political parties, including the KMT, have reduced influence and are less able to control the electoral process. Candidates themselves are increasingly responsible for their campaigns. They are more likely to be unknown self-starters than stalwarts of the party organization. They must form their own candidate support groups to supply the resources for increasingly expensive campaigns. Once elected, they are virtual free agents, even if they carry a party's nomination. A recently elected independent KMT legislator (and at 33 one of the youngest) remarked:

> In the past, the party's influence was strong, but now it is weak, and they can't push us (legislators) around. I was not nominated by the party; I was on my own. At last they said they agreed with my candidacy, but they didn't support me. . . . Now, your personal relationships are most important in the campaign. Few legislators are elected because of the support of any political party. Most of us are elected based on our personal characteristics.[62]

This individualization of electoral politics is the single most important factor in the recent volatility of Taiwan's councils, assemblies, and legislatures. Political parties are not yet irrelevant, but they have far fewer means to discipline politicians than previously.

Demise of the Party-State in Taiwan?

Taiwan has entered its democratic transition as a mature, industrialized state. By 1997 it possessed these defining characteristics of democracy:

- Party competition for all offices, races that determine significant   outcomes for the population
- Free elections, regularly scheduled, without obvious discrimination against individuals or groups based on gender, ethnicity, religion, or class
- Print media free from government control
- Protected rights of political speech and writing
- A highly educated and attentive public
- A thriving economic system not dominated by any of the parties in competition

However, the critical stage in democratization, *consolidation,* has not yet been completed. Troubling factors include the KMT's enterprises, its continued control over electronic media, and the lack of administrative neutrality in the state. Recent challenges point to continued tension over the party's control.

KMT Enterprises

Over its long life, the KMT has accumulated vast wealth. The party has sizable holdings of land and buildings. Most important is party control over business corporations. In 1997, there were nearly 150 KMT enterprises. Some were quite small, but others were large trading companies, investment houses, and manufacturing firms. The total amount of party assets in December 1995 was US $3 billion, and profits during 1996 were about $300 million.[63]

KMT enterprises expanded aggressively from 1988 to 1993, a period when the party opened new enterprises at a rate of one every two months. One explanation for expansion was the democracy movement and opposition criticism of the mixing of national and party budgets. This led to the 1993 law on the Organization of Civic Groups, which required the party to register its firms with the government. A second explanation for expansion was economic liberalization, which led to revisions in the banking and finance services laws that had protected KMT enterprises. At the 14th party congress in 1993, Liu Tai-ying, chairman of the KMT-invested China Development Corp., became head of a new business management committee. A former Cornell classmate of Lee Teng-hui, Liu developed the aggressive, profit-driven expansion strategy. He directed a reduction in the percentage of shares held by the KMT in individual companies, shifting toward portfolio investing and overseas projects.[64]

Economist Chang Ching-hsi calls the KMT's business network "the most important economic problem in Taiwan". In his view, party enterprises continue to skew Taiwan's economy through their connection to political leadership. Their privileged position makes it difficult for other firms to compete with them.[65] Critics allege that even with a minority of shares, the party can gain easy access to government contracts. The KMT also is able to influence the stock market through coordinated purchases and sales, most recently displayed when reports that the KMT was buying shares in the construction industry drove the share index up 3 percent.[66] Moreover, in the view of critics, the possession of enormous assets by the KMT has corrupted the morality of party members and the party itself.[67] For these reasons, at the December 1996 National Development Conference, opponents of KMT enterprises adopted a "four nos" platform: "Party-run enterprises should not operate monopolies, undertake public projects, bid for government purchase contracts, or invest on the Chinese mainland".

The KMT's wealth constitutes an incomparable political resource. More important than the dollar figure of party assets is the economic control, which no competitor can match. Moreover, the party is linked with business conglomerates and state-owned enterprises, a three-legged gargantuan that, in the opinion of critics, threatens the democratic reforms of the last decade. At the least, in an era of money politics, with campaigns for office highly dependent on donations, the KMT is very difficult to beat.

Media Influence

The last remnant of party control over newspapers was its ownership of the Central News Agency, long a target of criticism from opposition parties. Early in 1997, the KMT transferred all its shares in the agency to the central government, not only to appease the opposition but to remove itself from a money-losing business. However, the party has not privatized the electronic media.

One of Taiwan's three primary television stations is owned outright by the party, the second by the military, and the third by the provincial government. Although the government pledged neutrality during the presidential elections of 1996, news coverage retained some bias against the opposition candidates. Scholars who conducted a content analysis of six TV stations found that state-owned broadcast stations were far more likely than privately owned cable TV stations to give greater coverage and more sound bites to the KMT presidential and vice presidential candidates. They tended to use ruling party officials as principal news sources, and covered more news favorable to the KMT candidates than to their opponents.[68] When the party sought renewal of its lease of Taipei city-owned land for station operations, Mayor Chen Shui-bian (Taiwan's most influential DPP leader) insisted on TTV's neutrality; he also directed a city employee to count the minutes and seconds in the channel's coverage of opposition leaders.

Party spokesmen claim that KMT influence over the media is quite limited. On the one hand, they point to the popularity of cable TV, which reaches 70 percent of the market and is not under party control,[69] the planned development of a fourth broadcasting station by a group of DPP members, and the passage in late May 1997 of legislation authorizing the establishment of a public TV station in Taiwan. On the other hand, party defenders suggest that KMT defectors have greater influence in the broadcast media and are more likely to support the New Party than the KMT policy line. Members of opposition parties, however, are nearly unanimous in their belief that KMT influence over electronic media distorts the political marketplace.

Lack of Administrative Neutrality

An intractable obstacle in Taiwan's democratic consolidation is the lack of administrative neutrality due to party control over state functions. For example, the military and security apparatus of the state has not been fully depoliticized.[70] And there is continued interpenetration of party and state roles and functions in national policy-making.[71] Asked whether the last decade of democratization had reduced the role of the KMT central standing committee in setting the direction for state policy, a party official and senior bureaucrat said: "Nothing has changed".[72]

Separating the party from the state presents a huge challenge to Taiwan's rulers and population. Recent events, however, suggest that the changes in Taiwan's civil society will force a decoupling of party and state in the future.

Broadening the Civil Society

Taiwan's opposition parties have appropriated new social movements and made them relevant in elections. The women's movement gained influence in 1995, and women have demonstrated new electoral strength. In 1997, DPP candidate Annette Lu won a by-election to fill the Taoyuan county seat vacated by the gangland slaying of the KMT incumbent.[73] Annette Lu's victory brought 8 of 25 city and county governments under DPP control, in areas representing over 50 percent of Taiwan's population. The success of female candidates prompted KMT leaders to replace the Interior Minister with a woman in May 1997.

The decline of the party's ability to control social forces was dramatically revealed in two demonstrations conducted in Taipei during May 1997. On May 4, a crowd of 50,000 participated in a march dubbed "Walking for Taiwan" to protest the government's apparent indifference to deteriorating social order. (Protesters objected to the government's inability to solve three high-profile murders over the preceding six months. The most recent case was the kidnapping and brutal murder of Pai Hsiao-yen, daughter of TV celebrity Pai Ping-ping.) Demonstrators demanded that the president apologize and that Premier Lien Chan resign. The demonstration's chief organizer, You Ying of the Humanistic Education Foundation, pointed out that the event was not led by politicians, but expressed efforts of "concerned people".[74] No political speeches were delivered and no party's flags were flown, but opposition parties clearly supported (and had a hand in) the demonstration.

Two weeks later, on May 18, nearly 100,000 demonstrators marched on the presidential office and made the same demands. The crowd included members of more than 500 civic organizations representing students, college professors, Buddhists, and other groups. Protesters waved signs reading "shame", "grief", and "take a hike". In response to the protests, President Lee did apologize for the lapses in public order, but declined to accept the premier's resignation before the National Assembly concluded its revision of the constitution (scheduled for July 1997).[75]

KMT party leaders openly discussed the negative impacts that policy failures such as in crime control would have on electoral fortunes. Of equal importance is the serious deterioration of KMT ties to local factions at the county level. A DPP legislator commented on the usefulness of controlling counties for the mobilization of voters in elections for the legislature and the presidency:

> President Lee is now a lame duck. His popularity has plunged, and he can't help KMT candidates very much. The day is approaching when Taiwan will be under DPP control.[76]

Theoretical Implications

What explains the KMT's transformation, and how does it help us understand the process of democratization globally? A number of scholars have examined this issue, for example, Huntington and O'Donnell and Schmitter[77] and with specific reference to the Taiwan case Cheng and Haggard, Chu, Gold, Hood, Tien, Wu[78] and other scholars cited throughout this chapter. What is most clear from this literature is that the process of democratization is highly complex, and no single factor is sufficient and necessary to its development universally. Theories of democratic change are imprecise and cannot account for individual variation in the nearly 40 countries that have undergone democratization in the last quarter-century.

Three factors and conditions figure in most of the accounts of Taiwan's democratization: authoritarian withdrawal, American pressure, and the force of domestic opposition. Authoritarian withdrawal refers to a process of political reform initiated and directed by the state's rulers.[79] It defeats the immediate self-interest of ruling elites to withdraw from or share power, and the reform path, as Huntington reminds us, is filled with obstacles.[80] Scholars writing on Taiwan's political reforms correctly emphasize the strategic calculations made by the KMT elite. Increasingly, scholarly attention is focusing on the successful timing of Taiwan's democratization.[81] Regrettably, research has failed to turn up complete information on the motivation behind Chiang Ching-kuo's decisive actions in 1986, which made irreversible the movement toward competitive elections and functional democracy.

Potential US reactions figured in the calculations of both the ruling elite and the opposition. Taiwan relies on American support against pressures from mainland China, and for this reason its record on human rights is subject to greater scrutiny than that of the PRC. The United States reacted negatively to the extensive arrests and heavy sentences imposed on leaders of the Kaohsiung Incident of 1979, which was violent. Opposition leaders who established the DPP in 1986 gathered peacefully and appropriated potent cultural symbols: they formed the party on Teacher's Day in Chung-shan Tang, where Japanese surrendered to Chinese Nationalists in 1945. Although the Garrison Command urged the arrest of the organizers, Chiang Ching-kuo's course was clear: to do so would bring American pressure that the regime would be unlikely to counteract.

An even larger group of analysts points to the grassroots origins of Taiwan's political reform. Notwithstanding the repression of the regime in the White Terror, opposition leaders, often imprisoned or forcibly exiled, applied pressure on the regime to reform and took advantage of each opportunity to develop support and mobilize for political change. Moreover, they skillfully organized groups supporting liberalization in whatever venues permitted them. Opposition leaders also took great personal risks, and many spent precious years in jail for their courageous campaign to democratize Taiwan. For example, the decision of opposition leaders to found the Democratic Progressive Party in 1986 was a gamble, one they could lose only at great cost.

Cheng and Haggard's analysis of regime transformation in Taiwan attunes us to the importance of interaction between the agents of political change and their bargaining positions with both the state and possible coalition partners.[82] The outcome, they argue, depends on how the agenda for transition is set by different sides and how they exploit the different arenas—such as the Legislative Yuan or the streets—to accomplish their objectives.

Taiwan's rapid economic growth contributed both to authoritarian withdrawal and opposition pressure. At the top end, Taiwan's wealth allowed the KMT elite to make generous side payments to conservative opponents of reform (for example, retirement bonuses for elderly members of the National Assembly and Legislative Yuan who were retired involuntarily). At the bottom, economic growth and change spawned new social interests, which pressured the regime for institutionalized forms to accommodate their participation.

Events in both regional and international arenas encouraged Taiwan's democratic transition. The fall of first the Marcos regime in the Philippines and then the Chun Doo Hwan government in South Korea had important, though perhaps not decisive, repercussions for Taiwan's reform. The international climate of political change and liberalization encouraged reforms both within the regime and outside it.

Conclusion

Over a period of 12 years, the Chinese Nationalist Party has been transformed from the single party of a "soft" authoritarian state to the leading (and still dominant) party in a multi-party system. The party is now more open with respect to its rank and file and more pluralistic in its internal operations. The establishment first of the DPP, then the splitting off of the *non-mainstream* faction into the NP and, in late 1996, the formation of a new independence party from the DPP itself created a highly pluralistic and fluid political market in Taiwan. To compete successfully in that market, the KMT has had to emphasize cultivation of its political machine over ideological remolding. And the nature of that machine has undergone significant change as the *mainstream* faction of the party embraces both local factional leaders and conglomerate elites in Taiwan's new political economy.

The dominance of the party frustrates the full autonomy of the state, but in recent years, Taiwan's government structures have become somewhat more independent, a subject to which we turn in the next chapter. Most noteworthy have been changes in the legitimacy of the Legislative Yuan, which is now fully elected, and in which the KMT had, in 1997, the slimmest of majorities. The party has probably withdrawn farthest from its previous pattern of corporatist control, the subject of chapter 5. Most observers have focused on democratic elections of officials, but there is now greater freedom for individuals and groups in society. This growing pluralism augurs well for the development of an autonomous society in Taiwan.

Taiwan now must complete the consolidation of its democracy. The greatest hurdle is the continuing penetration of the state by the KMT. Decoupling the party from the state is unlikely to be an easy or quick process, but at least now there exists a very broad constituency for democratic reform in Taiwan.

Notes

[1] Sections of this chapter are based on the author's article, 'Transformation of the Chinese Nationalist Party (KMT): Adjusting to Liberalization', in the *American Journal of Chinese Studies*, vol. 5, no. 2 (October 1997).

[2] Edwin A. Winckler, 'Institutionalization and Participation on Taiwan: From Hard to Soft Authoritarianism?' *China Quarterly* 99 (September 1984), 482; Tun-jen Cheng and Stephan Haggard, 'Regime Transformation in Taiwan: Theoretical and Comparative Perspectives', in Tun-jen Cheng and Stephan Haggard, eds., *Political Change in Taiwan* (Boulder, CO: Lynne Rienner Publishers, 1992), 6.

[3] Yangsun Chou and Andrew J. Nathan, 'Democratizing Transition in Taiwan', *Asian Survey*, vol. XXVII, no. 3 (March 1987), 286; Linda Chao and Ramon H. Myers, 'The

First Chinese Democracy: Political Development of the Republic of China on Taiwan, 1986-94', *Asian Survey*, vol. XXXIV, no. 3 (March 1994), 220; Steven J. Hood, *The Kuomintang and the Democratization of Taiwan* (Boulder, CO: Westview Press, 1997), 20.

[4] Jurgen Domes, 'The 13th Party Congress of the Kuomintang: Towards Political Competition?' *China Quarterly* 118 (June 1989), 355.

[5] Yu-shan Wu, 'Marketization of Politics: The Taiwan Experience', *Asian Survey*, vol. XXIX, no. 4 (April 1989), 395.

[6] Hood, 1997, 29.

[7] Hung-mao Tien, *The Great Transition: Political and Social Change in the Republic of China* (Stanford, CA: Hoover Institution Press, 1989), 75.

[8] Tien, 1989, 44.

[9] Harmon Zeigler, *Pluralism, Corporatism, and Confucianism: Political Association and Conflict Regulation in the United States, Europe, and Taiwan* (Philadelphia: Temple University Press, 1988), 176; Michael Ying-mao Kao, 'The Power Structure in Taiwan's Political Economy', *Asian Survey*, vol. XXXVI, no. 3 (March 1996), 289.

[10] Peter R. Moody, Jr., *Political Change in Taiwan: A Study of Ruling Party Adaptability* (New York: Praeger, 1992), 28.

[11] Chao-hsien Liu, *Research on the Republic of China's Law on Industrial Associations* (in Chinese) (Taipei: Ming-ho Publishing Co., 1993), 15.

[12] Liu, 1993, 32.

[13] Tien, 1989, 86.

[14] Laurie Underwood, 'Inside the Ruling Party's Moneymaking Machine—KMT, Inc', *TOPICS*, vol. 27, no. 4 (April 1997), 19.

[15] Tien, 1989, 86.

[16] Personal interview with Lin Yu-hsiang, Deputy Director, Department of Policy Research of the Nationalist Party, May 19, 1997.

[17] Tien, 1989, 92.

[18] Tien, 1989, 94.

[19] Winckler, 1984, 481.

[20] Wu, 1989, 398.

[21] See Jaushieh Joseph Wu, *Taiwan's Democratization* (Hong Kong: Oxford University Press, 1995), 90-97.

[22] Gerald A. McBeath, 'Taiwan in 1976: Chiang in the Saddle', *Asian Survey,* vol. XVII, no. 1 (January 1977), 32; see also Wen-cheng Wu, *The Kuomintang and Political Development in Taiwan since 1968* (Ph.D. diss., Columbia University, 1987), 151-55.

[23] Bruce J. Dickson, 'The Kuomintang before Democratization: Organizational Change and the Role of Elections', in Hung-mao Tien, *Taiwan's Electoral Politics and Democratic Transition* (Armonk, NY: M. E. Sharpe, 1996), 52; also see Kau, 1996, 291.

[24] Domes, 1989, 348.

[25] Ts'ai Ling and Ramon H. Myers, 'Surviving the Rough-and-Tumble of Presidential Politics in an Emerging Democracy: The 1990 Elections in the Republic of China on Taiwan', *China Quarterly* 129 (March 1992), 131.

[26] John F. Copper, 'The KMT's 14th Party Congress: Toward Unity or Disunity?' *American Journal of Chinese Studies*, vol. II, no. 2 (October 1994), 171.

[27] Personal interviews with officials in the KMT's organization and policy departments, February 25, 1996 and May 18, 1997; also see James A. Robinson and Julian Baum, 'Party Primaries in Taiwan: Reappraisal', *Asian Affairs*, vol. 22, no. 2 (Summer 1995).

[28] Wu, 1989, 398.

[29] After Chiang Ching-kuo's death in 1988, the *mainstream* faction initially was weaker within the party organization than the *non-mainstream* faction. Newly elected central committee members who supported Lee Teng-hui formed the *Chih-shih Hui* (Wisdom Club). This faction enrolled 54 members, mostly legislators, at its peak in 1991, and provided critical support to the consolidation of support for Lee within the party. Tien and Chu note the large number of conflicts between the factions on other issues pertaining to democratization. See Hung-mao Tien and Yun-han Chu, 'Building Democracy in Taiwan', *China Quarterly* 148 (December 1996), 1145-48; also see Ling and Myers, 1992, 145-47.

[30] Steven J. Hood, 'Political Change in Taiwan: The Rise of Kuomintang Factions', *Asian Survey*, vol. XXXVI, no. 5 (May 1996), 481; also see C. L. Chiou, *Democratizing Oriental Despotism* (New York: St. Martin's Press, 1995), especially his account of the National Affairs Conference of 1990, 105-137.

[31] *Republic of China Yearbook 1997*, 99.

[32] John Fuh-sheng Hsieh, 'The SNTV System and Its Political Implications', in Tien, 1996, 195; and Qingshan Tan, Peter Kien-hong Yu, and Wen-chun Chen, 'Local Politics in Taiwan: Democratic Consolidation', *Asian Survey*, vol. XXXVI, no. 5 (May 1996), 486.

[33] Andrew J. Nathan, 'The Legislative Yuan Elections in Taiwan: Consequences of the Electoral System', *Asian Survey*, vol. XXXIII, no. 4 (April 1993), 428.

[34] Alan M. Wachman, *Taiwan: National Identity and Democratization* (Armonk, NY: M. E. Sharpe, 1994), 207.

[35] Ming-tong Chen, 'Local Factions and Elections in Taiwan's Democratization', in Tien, 1996, 176-77. For an earlier treatment of local factions, see Arthur J. Lerman, *Taiwan's Politics: The Provincial Assemblyman's World* (Washington, DC: University Press of America, 1978), 99-180.

[36] Dickson, 1996, 47-48; see also Joseph Bosco, 'Faction versus Ideology: Mobilization Strategies in Taiwan's Elections', *China Quarterly* 137 (March 1994), 29-30.

[37] Ming-tong Chen, cited in Hung-mao Tien, 'Elections and Taiwan's Democratic Development', in Tien, 1996, 19.

[38] Joseph Bosco, 'Taiwan's Factions', in Murray A. Rubinstein, ed., *The Other Taiwan: 1945 to the Present* (Armonk, NY: M. E. Sharpe, 1994), 128-29.

[39] Te-fu Huang, 'Elections and the Evolution of the Kuomintang', in Tien, 1996, 127, 130.

[40] Personal interview with Ming-tong Chen, College of Law, National Taiwan University, May 24, 1997.

[41] Bosco, 1994, 130.

[42] Cited in Linda Gail Arrigo, 'From Democratic Movement to Bourgeois Democracy', in. Rubinstein, 1994, 152.

[43] Nathan, 1993, 429.

[44] Tien, 1996, 20.

[45] *United Daily News*, June 19, 1996.

[46] *China News*, June 19, 1997.

[47] Hsieh, 1996, 199.

[48] Shelly Rigger, 'The Risk of Reform: Factional Conflict in Taiwan's 1989 Local Elections', *American Journal of Chinese Studies*, vol. II, no. 2 (October 1994), 135.

[49] Yu-shan Wu, 'Taiwan in 1994: Managing a Critical Relationship', *Asian Survey*, vol. XXXV, no. 1 (January 1995), 68; Kau, 1996, 288, 302-03; Yun-han Chu and Tse-min Lin, 'The Process of Democratic Consolidation in Taiwan: Social Cleavage, Electoral Competition, and the Emerging Party System', in Tien, 1996, 88.

[50] Hsieh, 1996, 208.

[51] Personal interview with Robert Hsu, KMT legislator, March 23, 1996.

[52] Fu Hu and Ying-long Yu, 'Orientations of Voting', (in Chinese) *The Annals* 11 (Taipei: Chinese Association of Political Science), 225-79.

[53] I-chou Liu, 'The Behavior of Taiwanese Voters in 1992', in Tien, 1996, 239.

[54] Yun-han Chu, *Crafting Democracy in Taiwan* (Taipei: Institute for National Policy Research, 1992), 61.

[55] A large number of scholars has studied Taiwan's electoral behavior since democratization. In addition to party appeals and electoral issues, they also have investigated the importance of candidates' performance as compared to promises in voters' decisions. See, for example, John Fuh-sheng Hsieh, Dean Lacey, and Emerson M.S. Niou, 'Retrospective and Prospective Voting in a One-Party Democracy: Taiwan's 1996 Presidential Election', (Paper delivered at the 1996 annual meeting of the American Political Science Association, San Francisco, CA, August 30, 1996).

[56] Tun-jen Cheng and Yung-ming Hsu, 'Issue Structure, the DPP's Factionalism, and Party Realignment', in Tien, 1996, 157.

[57] Chu and Lin, 1996, 88.

[58] Chu and Lin, 1996, 89.

[59] Chu and Lin, 1996, 88.

[60] Shao-chuan Leng and Cheng-yi Lin, 'Political Change on Taiwan: Transition to Democracy?' *China Quarterly* 136 (December 1993), 832.

[61] Simon Long, 'Taiwan's National Assembly Elections', *China Quarterly* 129 (March 1992), 223.

[62] Personal interview with Hsu Shu-po, KMT legislator, April 16, 1996.

[63] Underwood, 1997, 19.

[64] Underwood, 1997, 18.

[65] Shih-meng S. Chen, Chung-cheng Lin, C.Y. Cyrus Chu, Ching-hsi Chang, Jan-ji Shih, and Jin-tan Liu, *Disintegrating KMT-State Capitalism: A Closer Look at Privatizing Taiwan's State- and Party-Owned Enterprises* (in Chinese) (Taipei: Taipei Society, 1991), 69.

[66] *Commercial Times*, June 24, 1997.

[67] Ching-hsi Chang, 'Party Enterprises, Members' Ethics, and Party Corruption', (in Chinese) *Taiwan Economic Review*, vol. 24, no. 2 (March 1995), 38.

[68] Ven-hwei Lo, Pu-tsung King, Ching-ho Chen, and Hwei-lin Huang, 'Political Bias in the News Coverage of Taiwan's First Presidential Election', (in Chinese) *Journal of Electoral Studies*, vol. 2, no. 2 (November 1996), 63-77.
[69] Illegal cable TV stations operated by DPP politicians were legalized in 1993. See Tien and Chu, 1996, 1155.
[70] Constance Squires Meaney, 'Liberalization, Democratization, and the Role of the KMT', in Cheng and Haggard, 1992, 111.
[71] Leng and Lin, 1992, 837; Hung-mao Tien, 'Transformation of an Authoritarian State: Taiwan's Development Experience', in Cheng and Haggard, 1992, 51; Tun-jen Cheng, 'Democratizing the Quasi-Leninist Regime in Taiwan', *World Politics* 42 (March 1989), 496.
[72] Personal interview with P. K. Chiang, Chairman, Council for Economic Planning and Development, May 31, 1997.
[73] The government's response to the slaying was to initiate a "spiritual reform" campaign, urging the press to print positive news stories instead of focusing on lurid murder cases.
[74] *United Daily News*, May 5, 1997.
[75] President Lee later changed his mind and extended Premier Lien's tenure until the conclusion of the KMT party congress in August 1997.
[76] Personal interview with Parris Chang, DPP legislator, May 19, 1997.
[77] Samuel P. Huntington, *The Third Wave: Democratization in the Late Twentieth Century* (Norman, OK: University of Oklahoma Press, 1991); Guillermo O'Donnell and Philippe C. Schmitter, *Transitions from Authoritarian Rule: Tentative Conclusions about Uncertain Democracies* (Baltimore, MD: Johns Hopkins University Press, 1986).
[78] Cheng and Haggard, 1992; Chu, 1992; Thomas B. Gold, 'Consolidating Taiwan's Democracy', (The Illinois-Taiwan Seminar Series, No. 1, Center for East Asian and Pacific Studies, University of Illinois at Urbana-Champaign), 1996; Hood, 1997; Tien, 1996; and Wu, 1995.
[79] Stephan Haggard and Robert R. Kaufman, *The Political Economy of Democratic Transitions* (Princeton, NJ: Princeton University Press, 1995).
[80] Samuel P. Huntington, *Political Order in Changing Societies* (New Haven: Yale University Press, 1968), 59.
[81] Christopher H. Achen, 'The Timing of Political Liberalization: Taiwan as the Canonical Case', (Paper presented at the annual meeting of the American Political Science Association, San Francisco, CA, August 30, 1996).
[82] Cheng and Haggard, 1992, 3.

4 Pluralism within the State

Introduction

The system of organizing political power in Taiwan is unique. Also singular is the changing role of constitutional government over the last five decades. Both have been deeply affected by Taiwan's economic and political liberalization.

Structure of the State System

The Republic of China is a republican and unitary state. The republican credentials of the state date to the 1911 revolution, which brought down China's last dynasty, the Ch'ing. In the 1947 constitution, republicanism was expressed in the "five-power constitution", the apparent invention of Sun Yat-sen.[1] Three of the powers or branches are based on the American system of separated powers: Executive Yuan, Legislative Yuan, and Judicial Yuan. The other two branches—Examination and Control (censorial)—are drawn from the Chinese tradition. These five branches, together with the president and the National Assembly, form the seven primary institutions of the state in Taiwan. Throughout Taiwan's modern history, the most important, however, have been the president and Executive Yuan.

 The state does not resemble exactly any other nation's system of government. Although it has some characteristics of the presidential system—independent election of the president, involvement in government, and strong military powers—it is not a presidential form of government. The branches do not have fully independent constitutional authority. Although it has some parliamentary characteristics—a premier whose selection was ratified by the national parliament (until constitutional amendment in 1997)—it is not a parliamentary system either. The cabinet is not selected from the parliament, and the parliament lacked the power to dissolve the government until 1997. Just what the system should resemble has been an issue of debate in constitutional revisions over the last decade.

 The state system, however, is clearly unitary. Provincial and local governments lack autonomy. The central government may exercise direct administrative control over provincial and local governments. The authority of sub-national governments is constrained by the constitution and by statutes; most serious in limiting autonomy of these governments is their fiscal dependence on the central government. There is a high level of redundancy between the national and provincial governments because they perform many of the same functions over the same territory. The KMT's one-China policy, under which Taiwan is both a province of China and a national identity, made it difficult until recently to consider streamlining the operation of provincial government.

Changes in Constitutional Government

The first article of the 1947 constitution founds the state upon the Three People's Principles of Sun Yat-sen and creates "a democratic republic of the people, to be governed by the people, and for the people".[2] The first principle, nationalism, advocates equality of sovereign status for the Republic of China in the world of nations, and it promises equality for all ethnic groups within the nation. The third principle, people's livelihood, dedicates government to the popular welfare.

The second principle, democracy, is most relevant to the design of the constitution. It is the guiding doctrine behind the organization and structure of Taiwan's government.[3] The constitution divides government powers among seven institutions and delineates a system of checks and balances between the government's branches.

The early articles (9-24) of the constitution list individual rights and civil liberties common to citizens living in democracies. Modeled after American constitutional concepts, these include rights to equality, work, livelihood, property, education, voting, and holding public office. Basic freedoms included are those of speech, residence, travel, assembly, confidential communication, religion, and association. However, the temporary provisions and martial law severely curbed the exercise of these rights and freedoms, as well as the limitations on government power, from the late 1940s to 1987.

Martial law was declared on Taiwan in May 1949, and remained in effect until July 1987, even though Taiwan was not an active combat area during that period. The government justified continued limitation on freedoms because of tense relations with China. The chief provision of martial law was to give military commanders, specifically the Taiwan Garrison Command, authority over administrative and judicial officials. It monitored entries into Taiwan, authorized citizens' trips abroad, reviewed and censored books and periodicals, and approved meetings and rallies.[4] In violation of the constitution, which guaranteed civilian trials for civilians, under martial law some 10,000 cases involving civilians were decided by military tribunals.[5] Moreover, the powerful Garrison Command restricted civil rights, such as free speech, and subjected the population to restrictions and surveillance, actions the constitution explicitly forbade. Martial law was wildly unpopular in Taiwan, and it was a critical issue in Taiwan's relations with Western states, especially the United States.

In even greater conflict with democratic aims of the constitution were "the Provisional Amendments for the Period of Mobilization of the Communist Rebellion", called the "temporary provisions". Adopted in 1948, these provisions gave unlimited authority to the president in order to deal with the national crisis represented by the civil war. He could stay in office indefinitely, change at will the organization and personnel of the government, and take any other emergency measures deemed necessary— without procedural restrictions mentioned in the constitution.[6]   An important institution that grew out of the temporary provisions was the National Security Council (NSC), formed in 1967 to coordinate military and security strategy. Because of the broad reach of emergency powers, the NSC could influence virtually any policy area and even approved the annual budget. It was not until 1986, under reformist directives of President Chiang Ching-kuo, that the emergency decrees were lifted. Under the national security act of 1993, the NSC's status became official (constitutionally mandated under the Executive Yuan) and accountable (subject to oversight by the Legislative Yuan).[7]

Sources of Pluralistic Change

Organizing political parties directly contravened martial law and the temporary provisions, and the formation of the DPP was thus the primary catalyst for change. In initiating the KMT's reforms, Chiang Ching-kuo said "the party must accommodate itself to the changing times and environment".[8] The growth of opposition to the KMT on Taiwan, and opposition demands for further political liberalization and democratization, created the domestic environment to which Chiang referred. Moreover, votes for opposition candidates in previous elections made it obvious that the democratization movement had broad support from Taiwan's increasingly wealthy population.

Taiwan's democratization campaign had strong support in overseas Chinese communities, especially those in the United States. It also had very strong allies in the US Congress. Foreign reaction to the Kaohsiung Incident of 1979 had been intense. Reaction in the US to the assassination of Henry Liu, a Taiwan-born United States citizen who had written a highly critical, unauthorized biography of Chiang Ching-kuo, was virulent, particularly when it was learned that the assassins had colluded with Taiwan's military intelligence agencies. Political reforms were a way to deflect foreign pressures and to raise Taiwan's international status.

In this chapter we review the institutions of the state for signs of growing pluralism. We focus on the presidency, Executive Yuan, and Legislative Yuan, paying less attention to the Examination, Control, and Judicial Yuans. We also examine the major proposals for constitutional revision that were at the forefront of discussions in late 1996 and 1997.

Presidency

Historical Evolution

The president of the Republic of China on Taiwan is the single most important official in the nation. The source of that power resides partly in the constitution, which makes the president head of state and grants sizable influence over government operations. Both the temporary provisions and martial law endowed presidents with extraordinary powers, which exceeded the limits of the constitution. The ability to lead the KMT is an indispensable asset for any president. Personal qualities such as rectitude, sincerity, and benevolence are equally important in new institutions of the state in any culture, and are especially prized in Confucian societies.

Taiwan has had four presidents since nationalist officials brought the government of the Republic of China to its shores in 1949. Serving first and longest was Chiang Kai-shek (1949-1975). It was Chiang who imposed the temporary provisions, and he benefited from their application. He headed the KMT throughout this period, using the exalted title of *Tsung-ts'ai* (director-general), which expired with him. Although Chiang's style of leadership was distant and aloof, he was generally accepted by Taiwan's population for his emulation of traditional Confucian leaders.

At the time of Chiang's death, his son Chiang Ching-kuo was premier. Serving as vice president was Yen Chia-kan, who had spent most of his career in the bureaucracy, with expertise in finance and economic policy-making. Yen completed the rest of Chiang's term, but he did not succeed him as chair of the KMT (which was Chiang Ching-kuo's inheritance). As president, Yen was colorless and forgettable.

Chiang Ching-kuo was elected president by the National Assembly in 1978 and served until his death from diabetes in January 1988. Chiang took full advantage of powers available under the temporary provisions, and used them to open up seats for Taiwanese in the Legislative Yuan. He was a popular leader, admired for his integrity and incorruptibility. Although no democrat, he launched the political reforms of both party and state in 1986. In selecting a vice president for his second term, Chiang opted for Lee Teng-hui. He also announced before his death that no member of the Chiang family would succeed him as leader of the Republic of China, thereby breaking the dynastic cycle.

Lee completed the remainder of Chiang's term and became the chair of the KMT; in 1990, he was elected president in his own right by the National Assembly. In 1996, he won his second term, this time in a direct election.

Lee Teng-hui is unlike Taiwan's previous presidents in two respects. He was born in Taiwan, in 1923, in a village outside Taipei, and most of his early career consisted of academic and research positions, not political ones. After completing high school in Taipei, Lee became one of a handful of Chinese admitted to Kyoto Imperial University in Japan during Taiwan's Japanese occupation. After the war, he studied agricultural economics at National Taiwan University (NTU), then completed a master's degree at Iowa State University. He returned to Taiwan and worked with the Taiwan Provincial Department of Agriculture and Forestry, taught part-time at NTU, and was a research fellow at the Taiwan Cooperative Bank. Lee received his doctoral degree, also in agricultural economics, from Cornell University in 1968, and his dissertation won the prize of the American Association for Agricultural Economics the following year.

Lee's central government service began in 1957, when he became a specialist for the Joint Commission on Rural Reconstruction (JCRR). He moved up the ranks to become senior specialist in 1961 and chief of the JCRR's Rural Economics Division in 1970. Chiang Ching-kuo moved Lee into the cabinet in 1972 as minister without portfolio. Lee demonstrated his competence, expertise, and loyalty, and in 1978, was rewarded with the post of Taipei city mayor, followed, in 1981, by the governorship of Taiwan province. At the conclusion of his term as governor, Chiang selected him to be his vice president.

Today, supporters of President Lee describe him as charismatic and a champion of democracy; opponents (the most strident were members of the *non-mainstream* faction and now are New Party members) label him corrupt and disingenuous. Before his elevation to the presidency, however, Lee acted as an important liaison between the KMT and the opposition. As a member of the Presbyterian church, which has strongly supported indigenization and democracy, and as a person, Lee was regarded as incorruptible and diligent, and therefore worthy of opposition respect.

Powers

The president's powers are extensive. As chief of state, he represents the Republic of China in its foreign relations and state functions. He concludes treaties, and promulgates laws and decrees (with the assent of the premier and relevant minister). As the chief national security officer, he commands the army, navy, and air force. He declares war and cease fires. He also convenes the National Assembly, grants amnesty and commutations, and confers honors and decorations.

The presidential powers of appointment are more inclusive than those in most presidential systems. He has broad powers of appointment and removal of civil service officers and military officers. He appoints the premier and the auditor-general of the Control Yuan (with the assent of the legislature), the president, vice president, and grand justices of the Judicial Yuan (with the consent of the National Assembly), the president, vice president, and members of the Examination Yuan, and the president, vice president, and members of the Control Yuan.[9]

The president also may issue emergency orders, but unlike the temporary provisions, the president's power requires the confirmation of the Legislative Yuan within 10 days. The president is assisted in his responsibilities by the office of the president, directed by a secretary-general and deputies, and serviced by several bureaus and offices. Four additional offices are associated with the presidency: Academia Sinica, Academia Historica, the National Unification Council, and the National Security Council. The National Unification Council was established in 1990 to recommend unification policies to the president. It has approved guidelines for national unification, which express Taiwan's policy toward the Chinese mainland.

Direct Election of the President

Prior to 1996, presidents of the Republic of China were elected indirectly. The National Assembly performed this leavening role, along with its duties in amending the constitution.[10] By the late 1980s, however, the National Assembly was an anachronism. Its members were last elected in 1948; many had died, and the remainder were elderly and grossly unrepresentative of Taiwan's population.

President Lee convened a National Affairs Conference in mid-1990 to make proposals for further political reforms. Among its priority recommendations were the retirement of elderly parliamentarians and new elections for Taiwan's parliamentary bodies (chiefly for the Legislative Yuan and National Assembly). With this establishment of consensus and political support, and with a favorable opinion of the Council of Grand Justices, National Assembly representatives left their seats involuntarily, and new elections were held in 1991. At this time, Lee also proclaimed the end of the Period of National Mobilization for Suppression of the Communist Rebellion and repealed the temporary provisions.

The newly elected ("Second") National Assembly evaluated many proposals for amendments to the constitution to further democratize Taiwan's polity. Among the most hotly debated was the proposal to directly elect the president, finally approved in 1994, with the first election scheduled for 1996. The following year the Legislative Yuan passed laws outlining electoral procedures: any political party winning 5 percent of the vote in a recent election, or collecting signatures of 1.5 percent of voters in recent parliamentary elections, could nominate candidates. The law also provided for 30 minutes of TV time for each candidate and for presidential debates.

Four teams of candidates contested Taiwan's first democratic presidential election. The KMT nominated incumbent president Lee Teng-hui, who selected premier Lien Chan as his running mate. In a fierce primary contest, the DPP selected professor and long-time political refugee Peng Ming-min as its presidential candidate. Peng chose popular legislator Frank Shieh (Hsieh Chang-ting) as his vice presidential candidate.

The other teams were former high officials of the KMT who entered the race via petition. Lin Yang-kang, Taiwanese and former head of the Judicial Yuan and vice-chair of the KMT, paired with Hao Po-ts'un, mainlander, former premier, and also vice-chair of the KMT, as vice president. They were endorsed by the New Party. The fourth team was Chen Li-an, KMT member, president of the Control Yuan, prominent Buddhist, and son of Chen Cheng, who introduced as his running mate Wang Ching-feng, the only female candidate in the race and a member of the Control Yuan.

The presidential elections occurred while the PRC conducted military exercises off Taiwan's shores to attempt to dampen support for Lee Teng-hui and what mainland authorities perceived to be a further movement toward Taiwan independence by holding democratic elections for the island's leadership. This attempt was counterproductive. The United States, whose position on Taiwan-mainland relations had been less than clear, dispatched two aircraft carrier groups to the Taiwan Strait (one carrier, aptly, was the Independence). In the opinion of most observers, tensions over the strait contributed to Lee Teng-hui's impressive 54 percent of the vote (for which over 76 percent of eligible voters turned out). Peng Ming-min gained a disappointing 21.1 percent, which caused the DPP to re-evaluate again its electoral strategy. Lin and Chen won 14.9 and 10 percent of the vote respectively.

Pluralism within the state is demonstrated emphatically in the process through which Taiwan's population has become directly connected to the presidency through democratic elections. Lee Teng-hui made a consistent set of appeals to the electorate throughout the long campaign, repeatedly emphasizing, *Ni shih wode Laoban* (You are my bosses). However, to stage the first successful campaign in China's history required immense resources. The KMT supplied many of these, but notable in this election were the huge financial contributions of business interests (mostly conglomerates) and the dedicated but equally expensive work of local factions. The contours of Taiwan's new political economy emerged during the first presidential elections.

Executive Yuan

Premier

Second in influence to the presidency is the Executive Yuan, headed by the premier. Taiwan's premier in 1997 was Lien Chan. Born in China's Shenhsi province, Lien came from a wealthy Tainan family. (In June 1997, *Forbes* magazine ranked Lien the 263rd richest Chinese worldwide and the richest Chinese politician.) He graduated from National Taiwan University with a degree in political science in 1957, then studied at the University of Chicago, receiving a master's in international law and diplomacy in 1961, and a doctorate in political science four years later. Lien taught at two US universities before returning to chair NTU's political science department in 1968.

Lien's political career began in 1975, when he was appointed ambassador to El Salvador. The next year, he became director of the youth affairs department of the KMT; in 1978, Lien became deputy secretary-general of the party but within a few months began serving as chair of the Executive Yuan's national youth commission. Other posts in Lien's quick rise to power included minister of transportation and communications (December 1981), vice premier (1987), minister of foreign affairs (1988), and governor of Taiwan province (1990).

The president nominates the premier, who serves at his pleasure. The Legislative Yuan held the authority to confirm the president's appointment of premier until the constitution was amended in 1997; it lacked the power to dissolve the cabinet until then. The legislative confirmation power became an issue in 1996-97. Lien Chan had served as premier since February 1993. After his cabinet resigned in January 1996, the president renominated Lien, and the legislature confirmed him. However, Lien was President Lee's running mate and won election as vice president in March 1996. After the inauguration, the president asked Lien to continue as premier, but he replaced most members of the cabinet.

The Legislative Yuan cried foul, protesting that the same person could not serve as both vice president and premier (on two previous occasions in the Republic of China's history, one person concurrently has held both posts). Also, legislators called on the president to forward Lien's nomination to them for approval. President Lee demurred, stating that Lien had already been confirmed. The Legislative Yuan asked the Council of Grand Justices for a ruling on the constitutionality of the president's actions. In an ambiguous ruling, the council admitted that the action was ill-advised but did not violate the constitution. For the next year, the premier did not attend sessions of the Legislative Yuan.

The premier supervises the operations of all agencies in the Executive Yuan. He becomes acting president if the presidency and vice presidency are vacant. He also countersigns laws and decrees proclaimed by the president.[11]

The premier directs relationships between the Executive and Legislative Yuans. He presents administrative reports and policies to the Legislative Yuan, and he responds (with ministers and chairs of commissions) to interpellations of legislators. The Legislative Yuan has the power to request the Executive Yuan to alter an administrative policy it finds objectionable; with the president's approval, the premier may ask the legislature to reconsider such a resolution. If, after reconsideration, two-thirds of the legislators uphold their resolution, the premier must either adhere to it or resign (unprecedented in the history of inter-branch relations). Similar procedures apply if the premier finds statutory, budgetary, or treaty bills passed by the legislature difficult to execute.

Cabinet

Other important figures at the pinnacle of administrative power are the vice premier, ministers and chairmen of commissions, and a half dozen ministers of state. Most of these officials, together with the premier, compose the Executive Yuan Council or cabinet. The president also appoints the members of the cabinet on the recommendation of the premier. With the exception of the premiership of Chiang Ching-kuo from 1972 to 1978, presidents have hand-picked members of the cabinet. In the last cabinet shuffle of 1996, President Lee selected all but two new cabinet members.

The cabinet is a policy-making and implementing body, and it meets every Thursday morning. Cabinet meetings follow by one day the KMT central standing committee meeting, and the latter (and, of course, the president) is the source of important policies. The premier presides, and cabinet members may be joined by heads of the office of the president and commissioners who are not of cabinet rank. The cabinet discusses and decides on statutory measures to be submitted to the legislature. It debates changes to the next fiscal year's budget proposal, which must be presented to the Legislative Yuan three months before the end of each fiscal year. It also discusses matters of common concern to several ministries and commissions, such as changes in investment policy or responses to rising crime rates.

Of 38 cabinet-level officials in 1997, the majority were male (five officials, or 13 percent, were female). All but one were members of the KMT, and one-third were central standing committee members. The balance between mainlanders and Taiwanese was almost even: eighteen were born in mainland China, and 20 in Taiwan province. The average age of these high officials was 58. The oldest was 75, the youngest 48. Most had direct experience of the post-war reconstruction of Taiwan.

Taiwan's high officials tend to be remarkably well-educated. Only one stopped his training at high school, four at college. Twenty (53 percent) had doctoral degrees (including three in law), and the remaining 12 (or 32 percent) had master's degrees. Most of these officials studied abroad. Of the 23 with foreign degrees, the vast majority (17 or 74 percent) studied in the United States. Three studied in Japan, two in Europe, and one in Canada.[12]

Executive Organization

There are eight ministries under the Executive Yuan: interior, foreign affairs, national defense, finance, education, justice, economic affairs, and transportation and communications. Ministries dealing with defense, finance, economic affairs, foreign affairs, and education are regarded as the most important.[13]

Also, there are 19 commissions, councils, and bureaus in the Executive Yuan. These include the Central Election Commission, Overseas Chinese Affairs Commission, Mongolian and Tibetan Affairs Commission, Directorate General of Budget, Accounting and Statistics, Government Information Office, Central Personnel Administration, Council of Agriculture, Council for Economic Planning and Development (CEPD), Council of Labor Affairs, the Research, Development and Evaluation Commission, Council for Cultural Affairs, National Science Council, Atomic Energy Council, National Youth Commission, Vocational Assistance Commission for Retired Servicemen (VARS), Mainland Affairs Council, Environmental Protection Administration (EPA), Fair Trade Commission, and Department of Health.[14] Finally, since 1969, the Central Bank of China has been placed administratively under the Executive Yuan.

Most of the commissions were formed to deal with new circumstances and demands. For example, the cabinet established the EPA in 1987 to address rising public demands for pollution control, and in 1990, it founded the Mainland Affairs Council to help manage the thawing of relations between Taiwan and mainland China. Proliferation of councils, commissions, and bureaus has made policy coordination imperative, and this is achieved through the cabinet's secretariat, CEPD, and task forces.

The secretariat staffs meetings of the cabinet. Its primary responsibility, however, is to coordinate the development of proposed laws and regulations for the Executive Yuan. The secretariat is divided into seven divisions, each of which works with a group of cognate ministries and commissions. For example, the fifth division covers the Ministry of Economic Affairs, CEPD, Council of Agriculture, and the Fair Trade Commission. Its director was placed in charge of developing responses to the outbreak of hoof-and-mouth disease in Taiwan's pig population in February 1997. She formed a task force of affected agencies to resolve such issues as environmental concerns over disposal of pig carcasses, thus restoring confidence in the industry and protecting pork prices.[15]

The CEPD is responsible for coordinating national economic planning and for setting economic priorities and targets. It conducts economic research and supervises major construction projects. Tien Hung-mao calls CEPD and its predecessors instrumental in promoting Taiwan's economic modernization:

> Technocrats in these agencies generally are well educated and professionally competent. Compared to their counterparts in some of the high-growth countries of the Third World, such as South Korea or Brazil, ROC technocrats are cautious planners . . . Their educational background appears to have contributed three important elements to their work style: a commitment to the market economy, a receptivity to modern management, and a style of planning that emphasizes steady growth, reflecting in part their engineering and science backgrounds.[16]

In 1997, CEPD was in charge of some of the most important tasks of government administration in Taiwan: plans for the Asia-Pacific Regional Operations Center (APROC, discussed in chapter 7), legal revisions necessary for privatizing most remaining state-owned enterprises (discussed in chapter 6), and revisions to the national pension system.[17]

The president frequently forms large task forces to coordinate policy planning. He also calls national policy-making conferences, such as the December 1996 National Development Conference, to form consensus on controversial issues.

Signs of Growing Autonomy in the Executive Yuan

The independence of government institutions in Taiwan has been compromised by the KMT, a Leninist party that directed the action of the state by dominating both political and government institutions. In Leninist states, the cabinet and party standing committee form an interlocking directorate. During its first four decades in Taiwan, the KMT charted the state's course by selecting and cultivating all political and institutional leaders. Most government officials, in fact, held party membership; however, the use of examinations to qualify officials up to the sub-cabinet level curbed party control somewhat. In Taiwan, all cabinet proposals excepting economic policies (on which there tends to be a high degree of consensus) have been screened by the party before adoption and implementation.[18] Nevertheless, the party's central standing committee increasingly meets in a fish bowl. Reporters and camera crews flock to the Wednesday meetings, and even the results of closed meetings are leaked quickly to the media.

Chiang Ching-kuo's endorsement of economic reform led to increased autonomy of state agencies in the 1970s. As premier, Chiang cultivated in the Executive Yuan (particularly in the economics and finance ministries, CEPD, and Central Bank of China) a cadre of technological and intellectual experts who responded to him politically and shared his developmental goals. They were loyal to Chiang, who used them to replace supporters of Chiang Kai-shek in the central committee, but they had a secondary root of power in their expertise. This 1970s constellation of younger, Western-trained, technocratic elites was the first step toward development of autonomy in the national executive.

On his election in 1996, President Lee Teng-hui called for the formation of a "grand coalition" cabinet and said he would include members from the DPP and NP. Thereupon, he proceeded to hold interviews with a succession of non-KMT party representatives. Opposition party leaders criticized this objective and the process, and both DPP and NP leaders said that any member of their party accepting a position in the new cabinet would lose party membership. The cabinet presented to the Legislative Yuan in May 1996 contained no members of the DPP or NP. Even though his overtures were rebuffed, Lee made history by reaching out to the opposition the way he did.

The previous cabinet's gestures toward administrative neutrality would have been impossible before the advent of competitive party politics. For example, ministers of the first Lien Chan cabinet (1994-96) briefed DPP and NP members on major items of the Executive Yuan legislative agenda. At least twice a year ministers appear before the Legislative Yuan to make reports and to respond to interpellation from legislators. During the second Lien Chan cabinet (1996-97), the premier did not attend any legislative sessions, and thus the influence of cabinet ministers grew. They may supply legislators with administrative studies and policy analyses, which are valued given the minuscule staff of the Legislative Yuan and its lack of independent research capability, a proficient library or other data resources. Again, party competition has sparked a degree of dynamism—in the form of cooperation as well as conflict—between executive and legislative bodies that was minimal in the 1980s.

Legislative Yuan

Historical Evolution

Under the 1947 constitution, 760 persons were elected to the Legislative Yuan. Two years later, 470 legislators retreated with the government to Taiwan. These seats were frozen for the next 40 years, as no new elections could be held on the Chinese mainland; the average age of the 216 permanent legislators in the late 1980s was in the 80s, making this Chinese legislature the one with the world's oldest representatives.

To accommodate demands for increased political participation and to replace original representatives when they died, the temporary provisions were amended to add legislators from Taiwan through supplementary elections. The first was held in 1969, and it added 11 new members. A second election in 1972 added 51 seats; a third, in 1980, brought the number of representatives selected on Taiwan to 97. One interpretation of the expansion of the legislature is that each time Taiwan suffered a diplomatic loss, it liberalized representative institutions in order to improve political harmony and silence critics of the regime.[19] After the National Affairs Conference, called by President Lee in mid-1990 to make recommendations for democratic reform, the senior remaining parliamentarians were involuntarily retired. Elections for all seats in the new, 184-member Legislative Yuan were conducted in 1992.

During the period when mainland representatives dominated the Legislative Yuan, it functioned as an efficient rubber stamp for the KMT and lacked autonomy. On no occasion did the body veto initiatives of the Executive Yuan. Non-KMT members of the legislature provided only token opposition until development of competitive party politics in the late 1980s. Legislators such as Kang Ning-hsiang could use the parliamentary power of *chih-hsun*—interpellation, or questioning the government—to criticize decisions, to embarrass officials, to make the regime more accountable to the public. However, constitutionally, the opposition could not introduce legislation on its own without controlling a greater number of votes. To establish a presence on most committees, and to deny a quorum to the KMT majority (thereby halting action), required more seats.

Opposition parties reached the threshold of influence in 1992, when, for the first time, all seats in the Legislative Yuan were up for election. In that election, the DPP won 50 seats, or 31 percent of the Legislative Yuan membership. Moreover, nearly two-thirds of those elected were new to the body, reducing influence of the executive branch and KMT central leadership. In the 1995 elections, the DPP, NP, and other parties took nearly 50 percent of the seats in the Legislative Yuan. The KMT lacked a working majority (of 164 seats, it controlled a majority of two only) and in fact did not control three of the 10 committees in the legislature. The legislative coalition of DPP and NP members required the KMT to cooperate in order to conduct legislative business. (Analogous developments occurred in Taiwan's second parliamentary body, the National Assembly, when the KMT took less than 50 percent of the vote in 1996 elections. To gain DPP support for its proposals to strengthen presidential powers at the expense of the legislature's, the KMT had to accept the "freezing" of Taiwan province, an objective long sought by the DPP.) Although party competition increased dramatically the partisanship (also passion and antics) in legislative deliberations, it also brought new concerns within the purview of legislative committees and floor discussions. For example, during discussion of the three telecommunications laws (*Dian-hsun San-fa*) in January 1996, DPP legislators were able to place the issue of worker pensions and benefits on the agenda for all privatization plans, when previously these issues had been omitted.

Party competition brought an increase in visibility and legitimacy of the Legislative Yuan. The first wholly elected Legislative Yuan attracted younger candidates and those less likely to be mainlanders than Taiwanese (78 percent elected in 1992 as compared to only 20 percent in the former Legislative Yuan); the increased prominence of the Legislative Yuan in policy making gave constituents an interest in the branch and gave legislative candidates a stake in reaching out to voters. Once elected, legislators were far more likely to use their positions to bring government projects and services to their constituents and to address their problems with government. Again, party competition established this vital linkage between constituents and legislators.

The Legislative Yuan reached its pinnacle of influence in the sessions following the 1996 presidential election. The KMT could not produce a clear majority in support of President Lee's nomination of Lien Chan, the newly elected vice president, as premier. Legislators declined to invite the premier to attend sessions for interpellation, which hobbled the executive seriously in budget deliberations. Supporters of Lee Teng-hui called the situation a gridlock, which justified constitutional revision to clarify and enhance presidential powers.

Functions and Powers

Under the 1947 constitution, the Legislative Yuan exercises general legislative powers of law-making. Because the Executive Yuan initiates most proposals for changes in law, the role of the legislature is largely reactive. However, party competition in the Legislative Yuan has increased greatly the development of new legislative proposals by legislators.

The legislature's most important confirmation power is its right of consent over the president's nomination of the premier and of the auditor-general in the Control Yuan. Also, the legislature has the power to confirm the president's proclamation of emergency orders and measures within 10 days of their issuance. This amended provision of the constitution spells out an emergency as an imminent threat to national security or a serious financial or economic crisis.

Article 75 of the constitution prohibits dual office-holding: legislators may not hold another government post. This make's Taiwan's government system dissimilar from cabinet governments, where cabinet members hold elected positions in the parliament. It was designed to make the legislative branch independent of the executive, thereby avoiding the "monopolization of power by members of the Legislature".[20]

Opportunities for legislative oversight of the executive are provided through two additional powers. The Executive Yuan is required to present the legislature with a statement of its administrative policies and a report on its administration. Also, the premier and cabinet members are required to respond in writing or orally to legislative interpellations. Legislators increasingly have made effective use of interpellations to draw attention to lapses in administration or to focus on policy disagreements.

A second area of legislative oversight is the budget. The executive must present a budget to the legislature three months before the beginning of the fiscal year. During budget deliberations, legislators have opportunities to investigate administrative policies and practices. The constitution does not allow the legislature to increase the budget. It can approve the bottom line presented by the executive or reduce it. A recent court ruling disallowed the legislature from raising one budget program category while reducing others, a ruling that limits legislative budgetary power. Moreover, the legislature must complete budget work by the end of its first session (normally the end of May). The legislature also examines audit reports prepared by the auditor-general and delivered within three months of the executive's final accounts of revenues and expenditures.

A recent popular source of legislative ideas is the petition, a direct method for citizens to express their views. Legislators consider written petitions in committees, and if they pass through this process, they are considered the same as other bills.[21]

The legislature also may propose constitutional amendments to the National Assembly. Too, it has dispute settlement powers concerning matters of self-governance in provinces, municipalities, counties, cities, and other administrative units.

Summing up the main roles and powers of the Legislative Yuan in 1997, the vice president said:

> The executive depends on us to pass critical legislation, and they need to work with us. We are the national policy center, and the last place for action. Also, we are a platform for popular reactions to government.[22]

These are significant powers for a body that was once Taiwan's primary laughing stock.

Legislators and Their Roles

In recent years, most of Taiwan's legislators have been in their 40s and 50s; the youngest in 1997 was 31 and the oldest, 65. The average age was 48.6 years, meaning most legislators were born after the war. Only 23 (14 percent) of the members were women, a number increasing gradually. And most of the legislators were Taiwanese. Fifteen (9 percent) listed birthplaces in other provinces of China than Taiwan, but this probably understated the number of mainlanders by half, as second-generation *Wai-sheng-jen* active in politics are likely to list their birthplace as Taiwan.

Members of the Legislative Yuan are quite well educated; 92 percent have received at least a college education. A majority has taken graduate work, and a very high percentage (27.4 percent) has completed doctoral work. Few legislatures have this degree of educational specialization.

About 44 percent studied abroad after college, and the choice for most was the United States. Far fewer studied in the next preferred country—Japan—or in European universities.

Table 6. Background Characteristics of Legislators, 1996

Highest Degree Received		*No.*	*%*
High school or less		12	7.3
Baccalaureate		59	36.0
Master's		48	29.3
Doctoral		45	27.4
	Total	164	100.0
Study Abroad			
United States		51	71.0
Japan		11	15.0
Europe		6	8.0
other countries		4	6.0
	Total	72	100.0
Previous Occupation		12	7.9
Teacher (K-12)		33	21.7
Professor/researcher		21	13.8
Businessperson		12	7.9
Lawyer		5	3.3
Medicine		21	13.8
Elected representative		23	15.1
Public official (appointed)		10	6.6
Media—print, broadcast		3	2.0
Labor		9	5.9
Social organizations		3	2.0
Other		152	100.0
	Total		

Source: Compiled from *Roster of Legislators* (Taipei: Secretariat, Legislative Yuan, January 1996).

Based on information supplied by legislators about their experience, it is possible to draw an approximate occupational profile. Before they entered the Legislative Yuan, most were either teachers (nearly 30 percent) or public servants (also nearly 30 percent). A larger number had experience teaching at the college or university level, or doing research, than teaching at the elementary or secondary level.

One out of seven launched his or her career from an elected office. Most frequently cited were service in the provincial assembly, as city or county councilors, or as county or township magistrates. More than one in seven had held appointed public office. These included three judges, three with military experience, two former cabinet ministers with extensive portfolios of government service, and administrators from the municipal to the national government level.

The number of lawyers, 12 (8 percent), underrepresented those trained in the law, some of whom had worked primarily as professors or who had held either elected or appointed government posts. The number of businesspersons was also relatively small, only 21 (14 percent) of the members who identified their occupational history. A change over recent years was in the number of reporters, broadcasters, or editors—nearly 7 percent. (The social organizations to which the table refers cover a range of mostly nonprofit organizations.)

Only 31 legislators indicated any previous service in the Legislative Yuan (in either the First or Second bodies), the most experienced of whom, Liu Sung-fan (current president or Speaker) had served seven terms at the time of this writing. The majority were serving their first terms, an indication that the Legislative Yuan is not a permanent career goal. In fact, by May 1997, some 35 legislators had contemplated or actually launched campaigns for county magistrate positions, elected in November 1997.

An interesting note is that only nine (11 percent) of the KMT representatives were members of the party's central committee; four were members of the central standing committee. While most of the other party members listed membership in a party work group or policy committee, about a dozen indicated no party organizational affiliation other than that they were KMT representatives. On the other hand, DPP representatives to a person mentioned party offices, positions, and history.

Legislators in Taiwan have less opportunity than those in other states to specialize in legislative areas because of the nature of the committee system (discussed below) and high turnover. Also, the Executive Yuan drafts most legislative proposals, and the legislative role is thus mostly reactive. Legislators also have limited opportunities to conduct oversight of the executive branch. Committee hearings have not yet become institutionalized, and neither legislative rules, the statutes, nor the constitution give the legislature investigative powers—the authority to, for example, subpoena witnesses or force them to testify under oath.

The primary role of most legislators is constituent service or casework.[23] The typical legislator receives requests from about five constituents a day. Most of the requests are for personal assistance: to secure a job in a government agency, get a loan at a preferred rate, receive assistance in requesting a promotion, arrange a military transfer, clarify and increase pension benefits, and the like. Legislators regularly hear from economic interest groups, which we discuss in chapter 5. They also hear from bureaucrats in the ministries and commissions their committees supervise.

To satisfy these requests requires a larger staff than the Legislative Yuan supplies (a minimum of two and a maximum of five). Also, legislators from outside Taipei (and even some within the city) believe it is essential to establish constituent offices in their districts. A number of legislators have more than six constituent offices, where both paid employees and volunteers process requests for assistance and collect information.

In modern Taiwan, people also expect their legislators to attend functions, such as weddings, funerals, festivals, and buy them meals when they visit the Legislative Yuan. It is not unusual for legislators to pay for the transportation of constituents visiting them from out of town, arrange housing in Taipei, and invite them to banquets.

Legislators perform these services because they are directly related to votes in elections. But the services are costly. Legislators are well-remunerated for their work, earning nearly as much as cabinet ministers (about the equivalent of US $5,000-8,000 monthly). This, however, is insufficient to maintain constituent offices and provide services. (Nor does this begin to provide funds needed for elections, and Legislative Yuan elections, running into the millions, are very costly.)

As a result, most legislators maintain candidate support organizations between elections. These groups give money to legislators, often on a monthly basis in exchange for access. The legislator will meet with members of the candidate support groups, briefing them on legislative agenda items of interest. They are more common for DPP than for KMT or NP legislators. Most legislators will also serve as advisors or consultants: to business corporations, social groups, and business, labor, and farmers' associations. Some will even enter business joint ventures or own family businesses. These are the ways in which they supplement their salaries to cover office expenses.

Organization and Operation

The Legislative Yuan does its business through sessions of the legislature, operations of the secretariat, and legislative committees. It holds two sessions a year, the first from February to the end of May, and the second from September to the end of December. Sessions may be prolonged, but this requires a majority vote. A quorum is one-third of the total membership.

Legislators meet for floor sessions on two or three days of the week and meet in committee sessions on the other days, including Saturday mornings. The president (equivalent to a Speaker) of the Legislative Yuan or his deputy, the vice president, presides over floor sessions; leaders are elected at the start of the three-year term from among the membership. Each party selects legislative whips whose job is to inform members of the issues and ensure that they are present for critical votes.

The DPP organizes its members best for voting, even fining those absent for more than five votes.[24] The KMT party organization is looser for several reasons. Some KMT members won election as independent candidates and feel they owe the party no loyalty. A number of KMT legislators are businessmen, and business affairs take them away from sessions. (There is no restriction on holding a job outside of government, which some legislators claim is necessary to cover their expenses.) In the Third Legislative Yuan, the KMT had a slim majority, and one or two dissident majority members on an issue could cause it to fail. With loose party discipline and a small majority, it was hard for party leaders to collect support for priority legislation.

Resolutions and legislative acts require a simple majority vote to pass, unless the legislature is reconsidering measures vetoed by the executive, in which case a two-thirds majority is required. Legislative acts require three readings before the vote. The first reading is pro forma, often a reading of the title, except for bills proposed by legislators. The second reading occurs after committee review, and it is the substantive one. This reading discusses committee deliberations, and amendments are considered. The third reading is usually only for final corrections of wording and not for substantive discussion.

The secretariat provides staff services to the Legislative Yuan, and these are quite meager. A small library and reference center houses legislative journals, but it has few research materials relevant to the legislation under discussion. A legislative research section, added recently, provides some assistance to legislators, but the secretariat lacks a fully equipped budget office that either can prepare revenue estimates for the legislature or give it detailed, ministry-by-ministry breakdowns on budget expenditures. In fact, poor central staff support makes the legislature dependent on the Executive Yuan for most information it needs to legislate. The secretariat also supplies staff to the legislature's committees. However, the committee staffs are small, usually from six to eight people, and poorly paid, with resultant high turnover and limited expertise.

Legislators spend much of their time at committee meetings, but the committee system differs greatly from that in America. The ten standing committees of the legislature are home and border affairs, foreign and overseas Chinese affairs, national defense, economics, finance, budget, education, transportation and communications, judiciary, and organic laws. The legislature also has set up five special committees: discipline, rules, accounts, publications, and constitutional amendment.

Each of the standing committees may have no more than 18 members. Although parties attempt to influence committee membership, increasingly, the choice has become free. When a committee is oversubscribed and, after negotiations, more than 18 still seek membership on it, resolution is achieved through a lottery. Therefore, a very knowledgeable committee member may lose a committee seat to an inexperienced member. This method of committee recruitment erodes the accumulation of expertise within the committee.

Legislators select committees because of their interest, and often this is economic. The most powerful money committees are economics, finance, and budget, and sitting on them are a disproportionate number of businesspersons, with economic interests at stake in committee deliberations. Defense and foreign affairs are also popular committees.

Committees select three co-chairs, so that no member is tied down to committee sessions within the week. Often, the co-chairs come from different political parties. This creates opportunities for the opposition to steer the committee agenda and votes in its preferred direction. Having multiple chairs also weakens the committee's leadership and power.

Because the KMT had such a small majority in the Third Legislative Yuan, it was not able to supply a majority to each committee. Both the education and judiciary committees lacked KMT majorities, which seriously disrupted the budget review of the agencies considered by the committees.

In 1994, the president of the Legislative Yuan called together a group of resident and outside experts on legislative processes to suggest reforms to improve legislative effectiveness. The committee proposed three areas of improvement. First, it recommended strengthening legislative committees by implementing a seniority system for committee chairs and by basing the committee power ratio on that of the chamber as a whole. Second, the committee proposed increasing committee staff to facilitate and improve committee work. Third, it proposed increasing research organizations in the Legislative Yuan, and it specifically recommended a research office resembling the American Congressional Research Service and a budget office resembling the Congressional Budget Office.[25]

When the proposals came before the membership, they failed to receive support. KMT members were uninterested in the proposals. DPP members were opposed because they have benefited most from the status quo. With a tightened procedure of committee assignment, they would be in the minority forever. In 1997, however, the legislature was considering a rules change that would allow members to sit on two committees.

Economic Interests in the Legislature

The increase in the Legislative Yuan's power has been accompanied by an increase in its penetration by economic interests. In 1985, financial tycoon Ts'ai Chen-chou, who had bought his way into the legislature, formed the "Thirteen Brothers Group", comprised of thirteen KMT legislators elected in Taiwan (all of whom Ts'ai had helped swing business deals or arrange low-cost loans). Ts'ai and his associates then proceeded to influence the revision of laws on credit cooperatives, trusts, and the banking law. Ts'ai was able to use his group to forestall investigation of his Tenth Credit Cooperative, which had overextended its loan capacity; he obstructed bureaucratic review of the credit cooperative. A major scandal brought down Ts'ai's Tenth Credit Cooperative, leading to Ts'ai's arrest.[26]

A second example concerns the Second Legislative Yuan, the first in which all seats were selected democratically. This election produced a large number of winners with business interests: 19 with ties to conglomerates, 27 with large banking investments, and 31 heads of monopolies, protected or licenses enterprises (with some overlapping of interests). The leader of a large group formed from these interests was Ueng Da-ming. (Ueng headed the Hua-lung conglomerate and was a large stock trader. He ran in the 1992 election from jail, where he was serving time for illegal stock exchanges.) Ueng's group in the legislature numbered two dozen members crossing party and factional lines, all of whom had some connection to the conglomerate—as employees, joint venture partners, secret loan recipients or partners in a huge, secret mutual fund.[27] By dominating the finance committee and collecting insider information, group members were able to reap windfall profits from short-term transactions. When, in 1994, a subsidiary of the Hua-lung conglomerate, Hong-fu Securities Co., was involved in illegal trading, the stock market crashed, and fingers pointed at Ueng. Eighteen Hua-lung group legislators from all three parties then rushed to Ueng's house and tried to interfere with evidence collection by the Bureau of Investigation. Journalists called this episode "Eighteen Disciples Rescuing the Buddha".[28]

Kuo Cheng-tian believes that the public uproar over this scandal led to an "authoritarian withdrawal" from the Legislative Yuan, which he attributes to Taiwan's democratization. There is no convincing evidence on this attractive thesis because systematic studies of interest groups in Taiwan's legislature are still in their infancy. A recent paper by Shiow-duan Hwang, however, contains some telling observations. She considered the deliberation of legislators in committee meetings over several legislative sessions, assessing influence of legislators based on a content analysis of the official bulletin of the Legislative Yuan (*Li-fa Yuan Kung-pao*). Hwang did find evidence of interest group influence. This influence was strong at the committee stage when the issue pitted two groups against one another (on legislation concerning credit union expansion, for example) or when one group clearly benefited, but the costs of the legislative change were broadly distributed. However, when economic interests conflicted with a large popular majority, they were less effective (at the committee stage).

A case study of the financial disclosure law also shows the changing sphere of KMT party power and business interests in the Legislative Yuan. The central party leadership opposed the compulsory blind trust provision of the act, which gave the measure enforcement power. However, the party was not able to enforce discipline on one-third of its members who joined opposition legislators in support of this very popular provision.[29]

Seasoned observers of Taiwan's Legislative Yuan, such as Tien Hung-mao and Chu Yun-han, find that KMT party discipline breaks down readily over public construction projects,[30] financial regulation, and social welfare. Those KMT members with ties to conglomerates and local factions select relevant committees (economic affairs, finance, communication and transportation) and seek a range of special benefits—below-market prices for public land purchases, public works contracts, loans from state-owned banks, etc. Those without business or factional ties compete with opposition legislators in bidding wars over popular measures such as farm subsidies, universal health insurance, or old age annuities.[31]

What can be said at this stage of research on Taiwan's new Legislative Yuan is that economic interests do indeed penetrate into public decision-making. Their success or failure, however, depends on the nature of the issue and the stage of the legislative process. Also, large-scale public opposition has been effective at curbing economic influences that do not appear to be in the public interest.

The Other Branches

Three other Yuan complete our review of the primary institutions of the state, the examination, control, and judicial branches.

Examination Yuan

This branch of government is unique to Taiwan. It reflects the importance of the examination tradition in Chinese history, for China was the first state to use merit examinations to select its officials, and it did so more consistently and for a longer period than any other state system. The branch is responsible for the examination, employment, and management of all civil service personnel in Taiwan. It oversees all examination-related matters, issues concerning qualification screening, security of tenure, financial aid in case of death, and the retirement of civil servants. It also supervises all legal matters relating to the employment, discharge, performance evaluation, scale of salaries, promotion, transfer, commendation, and reward of civil servants.[32] Covered by the Examination Yuan's provisions are more than 618,000 civil servants (in December 1995), 34.2 percent of whom worked for the central government. (Twenty percent worked for the provincial government, and the remainder, 45.8 percent, worked for local governments.)

The Examination Yuan has a president, vice president, and 17 members. All are appointed for six-year terms by the president with consent of the National Assembly. These officials comprise the council, which is a policy-making organ. Members chair various examination boards that write questions for and grade the examinations. They determine the number of successful candidates in each examination.

Control Yuan

The Control Yuan also is a unique Chinese governmental institution, and many of its functions resemble those of the censorate in imperial China. Formerly, this institution was a parliamentary body (the third after the Legislative Yuan and the National Assembly). Provincial and municipal councils elected its members. A constitutional amendment in 1992 transformed it into a quasi-judicial organization. Now the Control Yuan has 29 members (including its president and vice president) who are appointed by the president with the consent of the National Assembly to terms of six years. As a means of protecting the Control Yuan's independence and non-partisanship, Article 103 of the constitution states that no member "shall concurrently hold any other public office or engage in any other profession".

The chief function of the Control Yuan is to institute impeachment proceedings against public officials, up to and including the president (no president or vice president has been impeached yet), if the official is believed to be in violation of the law or guilty of dereliction of duty. A majority of members of the branch must agree on the motion for impeachment, which then goes to one of three bodies for trial: the Committee on the Discipline of Public Functionaries (within the Judicial Yuan) for civil servant cases; the Ministry of National Defense for military personnel; or the National Assembly for the president or vice president.[33]

A member of the Control Yuan, with the support of three other members, may file a censure against an official whose actions warrant immediate suspension. Under the Law on Discipline of Public Functionaries, the supervisor must resolve the issue within one month of the censure. The Control Yuan has investigative powers to review the operations of the Executive Yuan and propose corrective measures, to which the relevant ministry or commission must respond. Officials of the Control Yuan may conduct field investigations of public or private organizations based on the actions of citizens who file written complaints with the Control Yuan.

The Control Yuan has auditing responsibilities over provinces and local governments, and the National Audit Office is lodged in this branch. It received a new function in 1993 when the legislature, after much prodding from public interest organizations, passed the Public Functionary Assets Disclosure Law. The Department of Assets Disclosure receives reports from the president and vice president, presidents and vice presidents of the five Yuan, political appointees and elected officials.[34]

The workload of the Control Yuan does not indicate much vigor in the pursuit of its responsibilities. From 1950 to 1984, there was a steady decline in the total cases of impeachment, censure, and corrective measures,[35] with a modest revival after Chiang Ching-kuo took over the premiership. Moreover, in early years, high-level officials (including a premier, mayor, and two ministers) were investigated, compared in later years to middle- and lower-level officials.

The aging of Control Yuan membership may be a factor in its reluctance to prosecute cases, and a lack of staff may represent another. Of greater importance, alleges Tien, is growing KMT intervention in the work of the Yuan: "The ruling party uses it to patronize elected politicians who are seeking upward political mobility and who are not expected to rock the boat once in office".[36] This was a factor behind removing elections from the hands of provincial and municipal councils and making the positions appointed. Since this change occurred in 1993, there is no evidence to suggest that the Control Yuan has become more aggressive in ferreting out malfeasance. Indeed, in 1997, Control Yuan member Tsai Ching-chu was indicted for corruption and faced impeachment. Tsai allegedly pressured the Securities and Exchange Commission to list a company in exchange for cash and stock options and wheedled loans from a state bank. Taipower also accused Tsai of trying to exempt a company from paying penalties for delays in a construction project.[37]

Judicial Yuan

The Judicial Yuan is the highest judicial organ in Taiwan. It has a president, vice president, and 15 to 17 grand justices. All are appointed by the president with the consent of the National Assembly. All courts and their administrative agencies are subordinate organs of the Judicial Yuan.

Council of Grand Justices   This council's role is to interpret the constitution and unify the interpretation of laws and ordinances. In these respects, it exercises the power of judicial review. Its 16 members (from the start of the 1994 term) serve terms of nine years. From 1948 through 1996, the council made 412 interpretations of the constitution. Requesting resolution of conflicting interpretations of the constitution or judgments on the constitutionality of laws, regulations, and decrees have been government agencies, individuals, other courts, and political parties.[38] Perhaps the most significant council interpretation was that which brought about the mandatory retirement of senior parliamentarians elected on the Chinese mainland and serving in Taiwan for more than 40 years without facing voters.

The council received a new responsibility in 1993 when the judiciary established a constitutional court (identical in membership to the council) for the purpose of adjudicating cases concerning the dissolution of political parties in violation of the constitution. Previously, the interior ministry had most influence over this politically sensitive area; opposition leaders suspected it of seeing a danger to the republic in every whiff of independence rhetoric from the DPP.

Taiwan's court system Three levels of courts compose the rest of the court system. District courts and their branches at the lowest level are trial courts hearing civil and criminal cases. An intermediate level of courts is appellate, hearing judgments against district courts. The highest level of appellate courts is the supreme court, but it also is a court of first instance in cases of rebellion, treason, and offenses against other nations. Finally, an administrative court handles complaints about violation of rights by government agencies.

Judges in Taiwan are government employees who gain their jobs through competitive examination, similar to European practice. Critics of the judiciary complain that training of judges is uneven and that screening exams are far more lax than those for lawyers (whose passing rate is from 5 to 10 percent).

A Rule of Law?

Taiwan has made great strides in implementing a rule of law and abridging arbitrary personal rule. The chief early obstacles to rationalization of the system of laws were the temporary provisions and martial law, which left enormous power in the hands of military authorities and granted the president vast unchecked powers. Terminating both these extra-constitutional measures has significantly improved the transparency of legal procedures and their implementation.

Development of a competitive party system and a free press both have focused on remaining problems in the design of the legal and judicial system, in the uniform application of rules and laws, and in the non-discriminatory treatment of those guilty of infractions. The 1990s have seen a series of instances of official corruption that have not been successfully prosecuted. For example, in 1996, press reports focused on huge cost overruns in large public construction projects. Regime critics (and there are many) contend that the projects' costs were inflated up to 50 percent by kickbacks to business cronies of government officials and by protection money paid to gangsters. Allegedly, both construction company executives and "black" (or gangster) elements are interconnected with KMT party leaders.

A regime crackdown on public construction abuses netted a few lower-level officials, who were dispatched to Green Island (a major prison facility off Taiwan's east coast). No high-ranking official lost his job. Then, in early 1997, attention switched to the operation of gambling halls, clearly in violation of the statutes, in which police and local officials were compromised. Again, a few local administrators and operators were arrested, but evidence pointing to higher-level involvement led nowhere.

These instances of corruption in the state's administration helped fuel the mass demonstrations in May 1997 calling for an improvement of public order. Problems in personnel selection, legal ambiguity, and enforcement of the law continued to plague the government.

Personal relationships (*Kuan-hsi*) still dominate recruitment of appointed officials, meaning that those charged with administering state affairs may be personally tainted with corruption or unsavory associations and may use the law to improve the terms of their relationships.[39] In March 1997, Justice Minister Liao Cheng-hao remarked that even elected officials, including Legislative Yuan and National Assembly members, were implicated in corruption. He alleged that "10 percent of public officials . . . had connections with organized crime groups, a criminal record, or membership in a gang".[40] The media feasted on the selection of independent legislator Lo Fu-chu as chair of the legislature's judicial affairs committee, which screens anti-crime bills and oversees budgets for law enforcement units. Lo spent four years in jail and had confessed links to the Tiendaomeng, one of Taiwan's four major gangs, which he served as "spiritual leader". Lo's selection as committee chair was arranged by the KMT in exchange for his support of a KMT legislator's entry into the rules committee.[41]

Second, the law in Taiwan tends to be vague and ambiguous, which gives great discretion to executive officials who develop the implementation rules and may do so with favoritism toward individuals or firms in mind. Further, confusion arises from conflict between laws, rules, rulings, orders, decrees, and regulations. This makes the legal environment uncertain and unpredictable, though it has improved somewhat, particularly in areas affecting foreign businesses.[42]

Third, effective and consistent enforcement of the law is an equal, if not greater, problem in improvement of Taiwan's legal system. Supporters of the rule of law in Taiwan heralded the appointment of Harvard Law-trained Ma Ying-jeou as Minister of Justice in 1993. Ma designed a new anti-corruption approach by combining the forces of the prosecutors' offices, investigation bureau, and ethics officials in government agencies.

His targets were government corruption, organized crime, vote buying, and drug trafficking. He had early successes in cleaning up local legislatures where gangsters had acted with impunity, even to the extent of murdering enemies in cold blood and daring authorities to move against them.[43] His three-year campaign against vote buying also bore fruit in conviction of 981 people in a scandal involving a KMT candidate. However, Ma lost his job in a cabinet reshuffle after the 1996 presidential election, reputedly because he was too successful and his probes endangered KMT high officials. (As a handsome, charismatic mainlander with a following, Ma also posed a threat to Premier Lien Chan.)

To balance this assessment we must include successful upgrading of the law to international standards in several areas. For example, there has been striking progress in the elimination of pirating firms. An international banker said that "if you suspect an infringement of trademark or copyright, you can call out a police raid and they may go to jail, which is far different from years ago".[44] In recent years, too, the number of officials and ordinary citizens arrested on corruption charges has been high—about an average of four every day over the period 1994 to 1997. Nevertheless, Taiwan is some distance from establishing a system of law that citizens believe is fairly administered and rigorously enforced.

Constitutional Reform

For nearly a year in 1996-97, Taiwan's political leaders engaged in discussion and often acrimonious and rowdy debates over the constitution. In December 1996, President Lee called a National Development Conference (NDC), purportedly representing all parties, to discuss his proposals for constitutional reform. That conference agreed to the main items on Lee's list of changes and produced a rare two-party agreement between the KMT and DPP, which pledged to support the reforms at the meeting of the National Assembly, beginning in May 1997 and continuing through July.

We look at the three major elements of the reform to the Taiwan provincial government, National Assembly, and powers of the president and legislature. We also consider the motivation behind reforms and what the ensuing debate reveals about the democratization process in Taiwan.

"Freezing" Taiwan Province

Initially, President Lee proposed the elimination of Taiwan province, or its maintenance as a shell, much like the office of 34 that supervises the affairs of two small counties in Fukien province. Then, Lee moderated the proposal, this time to "freeze" (*tong-chie*) the province. This would mean that the provincial governor, James Soong, and the provincial assembly would serve out the end of their terms (December 1998), whereupon both governor and assembly would be appointed by the president. Following this, the provincial government, now employing 124,000, would be reduced and simplified. Governor Soong resigned after the NDC adopted Lee's proposal, but both the premier and president declined to accept his resignation. In protest, Soong absented himself from meetings of the KMT's central standing committee for five months.

In support of Lee's proposal, observers have questioned the need for a provincial government in Taiwan. Two overlapping governments—the central and provincial—rule over a virtually identical territory, and many of the functions and personnel are redundant. The province operates industries, such as the Taiwan Tobacco and Wine Monopoly Bureau and three of the wealthiest commercial banks, which stand in the way of economic liberalization of Taiwan (see discussion on privatization in chapter 6 and of TTWB in chapter 7). The province-owned industries and banks are even more infested with patronage and rent-seeking behavior than SOEs under central government control.

Defenders of the province have pointed out that most of the functions performed by the province would still be necessary. For example, the education department, which controls middle through high school education, would still need to exist. The transportation department controls most of Taiwan's ports and harbors, and its functions would still need to be performed. Only a handful of positions could be eliminated. Defenders identified two different motivations for freezing the province in 1997: Taiwan independence and removing James Soong as a political rival.

DPP support of President Lee's proposals was crucial to their successful implementation. Because the KMT controlled less than the three-fourths majority in the National Assembly required to amend the constitution, it needed DPP support. Eliminating or at least starting to eliminate Taiwan province was the price for that support. Without a Taiwan province, the DPP would be one step closer to declaring an independent Taiwan. No longer could critics say that Taiwan was just a province of China and point out the continued existence of a provincial governor and assembly. Defenders of the province saw this rationale as a great concern to mainland Chinese officials, who regard it as another step away from unification.[45]

The second and doubtless the strongest motivation for Lee to propose freezing the province was to remove James Soong, the primary political rival of both Lee and Lien Chan. If the province were frozen, Soong would, at the expiration of his term, no longer have a political base to use in the 2000 presidential election. Soong poses a threat for several reasons. His election to the governorship in 1994 was the first democratic election for an island-wide chief executive. He won 57 percent of the vote against four rivals, more than Lee attained in 1996. He did this as a mainlander who had learned to speak Taiwanese. In 1997, Soong was also the most popular politician in Taiwan. Newspaper polls in April and May 1997 gave him approval ratings of over 80 percent, compared to ratings of 30 to 40 percent for Lien Chan and ratings for the president that barely hovered above 50 percent. Soong also is a clean, competent official, commonly regarded as having unimpeachable integrity, whereas Lien's competence is challenged and rumors escalate about Lee's corrupt associations and his wife's grasping behavior.

Discussion and debate ranged over these points. Although the KMT and DPP held to their bargain on the issue of Taiwan province, the New Party strongly opposed all constitutional reform proposals. Its National Assembly representatives disrupted proceedings on several occasions and stalled deliberations by introducing more than 100 amendments as the session wound toward closure. This party's unification goal was damaged by freezing Taiwan province, and when the National Assembly approved the proposal, NP delegate walked out of the sessions.

Role for the National Assembly

The National Assembly is a limited-purpose parliamentary body. For most of its history, its main function had been to elect the president and vice president, but constitutional amendments in 1994 stripped it of this power. Its remaining substantive function is to amend the constitution. In addition, it confirms presidential nominations to several offices and has largely unused powers to fill the vice presidency when vacant, recall the president and vice president, and serve as a trial body for presidential or vice presidential impeachments. Four-fifths of its membership of 334 is elected directly, following the procedure for Legislative Yuan elections, and the remainder of seats are filled on an at-large basis. In 1997, a majority of its members were KMT, but as noted, this party lacked a three-fourths majority.

Proposals to change the National Assembly were embedded in a broader-scale reform to eliminate the "five elections", for provincial governor, assembly, National Assembly, town and township mayors, and village chiefs. The DPP often has criticized the large number of elections held in Taiwan's small jurisdiction and argued for elimination of elections for all offices except legislators, Taipei and Kaohsiung mayors, county chiefs and councilors, and the president and vice president. (No one except town and village chiefs came forward to support their continued elections; President Lee supported one final round of elections, allowing the chiefs a transition so they could find other opportunities.)

KMT and DPP party caucuses agreed to reduce the membership of National Assembly to 254, with all members appointed by parties according to the share each party received in the presidential election. One-tenth of the assembly seats will be reserved for women. An additional proposal to make the National Assembly the upper house of a new bi-cameral legislature, with limited legislative but large constitutional amendment powers, received some attention but was not enacted.

In addition to the rationale to reduce numbers of elections, two other arguments arose in the context of constitutional revisions. One generic argument concerned the corruption of local elections and the high costs of all elections. Reducing the number of elections presumably would facilitate their purification. Second, critics saw little value in having a nearly full-time legislative body for occasional tasks. Efficiency would be improved by assigning the functions elsewhere or by reducing the autonomy of the National Assembly.

After nearly two months of raucous demonstrations and uncivil debates in the National Assembly (from May through July 1997), which prompted its Speaker to resign in disgust (the president declined to accept), few observers could find strong reasons to continue the body in its existing form. Its role seems likely to be modified further in the future.

Legislative and Presidential Powers

The most controversial reform proposals concerned the relationships between the president, premier, and legislature. The models most frequently discussed were "duarchy", the strong presidential system of the French Fifth Republic and the American system of presidential government with a strong legislative body.

Over the course of discussion and debate, President Lee's proposal was revised several times. Dissension in both the KMT and DPP ranks, with intra-party disputes over both models, led to constant iteration of proposals. Major areas of proposed reform, on which agreement developed between the two parties, included powers to dissolve the legislature, the legislative no-confidence vote, legislative confirmation of the premier, legislative veto power, and impeachment of president and vice president.

Currently, the president has no power to dissolve the legislature, and this body may not vote no confidence in the cabinet. Initially, President Lee proposed that the president could dissolve the Legislative Yuan even if it had yet to raise a no-confidence vote against the cabinet. The final proposal accepted by the National Assembly empowers the legislature to raise a no-confidence vote against the cabinet if supported by more than one-third of its membership. If two-thirds approve, the premier would dissolve the cabinet and offer his resignation to the president, requesting that the president dismiss the legislature. The president would have ten days to dissolve the legislature, and new legislative elections would be held within 60 days.

In a second area of reform, the National Assembly removed the legislature's power to confirm the president's appointment of a premier. This represented a significant diminution in legislative power.

The third area of change concerned the legislature's veto power. Currently, the legislature may veto cabinet proposals for reconsideration of legislation only with a two-thirds tally on the second vote. The National Assembly reduced this percentage. If cabinet reconsideration motions failed to gain 51 percent support in two votes, they would die.

The fourth proposal concerned strengthening the Legislative Yuan by increasing its size, altering composition of at-large seats, and enhancing its auditing and investigative powers. National Assembly delegates did vote to increase the number of seats from 164 to 225, thereby providing new electoral opportunities for provincial assembly members. However, they declined to approve allocation of one-fourth of the at-large seats appointed by parties to women, or to transfer the power to audit national expenditures from the Control Yuan to the legislature. They also declined to grant the legislature powers to hold official hearings and investigations.

Finally, the impeachment proposal enacted by the National Assembly removed this power from the Control Yuan and placed it in the legislature, with the National Assembly continuing to serve as the trial body. The legislature could impeach only for sedition or treason, and one-half of the legislators would have to support the motion. Two-thirds support would be required to pass the motion on to the National Assembly for a final vote.

Two rationales were advanced to support these reform proposals: immobility and efficiency. Supporters pointed to the frayed relations between executive and legislature since early 1996, tension they claimed had produced gridlock and brought government to a standstill. They believed that Taiwan's international status and security were too vulnerable to allow inaction from the central government. Moreover, given the tense relations across the Taiwan Strait, they argued that the nation needed to be represented by one voice.

Domestic consequences of immobility were more important to supporters. They recognized that the cause of immobility was the slim majority the Kuomintang won in the 1995 legislative elections. They asked what would transpire if the presidency and executive were under the control of one party and the legislature under the control of another. Current institutional arrangements, in their view, would lead to chaos, very much as France under the Fourth Republic had been unable to address its national crises.

Inefficiency of legislative operations is a second rationale for constitutional change. Critics point out that in the first legislative session of 1996 only six measures were passed: legislators spent most of their time fighting over the selection of the Speaker and Vice Speaker; during the second session, only 20-odd measures were passed, and legislators occupied themselves in confrontation with the executive. The third session was somewhat better, with 30 measures passed, although confrontation continued. Only in the most recent session (ending by mid-1997), did the legislature show signs of productivity by passing 80 bills.

Moreover, critics objected to the power that one or two legislators had to halt legislative processes. Chairman of CEPD P. K. Chiang took the extreme position that if the legislature had not acted on an executive proposal within a year, it should be automatically enacted.[46] In fact, during 1996-97, the legislative process resembled the US Senate's unanimous consent procedure. If one member strongly objected to consideration of an act, he or she could call for an item-by-item reading. Although the Speaker could override by allowing a vote on the issue, he was reluctant to do so, for that would cause the objector to lose face and become a permanent enemy of the Speaker. For example, in the 1997 budget deliberations, the executive placed US $3 billion in the income budget to reflect proposed sale of shares in Chinese Petroleum Corporation. A KMT legislator with an interest conflict objected to consideration. He threatened to throw a cup of hot tea at the Speaker if he called for a vote. The Speaker relented, and the income was deleted from the budget, delaying privatization of China Petroleum.

Also, in 1997, the stack of unaddressed legislation was high. Included were more than 50 measures related to Taiwan's accession to the World Trade Organization (WTO). A continuation of legislative inefficiency would impair Taiwan's growth.

Supporters of the status quo found other reasons for the proposals. They saw an increasingly democratic legislature exercising legitimate legislative powers in a manner essential for the consolidation of democracy. Changes would, in their view, have the effect of curbing movement toward democracy. They imagined no difficulty in having a president from one party and a legislature from another and tended to find the US presidential system preferable to the French, because it did not reduce the legislature to a cipher.

The most vitriolic criticism was directed at Lee Teng-hui, whom opponents charged with dictatorial aspirations, intent on creating a new Chinese empire. The proposed reforms would reduce the premier to little other than a chief of staff, and the government would be dominated by the president, with all his flaws.

A third criticism concerned the structure of support for proposals, specifically the KMT-DPP alliance. This was the first major occasion since the development of the DPP as Taiwan's major opposition party in 1986 that the two parties had reached agreement on complex reform issues. That agreement threatened those who strongly oppose Taiwan independence and who support eventual reunification with the Chinese mainland. Thus, the major opponents of the changes were the New Party and the media and academic elite, with strong representation from mainlanders.

Although the National Development Conference attempted to produce consensus on political and constitutional reform, it succeeded only in opening controversy.   The KMT and DPP were able to reach compromise on most issues of constitutional change, which enabled them significantly to amend the constitution.   Opposing these changes, however, were four out of five newspapers and hundreds of academics (more than 1,000 signed petitions against the reforms).

Conclusions

In its 1947 constitution, Taiwan gained a basic law that was democratic in form. However, the form did not preclude adoption of martial law and the temporary provisions, under which the state exercised authoritarian power and prevented democratic change. The lifting of the emergency provisions ushered in an intense era of democratic reform: multi-party competition, demonstrations, strikes, riots, and a high degree of personal freedom to criticize the government and participate in its transformation.

The structure of the state in Taiwan is more complex and redundant than even the American state system.   Taiwan has four levels of government, two of which (the central and provincial) perform similar functions for the same people. Constitutional revision in 1997 started the process of eliminating the provincial government, with the promise of improving government efficiency.   Taiwan has seven institutions of government.   Two are residuals of imperial practices and five are based on modern Western systems, and they have been integrated only under conditions of the party-state system. Constitutional revision in 1997 clarified the important relationship between the president and the legislature, preparing for that day when the branches will be occupied by different parties.

In this chapter we have considered developing pluralism in the state. We have focused on the direct election of the president, which makes him subject to social forces that previously could not penetrate the institution. We have also considered some changes in the Executive Yuan. We have devoted most of our discussion to the legislature, once a rubber stamp to the executive but now a rival for influence in the direction of political and economic change on Taiwan.

Political party competition has made the legislature a newly vibrant institution of government. Reforms to the Legislative Yuan will alter the expressiveness of political party competition and require greater cooperation among parties in order to maintain a check on the executive.

Notes

[1] John K. Fairbank, Edwin O. Reischauer, and Albert M. Craig, *East Asia: The Modern Transformation* (Boston: Houghton Mifflin Co., 1965), 637.

[2] *Constitution of the Republic of China*, Article 1.

[3] *Republic of China Yearbook 1997*, 73.

[4] Hung-mao Tien, *The Great Transition: Political and Social Change in the Republic of China* (Stanford, CA: Hoover Institution Press, 1989), 110.

[5] Tien, 1989, 111.

[6] Tien, 1989, 109.

[7] See David Shambaugh, 'Taiwan's Security', *China Quarterly* 148 (December 1996), 1288.

[8] Cited in Tien, 1989, 112.

[9] *Republic of China Yearbook 1997*, 76.

[10] National Assembly functions also include filling the vice presidency when vacant, recalling the president and vice president, passing impeachment resolutions instituted by the Control Yuan, voting on referenda amending the constitution submitted by the Legislative Yuan, and assenting to personnel appointments nominated by the president. See *Republic of China Yearbook 1997*, 78.

[11] *Republic of China Yearbook 1997*, 79.

[12] Compiled by the author from *Profiles of the Cabinet Members & Heads of the Executive Agencies*, Government Information Office, Republic of China, September 1996.

[13] Tien, 1989, 119.

[14] *1997 Directory of Taiwan* (Taipei: *China News*, 1997), 109-29.

[15] Personal interview with Ho Mei-yuah, Director, Fifth Division, Secretariat, Executive Yuan, May 30, 1997.

[16] Tien, 1989, 129.

[17] Personal interview with P. K. Chiang, Chair, Council for Economic Planning and Development, May 31, 1997.

[18] Constance Squires Meaney, 'Liberalization, Democratization, and the Role of the KMT', in Tun-jen Cheng and Stephan Haggard, eds., *Political Change in Taiwan* (Boulder, CO: Lynne Rienner Publishers, 1992), 112.

[19] Tien, 1989, 145-46.

[20] *Republic of China Yearbook 1997*, 82; for a review of legislative powers and procedures, see Fu-hsun Luo, *Procedures and Techniques of Legislation* (in Chinese) (Taipei: Wu-nan Publishing Co., 1996).

[21] *Legislative Yuan, Republic of China* (Taipei: Legislative Yuan, 1994), 19.

[22] Personal interview with Jin-pyng Wang, vice president, Legislative Yuan, May 30, 1997.

[23] See Shiow-duan Hwang, *Constituent Services* (in Chinese) (Taipei: Tang-shan Publishing Co., 1994).

[24] Even among the DPP, however, discipline is often weak. DPP legislator Michael C. Chang remarked: "It is different from the past; nonpartisan influence is greater. Voters support me, not the party". Personal interview, February 15, 1996.

[25] Personal interview with Chu Tze-hung, Professor of Political Science, National Taiwan University, May 30, 1997.

[26] Tien, 1989, 150.

[27] Cheng-tian Kuo, 'Democratization and Economic Development in Taiwan', (Paper presented at the annual meeting of the American Political Science Association, San Francisco, CA, August 30, 1996), 37.

[28] Kuo, 1996, 37-38.

[29] Chian-chung Chen, 'Legislative Politics of the Financial Disclosure Law', (in Chinese) (Taipei: M.A. thesis, Department of Political Science, National Taiwan University, 1995).

[30] Minister of Transportation and Communication Liu Chao-shiuan admitted in 1996 for the first time that legislators used their influence to gain construction projects for business cronies. At a legislative hearing, he said there was collaboration among officials, businessmen, and gangsters (*United Daily News*, May 2, 1996).

[31] Hung-mao Tien and Yun-han Chu, 'Building Democracy in Taiwan', *China Quarterly* 148 (December 1996), 1164-65.

[32] *Republic of China Yearbook 1997*, 85.

[33] *Republic of China Yearbook 1997*, 88.

[34] *Republic of China Yearbook 1997*, 89.

[35] Tien, 1989, 153.

[36] Tien, 1989, 155.

[37] *United Daily News*, June 5, 1997.

[38] *Republic of China Yearbook 1997*, 83.

[39] See Jane Kaufman Winn, 'Not by Rule of Law', in Murray A. Rubinstein, ed., *The Other Taiwan* (Armonk, NY: M. E. Sharpe, 1994), 209-10.

[40] *United Daily News*, March 4, 1997.

[41] *United Daily News*, February 27, 1997.

[42] Matei Mihalca, 'From Practice to Theory', *TOPICS*, vol. 26, no. 10 (December 1996), 16-18.

[43] Thomas A. Gold, 'Consolidating Taiwan's Democracy', (The Illinois-Taiwan Seminar Series, No. 1, Center for East Asian and Pacific Studies, University of Illinois at Urbana-Champaign, 1996), 11.

[44] Personal interview with Chris Murck, president of the American Chamber of Commerce, May 23, 1996.

[45] Personal interview with Yih-jiau Hwang, Director, Department of Information, Taiwan Provincial Government, May 31, 1997.

[46] *United Daily News*, March 28, 1997.

5　Changing Status of Economic Interests

Introduction

The Plural Society: A Metaphor or a Fact?

In chapter 2, we concluded that the client and corporate state approaches provide the best understanding of Taiwan's political economy from 1945 to 1986.　Although small- and medium-size enterprises (SMEs) were increasingly vital economic agents and were indispensable to Taiwan's export promotion strategy, the KMT party-state selected strategies and provided the incentives for each change in political economic direction.

In chapters 3 and 4, we evaluated the political reforms that weakened the state's control over social forces.　State leaders, and particularly Chiang Ching-kuo, launched a course of political reform.　This included lifting emergency decrees and martial law and reforming the KMT itself.　Equally, reforms included development of grassroots and elite pressures for political change, culminating in legitimate opposition parties.　Within 10 years of the chartering of political parties, two parties (DPP and NP) had gained nearly 50 percent of the vote in Legislative Yuan elections.　By acting as a coalition within the legislature, they were able to initiate additional democratic reforms and stall government action.　This division of power within the Legislative Yuan, and competition between it and the executive, were the clearest signs of increased autonomy of institutions in the state.

Another form of political liberalization accompanied these reforms: increased cross-straits relations.　Noting that cross-straits tensions had declined in the previous two decades, Chiang Ching-kuo lifted the ban on travel to the mainland in 1987. Over the next three years, more than 3 million Taiwan residents traveled to mainland China, and about 20 thousand mainland residents visited Taiwan. Indirect trade (mostly via Hong Kong) and investment followed these visits, and by 1991,[1] bilateral trade had reached $5.8 billion and investment at least $3 billion. This flood of social, economic, and cultural contacts opened the subject of Taiwan's relations with mainland China to political discussion and debate. Initially, the old "three no's" policy (no contact, no negotiation, no compromise with the Chinese communists) slowed the normalization of relations. So did the PRC's adherence to the "one country, two systems" modality, while Taiwan insisted it would make progress toward reunification when China became democratic. However, both sides used a series of unofficial means to increase relations, motivated by incidents needing to be resolved (return of hijacked aircraft, for example) and timed by the clock of Hong Kong's transfer from British to Chinese sovereignty (accomplished on July 1, 1997). Despite Chinese military exercises near Taiwan in 1995 and 1996, negotiations concluded successfully on the establishment of direct shipping links between Hong Kong and Taiwan in April 1997.

The range of political reforms in domestic politics and in Taiwan's most important foreign relationship represents a new stage in the development of political pluralism in Taiwan, and it raises the question of whether there are parallel forms of pluralism in Taiwan's economy and society. Pluralism is a metaphorical concept without a basis in free-standing, voluntarily organized social groups that can pressure the state, compete and cooperate with its agencies and institutions. Invariably pluralism requires an economic basis. In this chapter we examine the development of autonomy in economic interests.[2]

Changes in the Marketplace from 1986 to 1997

The trade promotion policy has now been in place for more than three decades and is responsible for Taiwan's growth miracle and rapidly expanding wealth. The government made structural adjustments in the late 1970s and 1980s to encourage realignment of economic sectors. Economic pressures continued and intensified, however, and it became necessary to make further structural adjustments. Pressures emerged from domestic and international sources.

Early in its industrialization strategy, Taiwan benefited from low labor and relatively inexpensive land costs. As industrialization proceeded, labor costs rose as productivity gains were returned to workers. Moreover, with rising living standards and higher quality of life expectations, labor shortages developed, especially for public construction and manufacturing jobs. As plants expanded and housing stock increased, pressures on Taiwan's limited landscape also intensified. A bubble economy with speculation in land and real estate figured in stock market booms in the 1980s and early 1990s, further increasing the costs of production in Taiwan.

Meanwhile, Taiwan faced growing trade competition for markets from other Asian NICs and, increasingly, from mainland China. In areas of labor-intensive production, such as textiles, Taiwan's firms lost their comparative advantage. SMEs began to move production offshore or to close shop. They also put pressure on the state to assist with the expensive R&D needed to help them move into new market niches. Domestic firms thus pressed the state for greater assistance in capital and technology to substitute for labor-intensive production.

The scandal of Taiwan's economic development success was her growing trade surpluses, and these increased international reactions. By 1987, Taiwan's trade surplus was a whopping US $18.7 billion. The trade surplus declined regularly after that high point, but in 1995 it still stood at US $8.1 billion. (Movement of industries to mainland China has also exported some of Taiwan's trade surplus there.) Taiwan's cumulative trade surpluses exceeded US $100 billion by 1996 and were then the second largest in the world (after Japan).

Permanent trade surpluses evoked protests from Taiwan's major trading partners, in particular the United States. When the United States became a global debtor nation in 1985 because of its high trade deficits, pressures mounted to "level the playing field", and Taiwan was a prominent East Asian target. Since the late 1980s, the United States has demanded that Taiwan remove trade barriers and allow a greater amount of foreign products to enter its domestic market at reduced import tariffs. The United States also pressured the Taiwan government to appreciate the NT dollar, which it did in the mid 1980s.

Pressures by the United States were soon echoed by Taiwan's other trading partners. Market opening pressures were also linked to changes in the global trading system, as negotiations in the Uruguay Round of the General Agreement on Tariffs and Trade (GATT) moved toward conclusion. The new global trading regime inaugurated by the World Trade Organization (WTO) required members to lower tariffs, remove discriminatory quotas and other restrictions, and liberalize trade in agricultural products, industrial areas, and (for the first time) in services.

The combination of pressures squeezed Taiwan's smallest firms uncomfortably tightly. It created new opportunities for Taiwan's large corporations, conglomerates, and medium-size firms. It increased requests for government facilitative assistance and for a change in rules of export. And it increased the pressure on the government to encourage large-scale capital investments abroad.

The state's investment in industrial technology research labs brought it into closer contact with large firms.[3] Large trading firms also were better able to use economies of scale to face increased foreign competition in domestic markets. Firms in low-end assembly operations without the capital or technology to ratchet up to new market niches continued to move overseas. Because these firms were connected to middle and upstream manufacturers, they often drew the latter along in their movement offshore. The government eased the process by liberalizing rules for capital movements. It announced its "southward strategy" for investment of Taiwan's enterprises in high-growth regions of Southeast Asia. And it did not oppose the growing interdependence between Taiwan and southern Chinese regions where factories established by Taiwan's entrepreneurs "exported intermediate goods from the island to China for labor-intensive assembly and then exported the final products to third markets, most prominently the United States".[4]

Vice chair of the Mainland Affairs Council Kao Koong-lian reported in mid 1997 that government policy did not encourage investment in the mainland, but he admitted it could do little to restrict such investment as it lacked the capability to conduct close scrutiny of activities of Taiwan investors there.[5] The general pattern, however, was a shift in Taiwan's trade dependence on the United States to growing investment and investment-led trade in neighboring economies, especially in Southeast Asia and mainland China.

A final change was a response to the insufficient level of domestic investment, contributing to an excess rate of domestic savings. In 1991, the Executive Yuan inaugurated a six-year National Construction Plan with a target investment of US $300 billion. This plan included procuring land for public use ($40 billion), expenditures on welfare, education, and health ($70 billion), and capital formation in the areas of power plants and refineries, transportation networks, infrastructure, and environmental protection ($190 billion).[6] By 1997, the six-year plan was not finished. It had reduced excess domestic savings and part of Taiwan's excessive trade surplus, but it had also, as noted throughout this study, increased opportunities for corruption in public construction projects.

We begin by reviewing the consequences of these economic adjustments in broad sectors of Taiwan's economy—agriculture, industry, and services—and then we consider briefly changes in the labor force. Most of the chapter focuses on business and commerce, which are the primary sources of pressure on the state in the 1990s. After examining the legal environment for economic organizations in Taiwan, we evaluate changes in the communication of business interests to government and government supervision of business associations. The chapter concludes with analysis of the changing direction of business associations in politics and some final observations on organizational autonomy and political influence.

Economic Sectors in the 1990s

Agriculture

Once farmers in Taiwan comprised over 90 percent of the work force. They lived in rural areas and cultivated rice, sugar, tea, sweet potatoes, and other crops, whose production formed most of Taiwan's GDP (and, in the 1950s, 90 percent of Taiwan's exports). Now farming is a diminished sector of the economy. Farmers comprise 10.6 percent of the work force (in the most favorable computation, including part-time employment) and produce only 3.5 percent of GDP.[7] Farm incomes fall relatively, while costs rise and farmers face increased foreign competition.

In 1995, about 2.16 million acres of farm land were worked by 807,000 farming households, leaving each household, on average, with just 2.67 acres of land to till. Fortunately, they have other means to sustain themselves: only 20 percent of the households farm full time, and the typical family derives 60 percent of its annual income from non-farming sources.[8] These mostly take the form of work in rural industries, which have transformed the rural economy and society of Taiwan since the 1960s and 1970s.[9]

The farm work force is also rapidly aging. Over the ten-year period from 1985 to 1994, the numbers of rural elderly increased 22 percent to 398,000, growing from 6.9 to 9.9 percent of the farming population. The government has rewarded elderly farmers, an important political sector, disproportionately. In 1995, the Legislative Yuan passed legislation (on a temporary basis) granting these farmers a monthly US $111 stipend if they were not covered by other pensions or social insurance. This increased the already extensive subsidization of farming.

Young members of farming families are unlikely to follow in their parents' footsteps. Most migrate to the cities and take industrial or service jobs. Although the government has developed training and counseling programs to retain youth on farms and improve farming efficiency, these measures have not reversed the trend of rural out-migration.

Farm land is a controversial political issue in Taiwan. Until 1996, restrictions on the alienation of farm land angered farmers because they reduced the value of this asset. An agricultural development measure in 1996 loosened these restrictions, allowing division of farm land into small lots as well as sales and inheritance by non-farmers. National restrictions on the rezoning of farm land also were loosened. Both measures have eased the crunch in housing construction, industrial and commercial expansion. They will also reduce the amount of cultivated land, which has implications for Taiwan's food security. Self-sufficient during the 1960s, Taiwan now imports more than 30 percent of its food supply.[10]

To increase the efficiency of agricultural operations, the government has developed a consolidation program to enlarge the average size of farms. The "Second Land Reform" enables farms to be enlarged through land consolidation, promotion of cooperative farming approaches, and mechanization.

Foreign competition in sales of rice, cereals, fruits, and animal husbandry products in the domestic market have resulted in some diversification of crops. Taiwan's historical self-sufficiency has been at the cost of heavy price supports and other subsidies. Demand for rice has fallen as Taiwan's wealthy population eats less rice and more cereal products, and the government has encouraged farmers to put less land into rice cultivation. On the other hand, products such as exotic flowers, which abound in Taiwan's tropical and subtropical climate but were not exported until the 1980s, are now one of Taiwan's fastest growing exports.

Industry

Over the last decade, industry has declined relative to the service sector as a percentage of GDP. In 1986, industry accounted for nearly half of Taiwan's total production of goods and services, but the following year it dropped to slightly over 40 percent. In 1991, it began its slide into the 30 percent range, and in 1995, industry contributed only 36.3 percent to GDP.[11] The industrial workers in 1995 comprised 38.7 percent of the labor force; its largest component was manufacturing, which produced nearly 80 percent of total industrial production and employed 27.1 percent of the national work force.

The first- and second-stage, labor-intensive industrial sectors have been in decline in the late 1980s and 1990s. Processed foods, textiles, garments, leather products, and wood and bamboo products now contribute significantly less to export sales than previously. Capital- and technology-intensive industries—such as chemicals, petrochemicals, information technology, electrical equipment, and electronics—led the growth charts during the 1990s.

It is noteworthy that the movement of SMEs engaged in these growth sectors to mainland Chinese and Southeast Asian production sites has not yet hollowed out the industries. Parent companies (upstream conglomerates such as Formosa Plastics) and mid-stream intermediate firms have usually followed them to offshore sites, but most also have retained their Taiwan staging areas while emphasizing management and production efficiencies.

The brightest sector in Taiwan's 1990s manufacturing industry is information technology; its growth rate in production value has increased at least 25 percent annually. Three-fourths of this growth arose from the nearly 1000 computer hardware manufacturers on the island. In 1996, Taiwan was the world's third-largest computer hardware supplier. Locally produced computers and peripherals—such as monitors, mother boards, scanners, and keyboards—owned over 50 percent of the world market because of their high quality and competitive prices.[12]

Taiwan's information technology industry benefits from substantial government assistance through the National Information Infrastructure program. The structure of the industry is pyramidal. A small number of large companies, such as world giant Acer (the seventh largest), invest resources and time in R&D and product innovation. About 85 percent of the firms, however, are SMEs, and they lack the capital to invest in technology. Yet their flexibility and capability give the industry most of its dynamism, as they can adjust production quickly to changes in market trends.[13] As is the case in many other manufacturing sectors, the SMEs rely heavily on imports of important parts and the latest technology from Japan, the United States, or Europe. They then produce goods based on the manufacturers' original equipment and design and keep in close touch with the global technological market. Vincent Wang explains the profile of Taiwan's high-tech development as "shaped by a dynamic trio of entrepreneurial state, guerrilla capitalism, and accommodative technologists".[14] In his view, the large state role in promoting high-tech industries has not led to negative consequences often found in other countries.

Taiwan also has its share of slow-growing manufacturers, such as the automobile industry. Unlike Japan and Korea, the government did not develop a successful line of Taiwan-made vehicles. Instead, 11 manufacturers formed joint ventures with foreign producers, mostly from Japan, and sell primarily to the domestic market.

Services

Services have become the largest part of Taiwan's GDP. By 1995, over 50 percent of Taiwan's employees worked in the service sector. Also, this sector accounted for 60.2 percent of Taiwan's total production of goods and services, a percentage not greatly different from that of many advanced nations. The dollar value of service sector production reached about US $152.16 billion in 1995.

Leading sectors in the services are finance, insurance, and real estate (31 percent); commerce (26.4 percent); telecommunications (16 percent); and transportation and storage (10.8 percent). Much of the growth in the rapidly growing finance and insurance area is attributable to the liberalization of the domestic market and the development of foreign competition.

Labor Force Composition and Interest Representation

Composition and Protections

Taiwan's labor force in 1995 numbered 9.2 million people, about 61 percent of whom were males. Two-thirds were hourly or salaried workers, and the balance were self-employed. However, the composition of the labor force has changed significantly over the last several decades: industrial and agricultural workers have declined, relatively, while service workers have increased.

Taiwan's rate of unemployment has been among the lowest of any industrial nation, hovering just above 2 percent in most years. (During the economic slowdown in 1996 it reached 3 percent, causing some observers to speak about an "unemployment crisis".) This low rate of unemployment combined with changes in the work force have created labor shortages in several sectors. Under pressure from business leaders, the state liberalized its foreign labor policy in 1990, recruiting more than 200,000 Southeast Asians to work (mostly in manufacturing and construction) on two-year visas. The majority of foreign workers come from Thailand (184,000 in 1995); the second largest number is from the Philippines (about 12,000, mostly domestic workers); and most of the rest come from Indonesia.

Foreign workers have fueled large labor issues in recent years, with several demonstrations by unions against the Council of Labor Affairs, which has most responsibility in regulating foreign labor policy. The unions claim that businesspersons substitute foreign laborers for local workers, arguing that foreigners have become a permanent part of the work force. Lending support to this view is the tendency of the Executive Yuan to extend visas for a third year, as it did in February 1997.

A series of government protections reflect the paternalistic attitude of the state toward workers. A labor standards law, ratified in 1984 and revised in 1997, covers about one-half of the work force (including most agricultural and industrial workers but omitting many service workers and the self-employed). It protects against unreasonable work hours, establishes pension eligibility, and makes provisions on wages, work hours, leave benefits, and the employment of women and children. Equal opportunity legislation promises access to employment services for all. Labor insurance legislation provides ordinary benefit insurance and occupational injury insurance. However, in 1997 Taiwan lacked a comprehensive unemployment compensation system and pension system that would secure benefits for workers retired from liquidated enterprises.

Labor Organization and Political Representation

Taiwan's legal framework protects the rights of workers to organize labor unions, reach negotiated agreements on labor issues, and voice their grievances and opinions. However, little more than half of the 6 million paid employees belonged to a labor union in 1995,[15] and the number of industrial and craft unions had declined as firms transferred their operations overseas. In December 1995, Taiwan had 1,218 industrial unions and 2,414 craft unions. In 1997, the Legislative Yuan finally completed revision of the collective bargaining law. It designated labor unions as the sole labor representative in the signing of collective agreements (short of creating the right to a closed shop). Over the last decade, however, there has been no significant increase in the number of enterprises that have entered into collective agreements with employees.

Under martial law, strikes were illegal; since then, they have become common. In 1995, there were 2,271 labor disputes,[16] a 10 percent increase over the previous year. Yet fewer workers were involved in these disputes, and most labor disputes were resolved within the year.

The passivity of the labor force until the late 1980s is puzzling in Taiwan's economic and political development. This has been attributed variously to the prevalence of small- and medium-size firms with few employees (some of whom may be relatives); regime controls, such as prohibition of strikes until the end of martial law and prohibition of larger unions covering identical or similar trades; KMT corporatist control; and even the application of the "people's livelihood" ideology of Sun Yat-sen's Three People's Principles, which brought better wages and working conditions for labor.[17] Clearly, however, state and party management have been overriding factors, and they still inhibit labor's independence in society.

Political reforms gave workers the right to found their own unions and to strike. But, in response, business owners organized or attempted to dominate unions, and some curb labor by threats (realistic) to relocate to less expensive sites in Southeast Asia or on the Chinese mainland.[18] KMT corporatist control of labor was a less important factor in the "muzzling" of labor in 1997. Directors of the Chinese Federation of Labor believed that KMT officials could still influence outcomes in the elections for directors and supervisors; as one leader remarked, "the higher you go, the more KMT influence there is".[19] But labor was not among the party's "iron" votes. Moreover, opposition parties now compete for labor votes, and the revised labor legislation of 1997 promises to facilitate the organization and empowerment of workers.

In 1987, the Labor Party formed, but it enrolled only a small fraction of Taiwan's 6 million paid workers. In 1988, party chair Wang Yihsiung (the only Legislative Yuan member of the party) purged the party's confrontational faction, limiting the labor movement's development at the start.[20] The Labor Party became defunct in 1989; the Workers Party formed that year, but it has not attracted much labor support either. In frustration, labor activists formed the Taiwan Labor Front in 1992, which has rallied unions and activists to protest against the corruption and money politics that, in leaders' views, contribute to labor's subjugation.[21]

The Chinese Federation of Labor (CFL) is supposed to represent all workers, but its effectiveness is questionable. Labor activists complain that CFL leaders listen to the KMT or even big business before labor. They cite an agreement between the CFL and the National Federation of Industries to skip an adjustment to basic salary in 1997 and instead award workers an across-the-board 3 percent increase in 1998, an agreement supported by the state Council of Labor Affairs. Taiwan Labor Front members claimed the federation failed to represent labor and instead exploited them.[22]

The DPP draws some support from labor because of its populist line. DPP legislators and local administrators protected labor activists and served as mediators in several labor disputes.[23] DPP legislators also have defended employees of government enterprises facing privatization. This strikes observers as incongruous, for the DPP also has strongly urged the privatization of government enterprises. A limitation on DPP mobilization of labor, however, is the support it draws from small and medium enterprises. Michael Hsiao notes that the DPP's ambiguous class stand has given it an "unclear and passive role" in the surge of the labor movement since 1987.[24] Sociologist Thomas Gold, however, points to the low level of class consciousness of labor, in a social structure that "appears to be bulging around the middle".[25]

Farmers' Organizations and Political Representation

A number of organizations represent farmers' interests, but most still are supervised and guided by the state. In 1996, there were 304 local farmers' associations (*Nung-hui*), 17 irrigation associations, 456 agricultural cooperatives and stations, and 38 local fishermen's associations.

The KMT's penetration of *Nung-hui* has been pervasive, and the party approves key positions of general managers, directors, and supervisors. Even in the mid-1990s, the political affiliation of farmers' association representatives during organizational meetings has been staunchly pro-KMT. For example, at meetings of farmers' associations in 1995, only 25 of more than 2,000 representatives expressed support for the DPP.[26]

The value of seats in associations and credit cooperatives has increased as a stepping stone to mayor and county magistrate positions.

They are also conduits for channeling bribes to voters. Some candidates seek help of criminal syndicates to intimidate voters. Vote-buying was rife in 1997 elections for officials of farmers' associations. A roundup by local prosecutors produced cases of embezzlement, illegal loans, voter harassment, and vote-buying. One Changhua county association deputy admitted he had bribed each voter with US $77 in cash. An unsuccessful candidate said he sent out gold rings to those who agreed to vote for him.[27]

Yet two signs indicate relaxing KMT control over this sector. First, in 1987 (the same year in which the labor movement started), 3,000 fruit growers protested in front of the Legislative Yuan. They demanded a reversal of the decline in domestic fruit prices due to imported US fruit.[28] The following year, rice farmers protested in Taipei, and the demonstration became violent. Some protests appeared to be spontaneous, but most were organized. For example, a DPP member from Yun-lin organized the *Nung-chuan-hui* (Farmers' Rights Association). He gained a seat in the Legislative Yuan in 1992 and has been a vocal critic of national agricultural policies since that time.

Second, the formal affiliation of farmers' associations with the KMT does not mean that farmers vote only for the party. As elections in Taiwan have become more competitive, and as that competition has become more personal, favorite sons and daughters of the DPP often can attract farmers' support. In recent sessions of the Legislative Yuan, DPP members have stridently defended farmers' pensions, thereby enhancing their electoral support from agricultural interests.

Therefore, both farmers and laborers have higher economic status in Taiwan's new political economy, but they lack meaningful autonomy.[29] This is not the case for business and commercial interests, to which we now turn.

The Legal Environment for Economic Organizations

Economic organizations in Taiwan fall under a comprehensive system of legislation and regulations that dates from development of the Republic of China's legal code in the early 20th century.[30] The Chinese system follows that of the European continent, which is far stricter in the regulation and supervision of social organizations than the Anglo-American (or maritime) system. The legal environment for social organizations in Taiwan is one of the most stringent in the world, even after considerable social liberalization.

The law requires that all social units register with the government to operate legally. This means that factory and business owners, trading company partners, and individual businesspersons or professionals must be licensed in order to operate. The law further requires that activities with sufficient members (for example, five factories producing the same product, such as man-made fiber, or 30 members of the same profession) must join an industrial, commercial, or professional association. Special regulations apply to the three different kinds of organizations: socio-political, industrial/commercial, and professional. Socio-political organizations number in excess of 2,500; professional associations number around 400; and there are approximately 1,800 industrial and commercial associations.[31] Our concern primarily lies with the industrial and commercial associations, which formally represent most of Taiwan's economic activity.

Of these 1,800 economic associations, 10 are national federations, umbrella groups or peak associations representing hundreds of individual industrial or commercial associations. About 275 are provincial federations. Most are small associations, organized at city and county levels. The associations are further divided into three types.[32] The manufacturers and producers of industrial commodities are organized at the county, city, and provincial levels, and are highly specialized. They include, for example, the Steel Wire and Wire Rope Industries Association, Association of Fruit and Vegetable Juice Industries, Toy Manufacturers Association, and Transportation Vehicle Manufacturers Association. A peak association, the Chinese National Federation of Industries (*Kung-yeh Tsung-hui*, or *Kung-tsung*), represents the interests of all the industrial associations.

The second type of business associations includes firms engaged in commerce, such as the Rice and Corn Dealers Association, Taipei Meat Trades Association, Insurance Brokers Association, and the Photography Association. The commercial groups also are organized hierarchically into county or city bodies affiliated with a provincial or national federation. Also included in the second type are chambers of commerce, which operate at the county, city, and provincial levels and represent the common interests of businesspersons and their companies or firms. The General Chamber of Commerce of the Republic of China (*Shang-tsung*) is the peak association for chambers. A third peak association, the Chinese National Association of Industry and Commerce, numbers among its membership about 1,100 industrial and commercial firms; unlike the *Kung-* and *Shang-tsung*, its members join voluntarily.

The third type of business association consists of import-export associations organized along lines of trade. This type, too, follows the hierarchical pattern noted above, and there is a general import-export association promoting the interest of all Taiwan's firms engaged in international trade.[33]

Altogether, this system is remarkable for its high degree of specialization by function, type of industry or commerce, and locale of operations. The governmental and political infrastructure linking it is equally complex. Interpreting and enforcing national law on organizations is the Social Affairs Bureau of the Ministry of the Interior, which provides primary supervision over national associations but which also coordinates some activities of provincial associations. Comparable social affairs offices are found in the governments of Taiwan province, Taipei and Kaohsiung cities, and municipal and county governments. The Seventh Division in the Industrial Development Bureau of the Ministry of Economic Affairs (MOEA) also has a supervisory role with respect to the 136 industrial associations. The control agency for commercial associations involved in import-export trade is the Board of Foreign Trade (BOFT), a nearly autonomous agency of the MOEA. Finally, the KMT has a social affairs committee at each hierarchical level whose primary responsibility is to monitor business, labor, and agricultural associations.

The Taiwan system seems to correspond exactly to Schmitter's definition of corporatism:

> Corporatism can be defined as a system of interest representation in which the constituent units are organized into a limited number of singular, compulsory, non-competitive, hierarchically ordered and functionally differentiated categories, recognized or licensed (if not created) by the state and granted a deliberate representational monopoly within their respective categories in exchange for observing certain controls on their selection of leaders and articulation of demands and supports.[34]

However, Taiwan's system has loosened in recent years, particularly with respect to recruitment of organizational leaders and management of demands and supports. Before we review the weakening of corporatist controls, we turn to the process that economic organizations use in contacting the state.

Communication with Government

The primary rationale behind the state's requirement that factories, companies, and firms join industrial or commercial associations is the creation of a bridge between government and business: to use in transmitting government directives and regulations to individual companies and firms, to solicit opinions and views on proposed policies, to collect data on industrial and commercial development, and to serve as a channel for complaints. Associations also play a role in Taiwan's economic development through sponsorship (with government agencies or the China External Trade Development Council) of market-opening delegations abroad, displays and product exhibitions. Some associations remain "fingers of the government", for they clear imports (certify, price, and inspect barley, for instance) and administer export quotas (for textiles). All associations spend some time mediating intra-industry conflicts, and the creation of orderly industrial sectors was one of the objectives in establishing business associations.

Over a four-month period in 1996, we asked association leaders which government agencies they communicated with, how frequently, in what manner, and for what reasons.[35]

Locus of Contacts

Most of the associations we studied were national or Taiwan provincial associations, and they directed their communications primarily to ministries and agencies of the Executive Yuan. Association presidents and secretaries-general were three times more likely to turn to the Executive as to the Legislative Yuan, which reflects the continued executive dominance of the Taiwan state in the 1990s. Nevertheless, a number of veteran association leaders remarked that they recalled few occasions in the 1980s when it had been necessary for them to seek out legislators. Business associations then had designated representation in the Legislative Yuan before the composition of that body changed in 1992. The greatest increase in communication with government has occurred with the Legislative Yuan in the 1990s.

Within the Executive Yuan, three ministries had the greatest amount of contact with business associations. The MOEA was, for obvious reasons, the most popular. Nearly all associations had been in touch with the Industrial Development Bureau (IDB) or with the BOFT on issues concerning their members' businesses. A smaller number of associations made contact with the National Bureau of Standards, Medium and Small Business Administration, and Bureau of Commodity Inspection and Quarantine, smaller offices within MOEA. And most of the associations also communicated with the Ministry of the Interior's Social Affairs Bureau. The third office sought out by a majority of business associations was the Ministry of Finance (MOF), with questions about customs duties paid for different product lines and commodity tax issues.

One-third of the association leaders mentioned having contacts with at least one of four more specialized offices: the Council of Agriculture, on food product issues; the Council of Labor Affairs, for foreign worker issues; the Department of Health, on sanitary standards issues; and the Environmental Protection Administration, for pollution standards concerns. A small number of association leaders had contacts with the Ministries of Defense, Foreign Affairs, and Transportation and Communications, and in each case the contacts pertained to government procurement contracts.

Frequency of Contacts

Small associations, either with just a few factories or companies, or with low sales/manufacturing output, tended to have infrequent contact with government agencies (less than once a week). Medium- and large-size associations, almost all at the provincial or national level, communicated with government offices at least weekly, and usually several times a week, if not daily. The national federations on average had two meetings daily with government officials.

Association presidents and secretaries-general who had long (at least ten years') experience noted an increase in the frequency of contacts with government officials. They tended to attribute this to increased regulations over business, particularly in the areas of health, sanitation, and environmental pollution.

Modality of Contacts

The law on organizations requires that business and commercial associations at the provincial and national levels have offices in Taipei and that each association office be managed by a secretary-general meeting specified criteria. In the early days of business associations, up to the mid-1980s, most of the organizational bureaucrats were retired military and mainlanders, which both eased control of business activity and facilitated communication with government officials, most of whom (in the Interior, Economics, and Finance ministries) were mainlanders, too. In 1996, only one-third of the sample of association secretaries-general were mainlanders or retired military. The secretaries-general, however, remained pivotal in the communication loop.

Communications took similar forms across associations. For simple requests and questions, bureaucrats in both government and association offices used telephones and fax machines. For routine requests of information from business associations, transmission of proposed policy changes for review, and response to formal inquiries, bureaucrats used formal memoranda (*Kung-wen* and *Han-wen*). For major policy change proposals, ministries customarily invited association bureaucrats and presidents to attend informational meetings in government offices, usually in groups.

In almost all cases in which associations found significant problems common to the industry or trade, they requested formal meetings with officials, attended by the secretary-general and president and, on some occasions, by other directors, too. The national federations invite ministers and legislators to general meetings to discuss economic issues and to lobby them on changes they seek in labor and welfare law. For instance, the National Federation of Industries holds meetings every six months with members of the economics, finance, and budget committees of the Legislative Yuan. The National Association of Industry and Commerce organizes monthly breakfast meetings with major directors and the ministers of MOEA and MOF, where business leaders air concerns about issues such as the volatile stock market and trade with mainland China.

Reasons for Contacting Officials

Business associations sought government assistance for a variety of reasons, as indicated in Table 7:

Table 7. Business Association Contacting of Government Officials*

Reason	*Executive Agencies*	*Legislative Yuan*
Factory/company problem	37 percent	62 percent
Industry-specific problem		
Industrial development	87 percent	13 percent
Export/import trade	81 percent	11 percent
Foreign workers	64 percent	17 percent
Air/water pollution standards	48 percent	13 percent
Product safety standards	32 percent	4 percent
Health/sanitary standards	18 percent	3 percent
General, business problems		
Tax issues	58 percent	31 percent
Legal changes	46 percent	56 percent

*Column figures indicate the percentages of 99 association presidents or secretaries-general who had contacted government officials for different reasons.

Source: Author's interviews.

While little over one-third of the association leaders had taken problems of individual companies or factories to executive agencies, nearly two-thirds had met regarding such matters with legislators, usually those representing the district in which their factories or companies were located. Although business leaders reported that they often sought out KMT legislators, because of their pro-business orientation, they were most likely to make entreaties to legislators with whom they had a personal relationship, whether they belonged to the KMT, DPP, or NP.

As one would expect, association leaders made the largest volume of contacts in order to address problems specific to their industry or trade. They were far more likely to take these problems to the Executive Yuan agencies than to the Legislative Yuan, for several reasons. All had experience working with executive agencies and knew to which agency and official to turn. Most had a good opinion of the service they received from executive agencies. In contrast, business leaders were more critical of the effectiveness of legislators in addressing problems, and they frequently complained of the tendency of legislators to politicize straightforward economic issues. With just a handful of exceptions, business leaders believed that the responsiveness of government agencies had improved since liberalization began in the late 1980s (both with respect to speed and attitude of officials), and that they received better treatment than previously.

The industry-specific problems mentioned by the sample of business leaders are an index of difficulties encountered in economic growth and development in the mid-1990s. The industrial development category includes problems in acquiring land for factory expansion, restrictive zoning and regulatory practice, maldistribution of government R&D assistance grants, high prices of inputs from state-owned enterprises (SOEs), and restrictions on investment in mainland China. Foreign trade issues included burdensome import duties for raw materials needed in the production process, and particularly, difficulty importing raw materials from mainland China, as well as barriers to Taiwan's products in foreign markets. Restrictions on the importation of foreign workers, especially as Taiwan's unemployment rose to 3.2 percent of the work force in 1996, left plants at reduced capacity. Air and water pollution standards imposed over the past decade created adjustment problems for about two-thirds of the manufacturing industries represented in the sample, who wanted to repeal regulations or at least delay their implementation. Product safety standards that necessitated expensive retooling and industrial redesign, or that gave competitive advantages to newer products and firms, occasioned protest and search for relief from government, as did revisions in health and sanitation standards (which affected food service industries most).

Association leaders also contacted government officials on issues general to business and commerce, but at a reduced rate of frequency. Several associations objected to the way commodities were taxed. For example, producers of CD roms sought taxation as computer peripherals instead of electronics. As part of the modernization of its tax code, the Taiwan government assessed taxes on business and commercial associations in 1993. All associations charge dues to members, usually based on the size and production capacity or sales of the factory or firm. The older associations, particularly those in textile production, acquired extensive property holdings—land, commercial buildings, and residences—which they used to defray a large part of their organizational expenses. Business leaders, however, uniformly opposed the tax levy and have protested to both executive offices (MOEA and MOF) and the Legislative Yuan. Almost half of the business leaders were involved in attempts to relax the laws on organizations.

A remaining question about business-government contacts concerns the role of associations as compared to individual firms and factories, especially Taiwan's conglomerates. Conglomerates have the wealth and influence to approach government officials directly for resolution of problems, and have done so increasingly in the 1990s. A few business group owners are golf associates of President Lee Teng-hui and have direct access to cabinet ministers. In the 1994 KMT party congress, four conglomerate CEOs were selected for the central standing committee (doubling the number selected at the previous party congress). Both ministry officials and business association leaders admitted that on occasion conglomerates made direct contacts with high officials to gain benefits for their factories or firms, but opinion was uniform that this occurred infrequently. A shipping association executive remarked, "Access doesn't mean results". Bureaucrats endangered their positions if they did favors for conglomerates in Taiwan's porous and open business society because competitors eventually discovered and opposed such actions.[36] Conversely, several association bureaucrats pointed out ways in which they had promoted resolution of problems confronting conglomerates that were members of their association. For example, the general secretary of the Man-Made Fiber Industries Association recounted the assistance he was able to give Formosa Plastics in acquiring a license to establish a second factory, when the firm had been twice spurned by MOEA officials.[37]

The extensive pattern of contacts between business associations and government offices indicates the continuing presence of the state in the private sector, its relevance to business development, and the attention that industrial and commercial enterprises pay to it.

Government Supervision of Business Associations

The pattern of government oversight of industrial and commercial activities through business associations has changed significantly during the period of economic liberalization. Initially, business associations functioned as bridges sloped sharply upward toward state agencies; increasingly, private sector organizations have established some balance in the relationships with government. We explore government-initiated contacts with business groups in the form of licensing requirements, economic data collection, representational opportunities, monitoring of association activities, and election of association officers.

Licensing Requirements

From the 1950s through the late 1970s, business associations were extensively involved in meeting state requirements for export licensing, import controls, and certification requirements. The economic liberalization beginning in the 1980s greatly reduced these requirements. Presently, most export licensing requirements have been eliminated, and the MOF and Board of Trade in MOEA have reduced most import controls. (Friction remains over controls on imports from mainland China, especially raw materials.) Previously, the main function of city and county chambers of commerce was to issue certificates of origin. Deregulation has reduced this quasi-official function of chambers, but the larger chambers, such as those in Taipei and Kaohsiung, still are involved. For instance, the Taipei Chamber of Commerce issues 7,000 to 8,000 certificates of origin a month.[38]

Data Collection

Government agencies routinely request that business associations provide statistical information. The subjects of official interest are plant capacities, change in work force size and conditions, production/sales amounts, new product developments, market expansion/contraction data, and marketing distribution data. The MOEA has supplied funds to business associations to enable them to upgrade computers and purchase software to collect and transmit data. However, this function of business association activity has declined in influence.

There are two reasons for the decline. First, government officials in both MOEA and the Ministry of Interior, who are most knowledgeable about economic organizations, believe that there are too many business and trade associations, and their influence is too diluted. Repeated efforts to combine small associations have failed,[39] and a number of the smaller associations no longer represent well the industries, which have modernized. Second, associations increasingly tend to withhold what they believe to be sensitive industry data from government collections. One textile trade association leader remarked: "Our records are complete for all relevant areas of the government's huge export code book, but the data we have are proprietary. We do not refuse to supply these data, but we sometimes say we do not have them". As a result, government offices are more likely either to request data from individual factories and firms, or to collect data, such as on exports, through shipping ports.

Representational Opportunities

Liberalization has dramatically increased opportunities for business associations to influence government policy, both in the executive and legislative arenas. Previously, agencies would post notices on bulletin boards about impending regulatory changes, without notifying business groups or publicizing changes through the media. Now, agencies invite association bureaucrats and presidents to attend briefing and comment sessions on proposed regulatory changes, and, regularly, agencies transmit proposed changes to associations, with requests that they notify members and solicit comments.

Peak business associations now participate directly in policy-making. For example, in 1993, MOEA established a "Mainland Affairs Committee" to plan and evaluate the ministry's economic policy making on the mainland. It invited secretaries-general of the federations of commerce, industry, the Foreign Trade Association, and the Textile Association to participate in its meetings.[40]

Legislators also seek out reactions from business associations. Individual legislators will sometimes use business association criticism in their interpellation of government ministers and the premier.[41] More often, legislators will invite business association representatives to meet when they are considering legislation. For example, at the major revision of telecommunications legislation in 1995-96 (*Dian-hsun San-fa*), three telecommunications industrial associations, the National Federation of Industries, and the General Chamber of Commerce prepared testimony, as did foreign business associations, particularly the American Chamber of Commerce and the European Council of Commerce and Trade.

Monitoring of Association Activities

Government regulations spell out that the directors and supervisors of associations must meet quarterly and that members must meet at least once annually. Both the Ministry of Interior and MOEA must be notified of these meetings. MOEA officials are likely to attend annual meetings of the larger associations, primarily so they can familiarize members with the latest ministry objectives. Interior representatives attend annual meetings less regularly. KMT representatives attend only the meetings of large associations.

Both interior and economics ministry officials claim to spend some time helping associations interpret the law on organizations. Neither ministry, however, monitors carefully the membership profile of associations or pressures those firms that have declined to join (an increasing number in the 1990s). Overall, about 80 percent of industries and commercial groups participate in business associations, which is probably the highest rate of such participation in the world. Smaller industries and firms, which are disinclined to pay association dues, are left alone.

These practices suggest little governmental control over operations of associations, with a few exceptions. The Social Affairs Department of the Taipei city government evaluated the quality of the 150 commercial associations registered with it in 1995. The department assessed the number of activities groups scheduled, records of meetings, responses to requests, membership lists, and association budgets.[42] A remaining indirect influence is in the selection of secretaries-general, who must pass examinations. However, recently, this requirement has been liberalized, and those with experiences in other trade associations may assume new posts; alternatively, presidents of associations may select whom they wish to serve as secretary-general, with the concurrence of directors.

Participation in Association Elections

Most associations elect directors and supervisors to terms of three years, and the most critical election is for the president, who determines the agenda of the association. Until the 1980s, a range of officials participated in these meetings: representatives from the Interior Ministry, MOEA, and the KMT invariably were involved. Over the past 10 years, Taiwan's business associations have taken charge of their own recruitment, with only a few exceptions.[43]

Interior ministry officials observe the elections of some associations, to help ensure that they adhere to the election laws. With the advent of political party competition in 1986, the influence of the KMT over elections declined precipitously. In the view of government officials, most associations support the KMT. Business association executives concur, but, as one remarked, "We support the KMT formally, but we tend to ignore them in practice". The party now pays attention to only the largest associations. A KMT social affairs department official commented:

> We send representatives to assist them in elections, to help them avoid conflict. But now, KMT influence is rare. There are only a few, large organizations that we pay attention to—the national federations, the national chamber—we influence them. The rest we leave alone.[44]

In a recent contest for the leadership of the National Federation of Industries, the KMT stepped in to support the candidate it favored (a member of the party's central standing committee) over the challenger, who had ties to the DPP. The Chinese National Association of Industry and Commerce represents on its boards of directors and supervisors a larger number of conglomerates than other peak associations. Its officers admitted that chairs of committees needed KMT approval: "If candidates can't resolve this issue of support by themselves, the party steps in".[45] Secretaries-general and presidents of the provincial associations, however, were unanimous in proclaiming their ability to hold elections free from overt KMT influence.

Review of these four areas of communication initiated by the state suggests considerable loosening in corporatist controls. The state and party still pay attention to who leads peak associations, however.

Changing Direction of Business Associations in Politics

In some economic organizations, a majority of the directors are supporters of opposition parties. For instance, the Chinese Medical Association of Taipei is aligned with the DPP, which is typical of professional associations, only 30 to 40 percent of which support the KMT. Several observers of industrial and commercial associations suggest that 70 to 80 percent support the KMT. However, many staff members and directors indicated that they were unfamiliar with the political leanings of all directors and supervisors. They commented repeatedly that business leaders were more diverse politically now than at any previous time.

Table 8 presents findings on electoral support of business associations:

Table 8. Business Association Support for Candidates, 1995/1996

Party Supported/Election	Percentage Support*
KMT, Legislative Yuan, 1995	86 percent
DPP, Legislative Yuan, 1995	47 percent
NP, Legislative Yuan, 1995	13 percent
KMT, Presidential Election, 1996	96 percent
DPP, Presidential Election, 1996	24 percent
Other Candidates, Presidential Election, 1996	7 percent

*The percentage of 99 associations in which at least one director supported the party's candidate.

Source: Author's interviews.

Most business organization leaders support the governing party because they believe it to be in the association's interest, for three reasons: the KMT is the only party that has ruled Taiwan; it has been stable and provided the best guarantee of the social order required for commercial and industrial development; and it has supported the broader interests of business in economic development and planning.

During national election campaigns, parties call on business leaders to provide assistance.[46] Party liaisons ask them to sponsor banquet tables to attract voters, endorse party candidates, fly banners in support of candidates, call other meetings of employees to publicize their support, and help the party by supplying campaign paraphernalia (cigarettes, soft drinks, etc.). More give support to KMT candidates than to those of other parties, and this support increased during the March 1996 presidential election. However, some conglomerates donate in a non-partisan fashion. For example, the Evergreen Group supports more than 30 legislators, including mainstream KMT and DPP. Its contributions range from US $20,000 to $200,000, depending on the degree of relationship with the candidate.[47]

The scale of business has a bearing on party competition. For example, most of the leaders of Taiwan's conglomerates have close relationships with KMT party notables; an increasing number of central standing committee members are conglomerate executives. On the other hand, heads of small- and medium-size enterprises normally are as likely to support opposition candidates. Individual firms and business organizations are not isolated from party competition. In fact, the development of Taiwan's political market has increased the salience of business organization support. According to one estimate, during the 1989 Legislative Yuan and county magistrate elections, 70 percent of the candidates were supported by business groups.[48]

Pluralism: Organizational Autonomy and Political Influence

A number of the business leaders we interviewed in 1996 and 1997 had served in their posts for several decades, and could observe the transformation of the relationships between business associations and government, particularly since the onset of liberalization. Several believed that the influence of business associations had declined somewhat, while their autonomy (and the political influence of the private sector collectively) had increased. This paradox requires an explanation.

Increased Autonomy, Reduced Business Association Influence

The president of the Electronics Manufacturing Association remarked that his association had previously had power to approve the acquisition of materials by companies; it also issued certificates of origin. Today the association has no role in export or import licensing, and for this reason it is less influential. The secretary-general of the Taiwan Feed Industry

Association spoke enthusiastically about the democratic changes in Taiwan's society. Pointing to work in his association, however, he lamented that it was now difficult for him to gain cooperation from factories. Trade liberalization had weakened the association's influence over its members. A deputy director of the MOEA division who had supervised business associations for 18 years commented on the changes in his own work. He used to approve all foreign trips for presidents of business associations (and their directors and supervisors); now they can travel freely. Formerly, he attentively observed association meetings, and now he rarely attends them. A MOF director observed that his division once approved the amount of money association representatives took out of the country; now, the ministry sets no limits on foreign exchange. Liberalization has reduced the regulatory controls trade associations once exercised over their members. This process has weakened them as handmaidens of government, thereby reducing their leverage over members.

The national federations of industry and commerce never exercised the influence of Japan's *Keidanren*, but through sponsorship of international trade missions and quasi-diplomatic functions (especially after the Republic of China's derecognition by the United States in 1979), they were able to discipline uncooperative members. These federations retain influence in the 1990s because of their membership size. Some have increased it due to the political connections of their directors. For example, the chairman of the National Association of Industry and Commerce is Jeffrey Koo; his uncle, Chen-fu Koo is the honorary chairman. The senior Koo heads Taiwan Cement Corp., a major business group, chairs the Straits Exchange Foundation, and is a confidant of President Lee Teng-hui. Some 43 percent of the directors and supervisors of this federation head up Taiwan's largest enterprises.[49]

While business associations have less influence over members, industrial and commercial organizations have considerably greater autonomy from the government and greater success in influencing it. They now can refer complaints to agencies with a far greater likelihood that issues will be addressed. The evolving power of the Legislative Yuan, as an alternative arena for dispute resolution, enhances opportunities for factories, companies, firms, and for aggressive association leaders. Political party competition heightens the influence of business leaders who can supply campaign assistance by, for example, donating money, forming candidate support groups, or lining up votes of employees and associates. In short, those who can organize and represent industrial and commercial resources have new options in Taiwan's democratizing political system. However, associations no longer have a monopoly in representing the interests of business.

Now, associations face competition from SMEs, which in increasing numbers seek political support independently and decline to enroll in associations. Very small firms cannot easily afford the fees; firms with factories in mainland China or Southeast Asia require political support in those nations. Conglomerates remain members of associations but operate independently when their own interests are affected. They now control more assets than previously, and with relaxed ideological controls and democratic election campaigns relying on donations, they are more influential. In short, the business sector, including business associations, is increasingly autonomous from the state; its overall influence is greater than previously, but that of business associations has declined somewhat.

The Bargaining Leverage of Conglomerates

Two cases of investment in mainland China during the 1990s show the influence of conglomerates in relationships with the state. Both concern Taiwan's most prominent industrialist, Wang Yung-ching, 81-year old head of the Formosa Plastics Group. (This conglomerate is the world's leading producer of polyvinyl chloride [PVC], a widely used plastic.)

In 1990, Wang announced that he planned to build a US $5 billion petrochemical complex on Haicang Island near the city of Xiamen in Fujian province. The complex was to include an oil refinery, two naphtha crackers, and thirty-four mills to process ethylene into plastics. (A naphtha cracker is a plant that converts naphtha, a light fraction of crude oil, into petrochemicals.) The Chinese government would provide loans and invest billions in development of infrastructure.

The project directly contradicted Taiwan's mainland economic policy, which then banned direct investment in the mainland. Moreover, an investment of $5 billion equaled the total amount of domestic investment in Taiwan from 1980 to 1989. Government planners feared the project would undermine Taiwan's petrochemical industry by drawing mid- and downstream petrochemical enterprises to the mainland.[50]

This threat was Wang's trump card in his negotiations with the government. While he "postponed" the Haicang project because of high-level government pressure, he urged the government to renegotiate terms with his group on a proposed petrochemical project in Taiwan. This plan to build a US $2.2 billion naphtha cracker in Mailiao had been stalled because of high land costs and environmental opposition. The government approved the Mailiao project in June 1992, but at the same time mainland Chinese officials sweetened the pot for the Haicang project. Although the Taiwan government still prohibited Wang's investment in Haicang, it then tripled the size of the Mailiao project, gave Wang's group a five-year tax break, supplied water at a low rate, and agreed to develop a new port.[51]

The second case began in 1996 when Wang proposed to invest US $3.8 billion to build six thermal power plants in China's Fujian province. The proposal topped any investment of American multinationals in China and was 22 times larger than the next largest investment, by a Taiwan company in China.[52] The proposal came within three months of China's military exercises off Taiwan's coast. Critics of the project objected more to the effects on Taiwan's industry than the timing, saying that if the construction were completed, it would create a crisis of confidence among Taiwan's investors and lead to an exodus of plastics companies from Taiwan.

In this case, Wang began with support of the Chinese government, which has favored investments in basic infrastructure and particularly in power. It provided land for the project and offered financial and tax incentives to the Formosa Plastics Group. The Taiwan government insisted that Wang apply for the approval of the Investment Commission of MOEA, and it ultimately banned the proposed investment. Wang claimed to observe the ban, but construction of the power plants began in March 1997 in a joint venture arrangement between Formosa Plastics Group and a foreign partner. (Wang had earlier threatened to run the investments through a few of his ten subsidiaries in the United States.) Meanwhile, Wang urged the government to adjust its mainland China investment policy to improve the prospects for Taiwan's firms competing there.[53]

Wang enjoyed the support of most of Taiwan's business community, which had been interested in reducing investment barriers in preparation for increased direct mainland trade links after Hong Kong's reversion to Chinese sovereignty. By mid-1996, more than a quarter of Taiwan's listed companies were either committed to or contemplating large investments in the mainland. Some 30,000 firms had already invested more than US $30 billion, making Taiwan one of China's largest overseas investors and the China market more important to Taiwan than the US one.

President Lee had called for a reduction in mainland investments in August 1996, arguing that their size and rapid increase made Taiwan politically vulnerable to the mainland. However, until May 1997, MOEA had not put a ceiling on the size of individual projects. It promulgated new rules, forbidding investment in Chinese infrastructure projects such as water works, railways, harbors, airports, roads, and power plants. The ministry imposed a limit of US $50 million on single-project investments (except for larger projects that promoted "sound interaction" or benefited Taiwan's economy). The total permitted investments by any firm would vary according to its size.[54]

In the first case, Wang was able to use the plans for a large mainland China project to extract benefits from the Taiwan government for his group's development projects in Taiwan. In the second case, he was able to begin construction on the mainland by circumventing the Taiwan government, when that course was in the interest of his group. Wang was not able to change government policy on investment, and the state retained sufficient power to deny him use of Taiwan assets to construct projects in mainland China. Wang's action did, however, have the effect of clarifying policy.

Wang Yung-ching is Taiwan's most respected business leader and also among the richest. Although he does not represent business groups, his actions symbolize the evolution of conglomerate influence. Business groups have greater influence vis-a-vis the state than at any previous time. The state may still compel adherence to policies, when it controls or affects resources. When resources of conglomerates elude the grasp of the state, the businesses have the freedom to be defiant, a pattern one observes in the relationships between multinational corporations and headquarters states in Europe and North America.

Conclusions

Our investigation of business-government relations has focused on developments of the 1990s, when new forces and rules influenced the organization and behavior of social and political interests. The pluralist approach, an ill fit for the Taiwan of the 1960s through the 1980s, may explain the new-found power of business groups. Certainly, the state is now far less able to direct industrial and commercial development, primarily because of policy changes endorsing economic liberalization and deregulation.

Corporatist development was a better overall predictor of business association behavior, until the 1990s. The network of laws, regulations, and practices linking the state to private sector enterprises expressed the spirit of corporatism, and this spirit was observed in fact until the onset of democratization in 1986.

We have focused most of our attention on the way that business interests are communicated to the state and the reciprocal processes through which the state links itself with economic organizations. We have found strong evidence of developing autonomy in business organizations, which has weakened corporate control of their behavior. Although plural social forces in the economy are now less susceptible to penetration and direction by the state and more able to influence state policy, Taiwan does not yet have a pluralist society. However, under stable international conditions, Taiwan seems likely to move quickly in that direction.

146 *Wealth and Freedom: Taiwan's New Political Economy*

Notes

[1] Ralph N. Clough, *Reaching Across the Taiwan Strait* (Boulder, CO: Westview Press, 1993), 1.

[2] This study does not focus on social groups broadly construed. For recent interpretations of social pluralism in Taiwan, see Mau-kei Chang, *Social Movements and Political Transformation* (in Chinese) (Taipei: Institute for National Policy Research, 1989); Chyuan-jenq Shiau, 'Civil Society in Taiwan's Democratization', (Paper presented at the workshop on 'Democratization in Taiwan', Asian Studies Center, St. Anthony's College, Oxford University, 1996); and Thomas B. Gold, 'Taiwan Society at the *Fin de Siecle', China Quarterly* 148 (December 1996).

[3] Yun-han Chu, 'State Structure and Economic Adjustment of the East Asian Newly Industrializing Countries', *International Organization* 43 (Autumn 1989), 670.

[4] Cal Clark, 'Successful Structural Adjustment and Evolving State-Society Relations in Taiwan', *American Journal of Chinese Studies*, vol. 2, no. 2 (October 1994), 192.

[5] *United Daily News*, July 1, 1997.

[6] Chi Schive, 'How Did Taiwan Solve its Dutch Disease Problem?' *Asian Economic Studies*, vol. 5 (1994), 186.

[7] Council for Economic Planning and Development (CEPD), *Taiwan Statistical Data Book 1996*, 2, 20.

[8] *Republic of China Yearbook 1997*, 187.

[9] Jack F. Williams, 'Vulnerability and Change in Taiwan's Agriculture', in Murray A. Rubinstein, ed., *The Other Taiwan: 1945 to the Present* (Armonk, NY: M. E. Sharpe, 1994), 218.

[10] Williams, 1994, 221.

[11] CEPD, 1996, 2.

[12] *Republic of China Yearbook 1997*, 162; see also Christopher Howe, 'The Taiwan Economy', *China Quarterly* 148 (December 1996), 1173.

[13] One small toy manufacturing firm had nearly 3 million toy dinosaurs in US stores a week before the opening of *Jurassic Park*.

[14] Vincent Wei-cheng Wang, 'Developing the Information Industry in Taiwan', *Pacific Affairs*, vol. 68, no. 4 (Winter 1995-96), 553.

[15] *Republic of China Yearbook 1997*, 348.

[16] *Republic of China Yearbook 1997*, 349.

[17] Yin-wah Chu, 'Democracy and Organized Labor in Taiwan: The 1986 Transition', *Asian Survey*, vol. XXXVI, no. 5 (May 1996), 496.

[18] Chu, 1996, 509.

[19] Personal interview with Ho-sheng Yu, Assistant General-Secretary, the Chinese Federation of Labor, March 5, 1996.

[20] Yu-shan Wu, 'Marketization of Politics: The Taiwan Experience', *Asian Survey*, vol. XXIX, no. 4 (April 1989), 389.

[21] *United Daily News*, November 17, 1996.

[22] *United Daily News*, June 26, 1997.

[23] Personal interview with Feng-hsi Lin, DPP legislator, March 13, 1996.

[24] Hsin-huang Michael Hsiao, 'The Labor Movement in Taiwan', in Denis Fred Simon and Michael Y. M. Kau, eds., *Taiwan: Beyond the Economic Miracle* (Armonk, NY: M. E. Sharpe, 1992), 163.

[25] Gold, 1996, 1107.
[26] Personal interview with Fu-shan Liu, Deputy Director, Farmers' Service Department, Council of Agriculture, April 26, 1996.
[27] *United Daily News*, February 18, 1977.
[28] Hsin-huang Michael Hsiao, 'The Rise of Social Movements and Civil Protests', in Tun-jen Cheng and Stephan Haggard, eds., *Political Change in Taiwan* (Boulder, CO: Lynne Rienner Publishers, 1992), 64.
[29] Shiau provides an explanation by suggesting that the social movements so critical to launching Taiwan's democratization have now been absorbed into normal politics.(1996, 35).
[30] This and the following sections are based on the author's article 'The Changing Role of Business Associations in Democratizing Taiwan', *Journal of Contemporary China* (forthcoming).
[31] Chao-hsien Shih, *Research on the Republic of China's Law on Industrial Associations* (in Chinese) (Taipei: Ming-ho Publishing Co., 1993), 13.
[32] Hung-mao Tien, *The Great Transition: Political and Social Change in the Republic of China* (Stanford, CA: Hoover Institution Press, 1989), 52.
[33] Tien, 1989, 53.
[34] Philippe Schmitter, 'Still the Century of Corporatism?' in Philippe Schmitter and Gerhard Lehmbruck, eds., *Trends toward Corporatist Intermediation* (Beverly Hills, CA: Sage Publications, 1979), 13.
[35] A sample of business associations was drawn from lists made available by the Social Affairs Department of the Ministry of the Interior, the Seventh Division of the Industrial Development Bureau, and the *Directory of Taiwan 1996* (*China News*). The sample included all national federations, about one-fifth of the Taiwan provincial industrial and commercial associations, and about 5.6 percent of city/county-level associations—a total of 99 associations. Associations were selected to represent different industrial and trade sectors. Some 123 individuals took part in the interviews, all of which were conducted in Chinese. Thirty-nine were presidents of associations, 73 were secretaries-general, and 11 were other association officers.
[36] Personal interview with J. Yang, Secretary General, Taiwan Shipping Agencies Association, February 28, 1996.
[37] Personal interview with H. C. Y. Chen, General Secretary, Taiwan Man-Made Fiber Industries Association, January 21, 1996.
[38] Personal interview with S. L. Chen, General Secretary, Taipei Chamber of Commerce, April 14, 1996.
[39] Personal interview with S. C. Huang, Director, Seventh Division, Industrial Development Bureau, Ministry of Economic Affairs, March 7, 1996.
[40] Tse-kang Leng, 'State-Business Relations and Taiwan's Mainland Economic Policy', *American Journal of Chinese Studies*, vol. 2, no. 2 (April 1994), 55.
[41] Fu-hsien Luo, *Procedures and Techniques of Legislation* (in Chinese) (Taipei: Wu-nan Publishing Co., 1996), 47.
[42] S. L. Chen, 1996.
[43] Personal interview with D. W. Yang, President, Taiwan Vegetable Oil Manufacturers Association, April 10, 1996.

[44] Personal interview with T. C. Huang, Director, Social Affairs Department, Chinese Nationalist Party (KMT), April 13, 1996.

[45] Personal interview with Bryan T. Wang, Deputy Director, Chinese National Association of Industry and Commerce, June 2, 1996.

[46] Most of the respondents based their observations on the December 1995 Legislative Yuan elections and the March 1996 presidential elections.

[47] *The Journalist*, September 11, 1993.

[48] Yu-jen Chou, *The Relationship between the Economy and the Polity* (in Chinese) (Taipei: Wu-nan Publishing Co., 1993), 113.

[49] Chou, 1993, 122.

[50] Jonathan Moore, 'The Emperor Speaks', *Far Eastern Economic Review*, June 28, 1990, 82.

[51] Leng, 1994, 57-58.

[52] *Wall Street Journal*, June 12, 1996.

[53] *United Daily News*, March 29, 1997.

[54] *United Daily News*, May 28, 1997.

6 Policy-Making in a Democratic Era

Introduction

In the previous two chapters, we considered the development of pluralism within the state and society of Taiwan. Our focus in this chapter is more concrete. We look at the policies of the state with regard to its environment and its citizenry, and we focus particularly on policies at the intersection of the polity and economy. We begin by reviewing the characteristics of the policy-making process and stating the policy objectives of the first four decades of KMT rule. Then we summarize the changes, both domestic and international, which began to affect initiation and implementation of policy.

Policy-making Characteristics

Taiwan's policy-making system up to the late 1980s was highly centralized, specialized, and closed. The system was authoritarian, and a very small elite operated it. Most estimates place the size of that power elite at around a dozen individuals.[1] The president headed the elite, joined by the premier, and several experienced cabinet ministers (usually from the Ministry of Economic Affairs (MOEA), Ministry of Finance (MOF), defense, and foreign affairs). All were members of the KMT's central standing committee. On occasion, in some policy areas, a private businessman would participate. In no cases were legislators or other opinion leaders included within the elite. Because Taiwan has had only three presidents of long and stable tenure over the last five decades (Chiang Kai-shek, Chiang Ching-kuo, and Lee Teng-hui), it has been relatively easy to trace the movements in and out of this small elite.

    Centralized control was established through collective decision-making bodies at the pinnacle of party and state power: the KMT's central standing committee, which met on Wednesday, and the Executive Yuan Council (or cabinet), which met the following day. The president chaired the KMT committee and indirectly influenced the deliberations of the cabinet.

The policy-making system also was highly specialized. Each function had a separate office, with an elaborate system of monitoring its responsibility. Recruitment to specialized agencies and bureaus of the state was through competitive national examinations. The specialized bureaucracy gained a reputation for energy and technological competence; to work in a national government office increasingly brought pride and respect and was the first employment choice of university graduates. To avoid the bureaucratic rigidity that narrow specialization breeds, policy coordinating organizations developed. The cabinet secretariat organized proposals for legislative and regulatory changes, and it formalized working groups of cognate agencies. The Council for Economic Planning and Development (CEPD), essentially a consultant for the cabinet, spearheaded coordination work with ministries and agencies and exercised overall planning responsibilities for new policy initiatives. Within ministries, coordination offices were formed, such as the Industrial Development Bureau (IDB), the primary agency implementing industrial policy within MOEA.

The policy-making system during this period was also closed. Elites held decisional meetings out of public view. They did not admit outsiders or attempt to expand the small number who could participate in policy-making.

Policy Objectives

Policy-makers expressed three interrelated objectives: security, stability, and growth. Protecting itself from what was thought to be an imminent invasion from the mainland occupied the most attention and resources during the regime's early years in Taiwan. Then, leaders needed to address diplomatic shocks after mainland China assumed Taiwan's seat in the UN and when Japan and the United States derecognized Taiwan.

Stability, especially in the domestic economy, interacted with security. Avoiding the radical consumer price swings that had disrupted the mainland market and the first years of KMT control in Taiwan became a central economic goal. Also, leaders used the power and resources of the state to avoid high unemployment rates, another economic goal.

Growth policies initially were designed to enable security and stability. Economic growth became a free-standing objective of leaders in the 1960s. The focus on equality as reflected in the regime's slogan "growth with equity" was added, almost as an afterthought, when Taiwan's high economic development rate caught the fancy of observers. The negative externalities of high economic growth, such as pollution, did not emerge as policy concerns until the era of democratization.

Pressures for Change

Some international pressures helped liberalize Taiwan's policy-making system. For example, the United States encouraged the development of Taiwan's technocratic elite, and, during the 1970s and 1980s, US human rights organizations put heavy pressure on Taiwan's leaders to democratize.

However, most pressures to change the policy-making system were internal. The elite itself was divided with respect to the extent and pace of reform, but Chiang Ching-kuo staked out a clear position, initiating the era of democratization by allowing political opposition to form legitimately. The regime's opponents then criticized the objectives of the elite, particularly its definition of Taiwan's security threat. They, in combination with grassroots organizers and newly formed groups, launched large-scale social movements that placed new issues onto the national agenda.

Before political liberalization actually began, seven social movements organized: the consumers movement (1980), the local anti-pollution protest movement (1980), a natural conservation movement (1982), the women's movement (1982), an aboriginal human rights movement (1983), the students' movement (1986), and protests by the New Testament Church (1986). In 1987, the year that the liberalization drive formally began, an additional seven movements organized to expand rights and provide greater protection for laborers, farmers, teachers, the handicapped and disadvantaged, veterans, victims of human rights violations, and mainlanders who sought to visit their relatives in China.[2] New social movements gained momentum, including, by the late 1980s, opposition to nuclear plant construction and, by the mid-1990s, support of gay/lesbian rights.

These movements seriously crowded the policy space, and they changed the participants, processes, and outcomes of public policy. We look at three areas of economic policy-making—monetary policy, fiscal policy, and both economic and social regulation—to see what, if any impact, the democratization era has had. Then we turn to an important case with major ramifications for Taiwan's future political economy, the privatization of state-owned enterprises (SOEs).

Monetary Policy

Monetary policy refers to the actions taken by governments to attempt to regulate the money supply for the purpose of economic stabilization—reducing inflation, spurring employment, or both.

Participants

The Central Bank of China (CBC) is Taiwan's highest monetary policy-making and implementing agency. As a decision-making body, the CBC is composed of three parts. A board of directors sets overall parameters for monetary policy. In 1997, the board had 14 members, all of whom were nominated by the cabinet and appointed by the president. Two ministers (from MOF and MOEA) sit as ex officio directors. Directors serve five-year, renewable terms. Although the majority of board members are government officials, the board includes at least one member each from the agricultural, business, and banking communities. (The CBC board has more government officials than the American Federal Reserve. It is unlike Japan's central bank, which is tightly intertwined with large corporations.) The board meets four times annually and is chaired by the governor. A second, less important part of the CBC is its board of supervisors, a body of five, with the director-general of Budget, Accounting, and Statistics sitting as an ex-officio member.[3] Their primary function is to audit the CBC's accounts.

The most powerful figure at the CBC is the governor, who influences the passage of policy by the board of directors, executes board decisions, and oversees bank operations. The governor is appointed by the president on the recommendation of the cabinet for a renewable, five-year term. Unlike the premier and cabinet ministers, however, the governor cannot be removed from office by the president before the expiration of his term. Invariably, the governor is drawn from the banking community; the 1997 governor, Sheu Yuan-dong, worked for most of his previous career in the Bank of Taiwan.

Until late 1979, the CBC fell under the jurisdiction of the office of the president and ranked higher than MOF. Revisions in its organic law moved it to the Executive Yuan but did not change its independent role in monetary policy. The CBC has a close relationship with the MOF, which is now a parallel cabinet institution. In the division of responsibilities, the MOF administers and supervises all financial institutions while the CBC implements monetary and foreign exchange policy as well as foreign exchange management. The CBC cooperates with the MOF in the examination of financial institutions.[4]

In a process that compromises the independence of the CBC somewhat (while enlarging participation in monetary policy-making), the governor reports twice yearly to the Legislative Yuan to respond to interpellations on the current economic situation and monetary policy; once a year, the governor attends the Legislative Yuan to answer questions on the CBC budget. In 1997, the CBC sought to revise its organic law again, to give it greater independence as a separate legal entity with full control over its budget.[5] Although bank officials worry that special interests could take advantage of the CBC's budgetary dependence, there is little evidence that legislators have attempted to do so.

Monetary Policy Instruments and Processes

The Central Bank of China Act stipulates that the CBC follow four objectives: promote financial stability, guide sound banking operations, maintain the stability of the internal and external value of the currency, and foster economic development. Its chief function is stabilizing the market, and it uses five different policy instruments to accomplish this objective: open market operations, rediscount and temporary accommodation facilities, reserve requirements, policies related to accepting or releasing re-deposits of financial institutions, and selective credit controls.

The most important and flexible policy instrument available is open market operations—the buying and selling of securities. The CBC can influence the amount of reserves and the level of inter-bank call-loan market interest rates through open market operations. (A call-loan is a future right to purchase a security.) Open market operations are relatively new for the CBC because Taiwan has not had a large debt securities market allowing the CBC to move a high volume of securities. Before 1988, the government usually had a budget surplus, and there were few issues of government bonds and treasury bills. Moreover, after 1983, trade surpluses created a surge of liquidity in Taiwan's financial markets. What the CBC did was issue negotiable certificates of deposit and savings bonds in its own name, which allowed it to absorb excess funds.[6] Now, when bank excess reserves are high, promoting inflation, the CBC can issue certificates of deposit to reduce market liquidity; when reserves are low, it can purchase the securities it issued previously.

Rediscount and temporary accommodation facilities are a less effective policy instrument of the CBC. Changes in the discount rate do not have large impacts on banks' costs because the CBC rarely opens the discount window.[7] In most cases, then, the bank uses this instrument either to signal its intentions or in combination with open market operations.

The third policy instrument is change in the reserve requirements of banks. Because small changes in reserve requirements may cause a ripple effect on the money supply and market interest rates, the CBC has been reluctant to use this tool. It has adjusted reserve requirements only when high or low excess reserves are projected to continue for a long period.[8] When used at all, this policy instrument also has been accompanied by open market operations.

The fourth policy instrument is unusual in central banking systems. The CBC can accept or release deposits of banks or the postal savings system, which affects the amount of money in reserves. The postal savings system has the largest amount of depositors' funds in Taiwan. (Assets in 1996 were US $81.39 billion.) Much of the security of this system lies in the fact that it may not make loans to individuals or enterprises from the general public's deposits. The CBC retains most of the postal savings system deposits, which account for about half of the bank's reserve money.

The final policy instrument is selective credit controls. The CBC used these to curb asset price inflation in the late 1980s. The rise in asset prices resulted primarily from Taiwan's rapid accumulation of huge trade surpluses; it was manifested in soaring stock and real estate prices. To dampen this inflation, the CBC imposed credit controls on bank loans secured against vacant lots and on bank loans to investment companies.[9]

The CBC's adoption of these policy instruments, like that of most nations' central banks, is clouded in secrecy. When directors meet, they do so behind closed doors. Responding to criticism about the excessive confidentiality of bank operations, the governor has begun calling a press conference after board meetings. And in 1997, the CBC announced that it would attempt to increase the visibility of its policy-making process by disclosing, at least in summary form, the contents of all board discussions.[10] These actions came in direct response to democratization pressures.

Private influences on the CBC take several forms. Private industry representatives sit on the board. The bank also sends out estimates on the current economic and financial situation to important businessmen.[11] Too, in Taiwan's relatively small economy, everyone in business and finance observes movement in commodity prices, interest rates, and in the value of the NT dollar. In this sense, CBC decision-making occurs with a keen eye to adverse popular reactions. Before he was appointed deputy governor of the CBC, Shea Jia-dong (then director of the Institute of Economics at the Academia Sinica) commented that CBC policies were "more influenced by the cabinet and legislators in the late 1980s. As a result, promoting economic and export growth supplanted financial stability as the CBC's primary goal".[12]

The CBC plays important roles in foreign exchange management. Formerly, Taiwan had a fixed exchange rate system. With the establishment of the Taipei foreign exchange market in 1979, the bank implemented a flexible exchange rate system but still intervened in the market often. Then, when it attempted gradually to appreciate the NT dollar to deal with burgeoning trade surpluses after 1985, which led to speculative capital inflows, the CBC relaxed most of its foreign exchange controls. It followed this action by releasing controls on remittance of capital abroad, initiating a process of financial liberalization that continues.[13]

The CBC also is responsible for managing Taiwan's huge balance of payments surpluses, which reached a peak of US $100.4 billion in mid-1995 and which exceeds Taiwan's annual need for foreign exchange to meet import payments. It invests most of the reserves in government bonds issued by major industrialized countries. The remainder it has used to develop a foreign currency call-loan market in Taiwan, aid local enterprises in overseas investments, mergers, and acquisitions, and offer financial aid to other governments.[14]

Outcomes

The CBC takes credit for playing a "leading and significant role in conducting a monetary policy that is aimed at maintaining price and financial stability as its first priority objective".[15] This credit-claiming is based on highly favorable statistics. From 1960 to 1996, real GDP rose an average of 8.64 percent a year, while per capita GDP increased from US $143 to US $12,872. With the exception of the two global oil crises in the 1970s, consumer prices over this period rose an average of only 3.3 percent per year.

Equally notable is the effective use of monetary policy in dealing with systemic shocks. Following the first oil crisis in 1973, consumer prices rose by 47.5 percent in 1974. The CBC took several measures to absorb excess liquidity; most importantly, it sharply increased interest rates on deposits. Observers credit the aggressive CBC actions for the drop in the inflation rate to 5.2 percent in 1975.

After the second major oil crisis that began in 1979 and lasted into 1980, inflation shot up again to 13.8 and 21.5 percent respectively. Again, the CBC raised interest rates on deposits, which corralled inflation rates to their post-war average. (Since 1980, the CBC has used interest rate regulation infrequently, relying instead on open market operations and other instruments.)

A shock comparable to the oil crises resulted from cross-strait tensions in July-August 1995 and March 1996. These spurred huge capital outflows, a depreciation of the NT dollar, and a decline in stock and real estate prices in Taiwan. The CBC intervened authoritatively to stabilize the NT dollar exchange rate (using about US $20 billion of its foreign exchange reserves).[16]

The heavy selling of US dollars to shore up the value of the NT, however, tightened monetary conditions already complicated by runs on a few local financial institutions. The CBC then lowered required reserve ratios on deposits four times; it released postal savings re-deposits and conducted open market purchases of securities. It also bailed out several overdrawn local banks. These measures stabilized monetary conditions within three or four months.

Most observers credit the CBC for very cautious decision-making. They fault it with trading efficiency in banking operations for stability, but they also acknowledge its effective role in confronting systemic shocks and crises.

Fiscal Policy-Making

Fiscal policy refers to the development and adoption of national budgets, incorporating decisions on government spending over the fiscal year (with respect to amounts and categories), taxation policies to generate revenue, and whether the budget is balanced, produces a surplus or results in a deficit. We review participants in Taiwan's fiscal policy-making, the process, and the outcomes, emphasizing spending policy.

Participants in Fiscal Policy-Making

A host of agencies, interests, and individuals are involved in Taiwan's fiscal policy-making. In the Executive Yuan, a specialized office, the Directorate-General of Budget, Accounting, and Statistics, takes the lead in budget preparation. Each of the ministries, commissions, and agencies of the central government has an interest in its own budget for the next fiscal year. The cabinet deliberates on the budget and receives input from the KMT's central standing committee, which will often adopt a resolution pertaining to the budget.

The Legislative Yuan allocates more time to budget deliberations than to any other topic. The legislature's budget committee is most extensively involved, but the other nine substantive committees, each of which oversees executive branch ministries and commissions, also hold deliberations. Print and electronic media cover budget deliberations on the floor of the Legislative Yuan.

Political parties inspect budget allocations and tax proposals carefully, and the DPP has a dedicated budget office. Economic interests, in particular business associations, monitor the budget process. Labor organizations may be involved too.

The Budget Process

In general, the budget process in Taiwan is incremental, allocating a slightly higher budget for the next fiscal year than for the current one. Different processes occur in the two branches of government, but constitutional restrictions give the executive greater influence over the outcome than the legislature.

The Directorate-General of Budget, Accounts, and Statistics starts out the budget process nearly a year before the next fiscal year begins and administers it throughout. Its forecasting team prepares a two-year forecast of government expenditures, revenues, income growth, and prices. The finance ministry prepares its own revenue estimates, and the budget office consults with it before submitting the overall package to the Council for Economic Planning and Development. The CEPD arrives at its own estimates of the outcomes of different budget scenarios. The product of these consultations is the primary guide used by ministries and agencies in formulating their budget requests.[17]

The budget office then gathers agency budget requests and distributes them to subcommittees of the cabinet, each of which is chaired by a minister without portfolio, as one means to increase the impartiality of the process. Subcommittees may revise budget requests, and subcommittee chairs reconcile differences in preparing a final version of the executive budget for cabinet review. The constitution requires the executive to submit its budget to the Legislative Yuan by March 31, where the process takes a different turn.

The legislature holds one or two general budget sessions, attended by the director general of Budget, Accounts, and Statistics and the finance minister before sending the budget to committees. The Legislative Yuan has one budget committee, which gives the executive budget package the greatest scrutiny. The committee, however, has quite a small staff (eight in 1997) and little cumulative expertise. The budget committee is one of the more powerful legislative committees; it has a full complement of members (18) and a partisan distribution weighted toward the KMT (10 of 18), "escorting" it through the legislative process. Because the majority supports the Executive Yuan's request, the opposition parties figure more prominently and critically in budget deliberations in committee.[18] Most organized has been the DPP, which has a party budget center and a list of cuts it annually proposes in government expenditures.

Any member of the Legislative Yuan may attend the budget committee meetings. Usually, ministers and directors make budget presentations and answer questions at the committee stage. Only committee members, however, can vote on whether to advance the budget to a third reading. At this time, each of the other committees reviews budgets for agencies it oversees.

The constitution requires the Legislative Yuan to act on the budget by May 31st, the last day of the year's first session. The legislature rarely finishes before then. When the budget reaches the floor, legislators who have filed budget amendments in committee may speak to them. This process occupies the legislature for two to three weeks and is widely attended. In 1996, because of the political situation with Premier Lien Chan, the legislature did not finish the budget for national enterprises on time. (Effectively, this second executive budget request is to be enacted by the end of June.)

The constitution also limits the legislature's fiscal powers as compared to the executive. The legislature may not increase the budget over the executive request. It can accept the executive's budget, reduce it in total, or reject it; it lacks the authority to increase preferred areas at the cost of those it disapproves or dislikes.

An additional constitutional limitation on budgeting is the requirement that at least 15 percent of expenditures be allocated to education, science, and cultural programs. However, this restriction is observed infrequently; in the 1997 constitutional revisions, it was eliminated

The budget process in the executive is more interactive and involves a wider range of interests than is evident in monetary policy. The Legislative Yuan provides even more opportunities for participation of partisan, ideological, and economic interests.

Budget Outcomes

Over the period of democratization, Taiwan's fiscal policy has changed significantly in four ways: the composition of spending, increased expenditures over revenues, sources of revenue, and growth in size of the government.[19]

Table 9 compares expenditure categories in the central government budget over the ten-year period, FY 1985 through FY 1994:

Table 9. Changing Composition of Spending, FY 85-94

Expenditure Category	*FY 1985*	*FY 1994*
National Defense	38.2 percent	23.7 percent
General Administration	7.1 percent	9.2 percent
Education, Science, and Culture	11.5 percent	15.5 percent
Economic Development	18.5 percent	16.8 percent
Social Security	16.7 percent	20.9 percent
Debt Servicing	4.5 percent	10.4 percent
Other Expenditures	3.8 percent	3.6 percent

Source: Taxation and Tariff Commission, Ministry of Finance, *Government Finance of the Republic of China* (Taipei: 1995), 14.

Defense spending shows the greatest change over the ten-year period, declining from 38 to 24 percent of the budget. (The most precipitous decline in defense spending occurred earlier. In the 1950s and early 1960s, defense consumed about 75 percent of total central government expenditures, a far higher ratio than for any other country in Asia.) Defense spending increased by about 5 percent in the FY 97 budget, to respond to Chinese military exercises off Taiwan in late 1995 and early 1996. In the FY 1998 budget, the cabinet proposed a 3 percent increase (a smaller rate than for other budget categories; as a percentage of the total budget, defense slipped from 21.1 percent to 20.9 percent), primarily to purchase French and American warplanes to counter modernization of China's air force. The opposition DPP, which customarily seeks to cut the defense budget (but supported it after military exercises in 1996), found support to pare this request by US $140 million.

Economic development generally has been a stable expenditure. This includes public construction activity, which, under the six-year infrastructure development plan, expanded greatly and, along with social welfare spending, is a primary means of economic stabilization. Legislators find it hard to control the construction budget. Although estimates as to its size range to 30 percent of the overall budget, capital goods spending is distributed throughout many budget categories.[20] Critics blame the growing size of the public construction budget for Taiwan's recent increase in corruption; both the size of projects and their management—from primary to secondary and to tertiary contractors—provide ample opportunities for kickbacks, payoffs, and waste.

An area of steady increase in expenditures is social security, which includes social insurance, social assistance, welfare services, national employment spending, housing and community expenditures, medical health, and also environmental protection spending.[21] In 1995, the legislature adopted a comprehensive national health insurance program accounting for more than 50 percent of the total social welfare budget. At a total cost of US $10 billion annually, the program extends benefits to the elderly, children, students, and housewives. Still, however, Taiwan's spending on social welfare is lower than most other industrialized nations but is likely to increase significantly, as the government plans to become the first Asian NIC to provide unemployment insurance.[22]

The third area of change is in debt servicing, which now takes one in ten dollars of government revenues. Until 1989 (FY 1990), Taiwan's budget typically registered a surplus every year. Since that time, there have been annual deficits. The largest increase came in FY 1992-94, as the government issued bonds to finance the Six-Year National Construction Program. The ratio of government debt to GDP jumped to 16.4 percent, but it has declined since then; in the most recent, FY 1998, budget, the deficit declined by 40 percent from the previous year, with the expectation of attaining balanced books by the year 2001.

Taiwan's public debt is quite small relative to that of other industrial countries. The debt service ratio (the ratio of annual debt repayment to export earnings) is the generally accepted standard used by most countries to measure the repayment capability of the debtor country; a ratio below 20 percent is generally considered acceptable. Measured by this statistic, Taiwan fares well. Taiwan's debt service ratio has never exceeded 5 percent, and over the period from FY 1988 through FY 1994, it was less than 1 percent.[23]

The final area of change is in the size of government, which has increased greatly. In 1995, government expenditures consumed 31.5 percent of total GDP, which compared to an average of 23.1 percent in the 1970s. Moreover, a critical CEPD report in 1996 noted that the bureaucracy needed to be trimmed: salaries of government personnel took up 10 percent of GDP, about the same percentage as in Western developed nations but 4 percent higher than in Japan, Singapore, and Korea.[24] Given a high population density and relative ease of delivering services, the report concluded that a smaller government work force would allow cost reductions.

The sources of government revenue also have changed over the period of democratization. Economic liberalization—dropping tariff rates, reducing commodity taxes, and privatizing SOEs—has reduced customs duties and monopoly revenue as a share of revenue. Correspondingly, the shares of land tax,[25] value-added tax, and income tax have increased. The land tax is the most progressive of the three; overall, however, analysts do not find that the changing mix of government revenue has had much of an effect, either positive or negative, on income distribution.[26]

As the government plays a larger role in the economy through its expenditures, taxes have increased, but at a ratio corresponding to the rate of increase in state spending. Taiwan's tax burden (ratio of total tax revenues to GDP) remains among the lowest of the industrialized countries of the world. Its tax burden in 1992 was 19.1 percent. This compared to rates of 19.4 percent in Korea, 28.7 percent in the United States, 30.1 percent in Japan, 33.7 percent in Britain, 41.3 percent in Germany, and 42.4 percent in France.[27]

The Legislative Yuan plays a larger role in fiscal than in monetary policy, but it still operates at the margins. Although it focuses public attention on the budget, it does not change the bottom line more than 2 to 3 percent at most. Development of opposition to the government within this branch has led to heated criticism of defense spending and long-winded harangues on government waste, official corruption, and inefficiency. Opposition forces have increased the government's receptivity to spending more money on social welfare and to spurring economic recoveries. Nevertheless, even during the period of its weakest influence in the Legislative Yuan, the KMT was able to round up a majority in 1997 that supported all but $654 million of the Executive Yuan's US $46 billion budget request.

Regulatory Policy-Making

Monetary and fiscal policies can have either distributive or redistributive impacts. Distributive policies such as the government's provision of a public education system benefit everyone potentially. Policies that redistribute, however, rob Peter to pay Paul; they deliver benefits to certain groups or interests at the expense of others. For example, the development of the national health insurance system benefited lower income groups primarily and cost employers, who opposed it. Similarly, unabated inflationary price changes benefit asset holders at the expense of those on fixed incomes. In general terms, both Taiwan's fiscal and monetary policies have been distributive.

Regulatory policies place controls, limitations, or restrictions on areas of economic and social life. They have a different nature from distributive and redistributive policies.

Characteristics of Regulatory Politics

Because government regulations curb freedom, it is not simple to put them into effect in a democratic society. The politics of the regulatory process are influenced by who wins and who loses from the effect of regulations and by whether the costs and benefits are broadly dispersed or narrowly concentrated.[28] The nature of the regulatory issue structures the opportunities for groups and mass publics to organize; it must be kept in mind when considering policy-making in Taiwan's democratic era.

James Q. Wilson distinguishes between four types of regulatory policy: majoritarian, interest group, client, and entrepreneurial. Majoritarian policies are those from which all benefit a little and all pay a little of the cost. One example is highway safety standards. There is no large incentive for any group to organize in support of such policies, and for them to be enacted, appeals need to be made to the broad majority.

Interest group politics, however, pit the economic interests of one group against those of another. Both costs and benefits are concentrated but accrue to different parties. Collective bargaining regulations are an example of interest group politics. Client politics also benefit one small group, but in their case everyone pays some of the cost, as in agricultural subsidies. Finally, entrepreneurial politics refer to issues where everyone would benefit a little (broad dispersion of benefits), but one group would pay most of the costs. To organize a majority supporting this legislation (an example of which is pollution control) often requires a political entrepreneur to overwhelm pitched opposition from business interests.

Although studies of the Legislative Yuan in Taiwan are in their infancy, we are fortunate to have one good study of the impact of economic interests in the regulatory process. This is our base for reviewing economic and social regulatory policy-making and de-regulation.

Economic Regulation

During the first two decades of its rule on Taiwan, the KMT enacted controls over all areas of the economy. In addition to regulatory policies, however, the regime also owned vital economic interests outright. Possession of railroads, other transportation linkages, and the telephone, telegraph, and postal service gave the regime the ability to monitor the population's movements. Control over the banking and financial sector allowed the government to stabilize economic fluctuations, particularly inflation, capture scarce foreign exchange, and direct economic growth. Control over food processing, textile production, and trading in rice, salt, and oil completed the regime's monopoly over the basic necessities of life.

Typically, economic regulation involves either interest group politics or client politics. Hwang Shiow-duan describes one recent case concerning the land law that shows this process at work.[29] A section of the land law was revised in 1989 to require an occupational licensing examination for real estate agents; those without licenses had a transitional period of five years to attain one. At the expiration of the grace period, thousands of agents had not obtained licenses, and they petitioned the Legislative Yuan to loosen restrictions in the law. Those agents with licenses, however, objected, and they petitioned the legislature, too.

A joint meeting of the legislature's interior and judiciary committees evaluated the proposal and invited the rival groups to send representatives. A greater number of representatives of the unlicensed agents (who were more numerous than the licensed ones) attended the committee meetings; they lobbied furiously because they stood to lose their jobs if the restrictions were not relaxed. The licensed agents had fewer arguments on their side, as they would lose nothing if criteria were loosened.

Hwang reports that most legislators attending the meetings supported the unlicensed agents. Political parties took no stand because the issue had neither broad political nor ideological effects, and legislators were on their own. They sided with the largest, noisiest, most intensely committed group.

Most of the public was unaware of this issue concerning the licensing of real estate agents, and they had at the best a marginal interest in it. This is typical of most interest group and client politics cases as well as of much economic regulatory policy-making. Lobbying legislators (and bureaucrats) is critical to the favorable resolution of such issues; the economic interests of policy-makers themselves also bear strongly on the outcomes.

Social Regulation

Attempts to correct social problems such as environmental pollution became national issues in Western states during the 1960s and 1970s. They changed the politics of these societies because the issues cut across the liberal/conservative fault lines of democratic party systems. Also, they brought new groups of people into politics who focused on single issues to the exclusion of traditional bread-and-butter concerns.

Although deterioration in Taiwan's environment was clearly visible in the 1960s, an environmental protection movement did not form until the 1980s. The absence of opposition in the national legislature and strong KMT party control were major elements in retarding its development;[30] the Environmental Protection Agency (EPA) was not established until 1987.

The EPA drafted an environmental impact evaluation law and submitted it to the legislature in 1990. The proposed law would require public and private agencies to conduct environmental impact evaluations before construction of plants, housing, or golf courses. The issue was one of entrepreneurial politics, for everyone benefits marginally from evaluation of such impacts; however, it would cost businesses to conduct the evaluations, and possibly, developments would be delayed or canceled.

It took 15 months for the proposed law to reach the joint reviewing stage by three committees (interior, economics, and judiciary), which may indicate stalling by business-affiliated interests in the legislature. At committee review, only one business group representative, the Rebar conglomerate's Wang Ling-lin, opposed the proposal because it might retard economic development. Legislators in support of environmental protection dominated the process, and it quickly passed through the committee.[31] Once reaching the floor, however, it took nearly three years to complete the last two readings, again suggesting that the leadership opposed the legislation. They could not thwart an issue with broad popular appeal, but they could delay it.

Another entrepreneurial politics issue, that of opposition to expansion of nuclear power plants, reveals the tortured pace of some social legislation. Taiwan's fourth nuclear power project has been on the drawing board for over 15 years. Business leaders complain incessantly about the lack of sufficient power, and Taipower has sought the added capacity.

Opposition to nuclear power plants developed in Taiwan after the TMI and Chernobyl meltdowns raised safety concerns. Also, Taiwan lacks adequate toxic waste disposal sites (prompting the government to negotiate with North Korea in 1997 for disposal of Taiwan's waste there). When the Executive Yuan requested budget approval for construction of the fourth project in 1996, the legislature responded to energetic anti-nuclear power protests by overturning the request. That same day, however, General Electric won the US $1.8 billion contract for the plant's two reactors. With this *fait accompli*, KMT leaders were able to assemble sufficient votes to revive the project.

In the area of environmental protection, a high visibility issue with majority support may overcome the opposition of development interests. The nuclear power plant protest shows that when those interests are supported by the executive, development can be delayed but not easily denied.

De-regulation and Economic Liberalization

Economic liberalization became popular in Taiwan from the mid- to late 1980s, continuing through the 1990s, and de-regulation of the economy has been a prominent topic. Some cases of de-regulation express majoritarian politics; most, however, represent interest group and client group politics. For example, major loosening of government controls on banking and finance pit established banking interests against newer interests such as credit unions, a clear illustration of interest group politics.

A number of de-regulation decisions were made by state technocrats who acted in anticipation of foreign pressures on Taiwan to liberalize its services sector. For example, financial capitalists who stood to benefit from liberalization of banking laws in 1989 did not press the government to revise the laws. The critical decisions were made by technocrats and government bureaucrats who shared a neo-classical economics perspective and an institutional relationship (through the economics department of National Taiwan University). Yet the design of banking law de-regulation— the requirement that new banks have assets of more than US $370.3 million—raised an insuperable market barrier for SMEs.[32]

A case of client politics is a recent statute encouraging private participation in transportation infrastructure projects. The issue arose in 1993 when the Executive Yuan froze construction of the high-speed railway through Taipei because of alarming budget deficits. The executive then requested legal authority from the Legislative Yuan to allow private participation so the project could proceed. It quickly drafted legislation and urged the legislature to adopt it.

Interests that would benefit from the new legal authority were the construction industry, those who had speculated on land near the railway line (large businesses), and local factions operating in areas adjacent to the line. Of the KMT members of the joint committee of transportation, interior, finance, and economics who participated in deliberations, most represented districts near the railway, were involved in construction-related enterprises, or were supported by local factions. They backed the legislation, which also bore the imprimatur of party support. Fewer DPP legislators had financial interests in the issue or represented districts near future railway stops. The DPP opposed the KMT on the issue, and it blamed the executive for a rushed process that produced bad legislation.[33] In this case, the clients were interconnected with the ruling party, with support in both the executive and legislature, and the legislation passed quickly.

In the section below, we consider a larger and more complex case, that of privatization of SOEs. It shows aspects of both interest group and client politics.

Taiwan's Privatization Process

Throughout the world, governments are restructuring and downsizing in attempts to reduce costs, improve economic efficiency, and increase democratic legitimacy.[34] The most commonly used expression for this process of shifting government assets and functions to the private sector is "privatization" (in Chinese, *Min-ying-hua*). Initially, observers focused on western European privatization cases, as first the Thatcher government, then the French, German, and Italian governments denationalized state corporations and other assets. The tide of change sweeping across countries of the former Soviet Union and the once communist countries of central and eastern Europe brought sweeping privatization efforts. Reverberations were felt in Latin America and Asia, even mainland China. By 1994, the ten-year total of sales to investors of state-owned enterprises around the globe had reached $468 billion.[35] Only Africa and the Middle East experienced little restructuring of their political economic systems.

Taiwan presents a fascinating case study of the privatization process. It has had a sizable state-owned enterprise (SOE) sector,[36] dating to the Japanese occupation from 1895 to 1945. The state played a large role in the industrialization of Taiwan, and SOEs were pivotal in providing assistance to the export sector (mostly composed of small- and medium-size enterprises, or SMEs) and stabilizing the domestic economy. SOEs have occupied a larger share of the gross domestic product in Taiwan than in the economies of Japan and South Korea. Large business conglomerates in Taiwan correspondingly are less influential politically and economically than Japan's *keiretsu* and Korea's *chaebol*.[37]

Taiwan's privatization process is also more disjointed than that of most other states. After land reform in the early 1950s, the state partially compensated landlords with shares of government enterprises, reducing the public sector portion somewhat. Then, after the first oil shock, Taiwan's government created new public enterprises in a secondary import substitution stage. The main era of privatization, from 1989 to the present, occurred simultaneously with significant democratization of the polity, and the complex process reflects tension between the state and private sector, between die-hard and lukewarm advocates of economic liberalization, and between different economic interests in the national elite.

This case study analyzes Taiwan's privatization process in four sections. It begins by describing the origins and development of SOEs in Taiwan. Then it examines the political and economic forces which lay behind the government's 1989 plan to privatize Taiwan's SOEs. The early privatization cases, which led to revisions in the timetable and methodology for economic restructuring, compose the third section. The final section analyzes the obstacles to sale of government assets, particularly in Taiwan's capital, labor, and political markets.

Public Enterprises in Taiwan

When leaders decided to launch a large-scale privatization effort in 1989, they had some experience in selling government assets to the public. Also, they had an appreciation for the role SOEs played in economic development and nationalist control. This cycle of privatization, business concentration, then privatization implies a zigzag pattern in the role of SOEs in Taiwan's economy. However, this role has been declining steadily since the 1970s. As a share in gross fixed capital formation, SOEs have ranged from 31.7 percent in 1952, to a high of 40.3 percent in 1975, dropping to a low of 14.4 percent in 1995, and averaging overall 27.3 percent. As a share in industrial production, SOEs ranged from a high of 56.6 percent in 1952, to a low of 15.7 percent in 1995, and have averaged 24.3 percent. Finally, as a share in GDP, SOEs have ranged from 14.7 percent in 1952 to a high of 17.8 percent in 1969, dropping to a low of 10.8 percent in 1995, and averaging 15.1 percent.[38]

By the 1990s, Taiwan's SOEs were less critical economically and a smaller part of GDP than China's SOEs, but nevertheless they were larger and more significant than those of any capitalist competitor in East and Southeast Asia—Singapore, Hong Kong, South Korea, or Japan. The SOEs numbered among the largest corporations in the state, with an asset value larger than that of the conglomerates, a pattern that differed especially from that in South Korea and Japan. In the 1996 listing of the Top 500 corporations in Taiwan, public enterprises included 10 of the top 50 firms (and four of the top five).[39]

The organization of SOEs in Taiwan also differs from that in other Asian countries. In 1989, there were 122 public enterprises. Of these, 29 were national enterprises. Some SOEs were agencies of government organization, for example the Directorate General of Posts, Directorate General of Telecommunications, and the Ret-Ser Engineering Agency; but most were government corporations, such as the China Steel and China Shipbuilding corporations. About 40 fell under provincial government supervision, six controlled by Taipei city, four by Kaohsiung city, and eight by counties. An unusual feature is that 35 SOEs were governed by the Vocational Assistance Commission for Retired Servicemen (VARS), which itself is a quasi-independent agency of the Executive Yuan. This differentiation in control and supervision introduced difficulties into the privatization campaign.

We can summarize the economic and political functions of SOEs in Taiwan in six points: they allowed state control over strategic materials, assisted industrial upgrading and development, aided implementation of counter-cyclical and supply-side management policies, provided economic security for regime supporters, created a training base for the state economic bureaucracy, and extended the arms of the state through linkages with satellite suppliers and downstream firms.[40] Their indirect effects have been to check conglomerate and multinational control of Taiwan's political economy.

Preparation for the Privatization of Public Enterprises

The privatization process in the 1980s consisted of two phases: increased private participation in government-controlled sectors, and planning and preparation for the sale of government assets. Implementation of privatization in the "first-ranked" SOEs occurred largely in the early 1990s and is discussed in the next section.

A prolonged recession in 1984 and concerns over the future international competitiveness of Taiwan's enterprises spurred the creation of an economic reform committee under the Executive Yuan, with a mission to make proposals for economic rejuvenation. The committee proposed "economic liberalization, internationalization, and systematization" as fundamentals to be pursued in future economic development.[41] More specifically, it recommended reducing the public sector and increasing private participation in selected areas of the economy. This led to private competition in retail gasoline sales in 1987, importation and competitive distribution of foreign tobaccos and alcohol, and plans for construction of a private naphtha cracker. Earlier (in 1980 and 1981), the

MOF had released a number of shares of the three provincial banks (HuaNan, ChangHwa, and First Commercial) to the secondary market.

This first phase privatization effort did not change the economic structure significantly, but meanwhile two other streams of criticism joined in a push to accelerate privatization. Foreign trade partners of Taiwan pointed to her rapidly growing trade surplus, which reached US $14 billion in 1989. With exchange reserves in excess of US $73 billion, Taiwan's SOEs, particularly the Taiwan Tobacco and Wine Monopoly Bureau (TTWB) and government banks at the national, provincial, and local levels, were cited as major impediments to opening Taiwan's market. (Services trade was a primary subject for international negotiation at the Uruguay Round of the General Agreement on Tariffs & Trade [GATT].) The United States, the major trading partner among Western nations, became especially peevish about Taiwan's government monopolies and their trade-constraining behavior.

The mid- to late 1980s was also an era of significant political liberalization in Taiwan, producing the KMT regime's first opposition party, the DPP, in 1986. Opposition leaders recognized the role that SOEs played in maintaining KMT power and were eager to see them denationalized. The poor performance of a number of government corporations, which sparked opposition criticism in the Legislative Yuan, provided an additional incentive to speed up the privatization process.

In July 1989, the Executive Yuan formed a privatization task force, led by the CEPD. Its members included representatives from the ministries of finance, economic affairs, transportation and communications, budget, secretariat, and the Taiwan provincial government. Its primary responsibilities were to specify objectives of privatization programs, develop an overall plan, revise the 1953 "Statute for the Transfer of Public Enterprises to Private Ownership," and draft related regulations and rules.

The task force defined the primary objectives of privatization as: 1) enhancing the operating efficiency of public enterprises, 2) financing government expenditures, 3) developing the domestic stock market, and 4) alleviating inflationary pressures.[42] The most important of these objectives has been improving the efficiency of enterprise operations.

The task force then identified facets of the overall privatization process, including needed legislative changes, administrative preparations (such as pricing SOEs to be offered for sale and providing for transferring employees), and development of a priority list of SOEs and timetable for their privatization. The task force completed its plan within six months and was succeeded in overseeing the implementation process by the CEPD alone; however, much planning work continued, overlapping with the implementation of privatization, contributing to the disarray of the process.

Initially, the task force and then CEPD and ministry specialists submitted a revised draft of the statute to the Legislative Yuan in November 1989. The legislature did not enact the revised statute until 1991, and it was 1993 before guidelines and regulations were in place.[43]

Administrative preparations were cumbersome, as they involved pricing SOEs, developing guidelines to protect employees' interests, and determining a modality of transfer. Price appraisal committees drawn from relevant ministry/agency staff were formed for each priority SOE, whose recommendations passed the scrutiny of the Executive Yuan and audit ministry before transfer.

Intensive safeguards to employees' interests were still insufficient. These precautions took the form of compensation guidelines (including provisions for layoffs and pension rights) for employees of SOEs during the transfer to private ownership. Also, ministry specialists developed guidelines that allocated priority shares in the stock of privatizing SOEs to employees. In fact, up to 35 percent of the total capital of the enterprise could be reserved for employees' subscription. This gave workers the opportunity, through aggregating shares, to gain seats on the boards of directors of privatized companies.

Modalities for transfer of public enterprises were equally complex. Four methods were spelled out in the regulations: partial public stock sales, private placements, issuance of depository agreements, and auctions in the secondary market.[44] The sales process to be used most frequently in Taiwan's privatization process was designed to achieve equity by spreading share ownership as widely as possible. Institutional investors were not attracted by this format; foreign investors initially were excluded from purchase of shares because of trepidation concerning multinational ownership of basic enterprises.

Perhaps the most important outcome of the task force was a priority list of SOEs to be privatized. Each government supervising agency represented on the task force set its own criteria for target firms. While some listed enterprises the private sector could operate more efficiently, the rule of thumb seemed to be the relative ease of privatization. Thus, the Tobacco and Wine Monopoly Bureau, with US $5 billion in assets, 15,000 employees, sales in 1996 of $3.1 billion US, and a complex intergovernmental revenue distribution system, was not on the list. Nor were Taiwan's three large provincial banks. Of Taiwan's 122 SOEs in 1989, only 19 (later 22) were selected for the first priority list.

Most supervising agencies also prepared a list of SOEs for the second stage of privatization, a list including many VARS enterprises created for socio-political purposes, without any profit-making objectives. One SOE was designated for exclusion from the privatization process: Taiwan Sugar Corporation, in 1996 Taiwan's 30th largest corporation. Originally, Tai

Sugar seemed a very good candidate for privatization, as its operations were profitable and downsizing promised greater productivity. However, it is also Taiwan's largest landowner, and fear of bringing thousands of acres of land into the private market at a time of highly depressed real estate values—as well as government plans to use the land for public housing, industrial parks, and shopping malls—kept this large SOE off the privatization list.

The final action of the task force was scheduling the privatization of each SOE on the list. The government in 1989 felt pressure to produce quick results—both for the domestic political and the foreign audiences. For this reason, the original plan for the first stage of privatization scheduled completion of the process by the end of 1995, and the 22 enterprises were given staggered dates based roughly on their readiness to go private. (Table 10 presents the initial priority list and timetable.) These dates, for the most part, proved wildly optimistic, given the range of obstacles encountered.

Cases in the Privatization Campaign

By mid-1997, only six of the 22 SOEs initially targeted for privatization had become private firms. Sales of the half-dozen enterprises produced US $5.6 billion in revenues for the government, and the efficiency of the privatized firms seemed good. Some declared the sales of SOEs a success, but most observers were less sanguine in their assessment of Taiwan's latest privatization path.

The first two cases—BES Engineering and China Petrochemical Development Corporation (CPDC)—embroiled the privatization process in controversy from the outset. The Ministry of Economic Affairs (MOEA) intended to sell 60 percent of the total capital of BES through a public stock offering in January 1993. The price appraisal committee, with no appreciation for what the market would bear, set an unrealistic price, however, and less than 9 percent of the share holdings were sold. In June of the following year, a combination of public offering of shares and private placement reduced the state's interest to about 20 percent of the total BES capital.[45] CPDC fared much better. Nearly 20 percent of its total capital was underwritten in the first public offering in June 1991. Three years later, 29 percent of the firm's total capital was sold in a combination of public offering and private placement. The government's shares were reduced to about 36 percent.

In both cases, irregularities flawed the process. The underwriter that had been contracted to sell shares gained majority ownership in the firms. This enterprise was Core Pacific Securities Co., Ltd., the 22nd largest non-manufacturing corporation in Taiwan in 1995. The scandal raised the spectre of conglomerate takeover of privatizing public enterprises,[46] an issue that has dogged the privatization process.

Table 10. Privatization Priority List and Revised Timetable

Administrative Agency	Public Enterprise	Timeline
Ministry of Economic Affairs	China Petrochemical Development Corp.	June 1994
	BES Engineering Corp.	June 1994
	Taiwan Machinery Manufacturing Corp.	end/ 1994
	China Steel Corp.	fiscal 1995
	Taiwan Fertilizer Co., Ltd.	fiscal 1996
	China Shipbuilding Co.	fiscal 1997
	Chinese Petroleum Corp.	fiscal 2000
	Taiwan Salt Works	fiscal 2001
Ministry of Finance	China Insurance Co.	May 1994
	Farmers Bank of China	end/ 1995
	Chiao Tung Bank	June 1997
Ministry of Transportation and Communications	Yangming Marine Transport Corp.	fiscal 1996
Vocational Assistance Commission for Retired Servicemen	Ret-Ser Engineering Agency	end/ 1996
	Taipei Iron Works	June 1995
	Veterans Pharmaceutical Plant	June 1995
Taiwan Provincial Government	Taiwan Chung Hsing Paper Co.	end/ 1994
	Taiwan Agricultural & Industrial Development Corp.	June 1996
	Taiwan Navigation Co., Ltd.	June 1996
	Medium Business Bank of Taiwan	fiscal 1997
	Taiwan Development & Trust Corp.	fiscal 1997
	Taiwan Fire & Marine Insurance Co.	fiscal 1997
	Taiwan Life Insurance Co.	fiscal 1997

Source: Council for Economic Planning and Development, Executive Yuan, 1995.

The third case, the transfer to private ownership of Chung Kuo Insurance Co., under supervision of the finance ministry, went smoothly. In early 1994, 15 percent of its total capital was sold in a public offering. In March 1994, 40 percent of the outstanding shares were auctioned off on the Taiwan stock exchange.

The fourth case, privatization of China Steel Corporation, was the most complex. China Steel is the largest corporation listed on the Taiwan stock exchange, and its mammoth size made the sale especially difficult and time-consuming, requiring nearly six years to complete. MOEA conducted six different offerings from 1979 to 1995 and also used private placement and an issuance of 144A Depository Receipts.[47]

MOEA selected China Steel for the priority list because it was a profitable firm and had a solid reputation of productivity. Managers attribute this success to its having been a private firm before 1978, with a distinctly private business operating style.[48] The expectation was that its shares could be sold easily, and it could be privatized without deleterious effects. However, the size of the sale overburdened Taiwan's underwriting system. Also, global depression in the steel industry weakened interest in shares. Notably, China Steel is the only SOE for which the government has sought foreign purchasers. Approximately 3.5 percent of its shares were bought by overseas investors.

In November 1994, the MOF conducted a public tender for shares of Farmers Bank of China. Ministry officials believed that this bank, and the Chiao Tung (Communications) Bank, the second of three national banks, could be privatized easily. Official concerns centered on timing the sale to avoid hurting market liquidity. Also, price of shares was an issue as the audit ministry looked critically at sale prices. Some shares of the province's three commercial banks were sold, but no government bank had been privatized by mid-1997.

The sole SOE supervised by the Ministry of Transportation and Communications, Yang Ming Transportation Corporation (YMTC) was privatized in 1996. Two share offerings, in April 1992 and February 1994 (accompanied by a private placement), reduced state control of this asset; government shares were reduced to 49 percent by further share offerings in February 1996. The sixth and last privatized SOE was the Liquefied Gas Supply Administration of the Vocational Assistance Commission for Retired Servicemen. This small enterprise was sold to a KMT enterprise in March 1996.

These privatization cases succeeded in the sense that the government transferred its assets to new, profitable, private corporations. All but BES Engineering downsized and produced positive cash flows. However, the glaring flaw in Taiwan's privatization process has been the delay in sales of government corporations.

The slow pace of privatization prompted concerns at the National Development Conference (NDC) meeting in December 1996. The NDC urged the president to proclaim privatization of SOEs a national priority (he did so in April 1997); it asked the government to complete privatization within five years. Thereupon, the CEPD, under its new chair (and former MOEA minister) P. K. Chiang, issued a report calling for renewed government vigor in implementing privatization.[49] We now examine the large majority of public enterprises included on the initial priority list, asking why they remain government-controlled enterprises.

MOEA received most of the criticism concerning the privatization process. In 1989, it supervised ten of Taiwan's SOEs, which were among Taiwan's largest corporations, playing vital roles in both infrastructure and facilitation of the manufacturing activities of such commercial giants as Formosa Plastics and Acer. Only one-third of MOEA's enterprises privatized; two-thirds remain public, for several reasons.

Taiwan Machinery Manufacturing Corp. (Tai-chi) seemed a prime candidate for privatization. This Japanese-era firm was reasonably profitable from 1945 to 1985. Its four factories in Kaohsiung produce diesel and low-speed engines for both the domestic and international markets. Increased competition from the mid-1980s jeopardized its position, and it has lost money repeatedly since then.[50] MOEA planned to auction off 60 percent of Tai-chi's total capital in June 1993 and reserve an additional 34 percent for its employees. The Legislative Yuan's delay in approving the MOEA privatization proposal forced a postponement in the auction to March 1994, and then the auction failed. A survey of potential investors after the auction elicited four reasons for lack of interest: the high auction floor price, prohibitions against firing or laying off unneeded workers, the deteriorating financial position of the company, and the requirement to invest in all four of Tai-chi's plants.[51]

When strong employee opposition halted a proposal to close Tai-chi, MOEA decided to privatize the firm factory by factory. It sold the first, a steel products factory to President Enterprises Corp., Taiwan's tenth largest manufacturing concern, in April 1996. The following month, it sold the second factory (specialty boats and tugs) to Southwest Cement Corp. The remaining two factories are to be downsized and managed until they become profitable, with a sale of shares scheduled for 1998.

Chinese Petroleum Corp. (CPC) is Taiwan's largest firm, with a book value of over US $100 billion, and is the 20th largest oil company in the world. It is the only supplier of petroleum in Taiwan. Its annual income in 1996 was US $12 billion, and it employed 20,700 people. The initial date for sale of shares was 1996, but this was delayed to 1997, with the intention of selling 10 percent annually until the target of 50 percent was reached in 2001.

The enormous size of CPC makes it unfeasible to sell it in one action, and thus its business groups are likely to be sold off one by one. The divisions will include refining, petrochemicals, exploration, trading, natural gas, and marketing.[52] Speeding the pace of reform is Formosa Plastic's naphtha cracker, which will be completed in 1997 and will extend the conglomerate's reach far upstream into direct competition with CPC. In preparation for privatizing, CPC has downsized its work force, releasing more than 2,000 employees in recent years. It has mitigated employee resistance to privatization by agreeing to transfer employees to downstream enterprises and to CPC's investments overseas.[53]

Another arena in which cracking the government's monopoly might spur privatization is power generation. Taiwan Power Co., Ltd. (Taipower) is Taiwan's second largest corporation. It supplies energy to virtually all of Taiwan's households, but its monopoly on power generation will end by 1998. The MOEA has outlined an accelerated timetable for the development of private power suppliers. Political pressure has increased because of brownouts resulting from Taipower's inadequate reserve margins.

Taipower is not yet close to privatization. The *Dian-yeh Fa* is the controlling law for privatization of power. Submitted by the Executive Yuan to the legislature in 1995, the authorizing legislation has not yet been approved. The draft legislation requires several conditions for privatization, particularly with respect to transfer rights and benefits for employees. Taipower's more than 30,000 employees are opposed to privatization without firm guarantees for their conditions of employment.

China Shipbuilding Corp. builds supertankers and many of the cargo ships carrying Taiwan's trade products. Like several other SOEs, it has a role in Taiwan's defense, building ships for Taiwan's navy. Originally, the MOEA scheduled stock sales for 1997, but they have been delayed three years to 2000. The economic position of the corporation has deteriorated as the Keelung shipyard, producing smaller ships for which the market has worsened, has accumulated large debts. (In one year, the firm's ranking dropped from the 38th to the 52nd largest corporation in Taiwan.) Analysts say this yard is not competitive with those in Japan and Korea.[54] The firm plans to restructure and concentrate on more profitable operations in the Kaohsiung yards. From 1994 to 1996, 1,200 workers were laid off, and some 6,000 employees would face disruptions when the firm is privatized. Moreover, the corporation lacks the revenues to solve employees' transition problems.

Taiwan Fertilizer Co., Ltd. (Tai-fei) is now a collection of six factories producing chemical fertilizers and biotechnology products. Its privatization is scheduled for completion by mid-1998. Some of its factories have lost money for several years, and they are undergoing restructuring. Prospects for a successful stock offering are not rosy, and corporate planners anticipate the eventual sale of assets, factory by factory.

Taiwan Salt Industrial Corp. (Tai-yan) is the smallest SOE under MOEA supervision. It has only 600 employees in five factories. Tai-yan's operations too are unprofitable, and although the plan calls for a five-year transition to privatization, this plan hinges on an increase in industrial productivity and an improved company balance sheet. Labor problems will complicate its transfer to the private sector. Two-thirds of Tai-yan's employees are contractual workers with a long-standing special relationship with the firm.

The timeline for the two national banks under MOF supervision—Farmers Bank of China and Chiao Tung Bank Co., Ltd.—has been drawn for 1998, but it is speculative. The MOF withdrew one attempt to improve the Chiao Tung Bank's financial structure by increasing its capital because of criticism from the Legislative Yuan. A similar request from Farmers Bank has not been resolved.

The other national agency with enterprises scheduled for privatization is the Vocational Assistance Commission for Retired Servicemen (VARS), which contains about 100 organizations. Of 35 enterprises, 17 are scheduled for privatization.[55] VARS is an atypical government agency. Its mission is to provide services for retired military personnel. Many of its units are hospitals and home care facilities, and there are no plans to privatize them. The agency has forest preserves and mountain lands; the enterprises in these locations, mostly small agricultural factories, have not been projected for privatization because of land issues concerning agriculture and forestry.[56]

With the exception of Rung-yung, a pharmaceutical company employing 10,000 workers, the VARS companies are small in scale. Those scheduled for privatization are small factories with between 100 and 300 employees. Most are money-losing operations, with obsolete equipment, disorganized accounts, and a primitive entrepreneurial climate. But the lands on which the factories sit are valuable.

Most VARS enterprises are scheduled for privatization in 1998 and 1999. Unlike the majority of the national enterprises, shares of which have been sold in public offerings, the VARS companies will be sold through private placement. One small carpet factory already has been sold in this manner.

The pitfalls identified in the campaign to privatize national enterprises are minuscule compared to those surrounding provincial enterprises. In addition to problems of inefficient and money-losing operations, labor resistance looms large. Most significant, however, is the quasi-autonomous nature of provincial activities, with a separately elected provincial assembly jealously guarding its powers against perceived national government aggrandizement.

Taiwan province has about 40 monopoly enterprises. They include manufacturing concerns, communications services, banking and insurance firms, water suppliers, and miscellaneous companies. About 13 or 14 of these are targets for privatization, and a few have applied to be privatized. Most, however, are reluctant, and there is no fixed plan to sell shares in public offerings or to sell the firms through private placement.

The most controversial provincial enterprises have been three highly profitable banks—First Commercial Bank, HuaNan Commercial Bank, Ltd., and ChangHwa Commercial Bank, Ltd.—Taiwan's fifth, sixth, and seventh largest banks respectively. Sale of shares in the banks has been discussed repeatedly, but, until 1997, the provincial assembly was adamantly opposed. The banks were important sources of patronage for assembly members who could influence hiring and promotion of employees. Also, the banks offered low-interest loans to provincial politicians.

This issue was resolved in July 1997. Both the KMT and its primary opposition, the DPP, agreed at the NDC to streamline this redundant level of government, and the National Assembly agreed with President Lee's proposal to suspend elections for the governor and assembly and "freeze" provincial government. A bright spot for Taiwan's privatization process was the decision of provincial assemblymen to dilute assets before they could be taken over by the central government. In April 1997, they voted to sell sufficient shares in the banks to reduce government holdings to below 51 percent.

Finally, ten municipal and eight county enterprises round out the list of government monopolies in Taiwan. None of these has entered the priority list for privatization, and there are no plans for their moving to the private sector soon.

Obstacles to the Privatization of Taiwan's Public Enterprises

Four impediments stand in the way of Taiwan's successful privatization of its public enterprises. These pertain to administrative planning, financial market capacity, employee resistance, and legislative foot dragging.

The rapid schedule to privatize 22 enterprises by the end of the century (amended in 1993 to include an additional 11 firms) overwhelmed the government's ability to coordinate and plan. Because Taiwan's SOEs are more diversified than those in other industrial economies, relevant ministries, particularly MOEA, often lacked managers knowledgeable about the wide range of problems likely to be encountered in privatizing SOEs (for example, legal, financial, engineering, and property expertise) and the interactive effects of expedited sales. Moreover, the government supervising agencies lacked managers with experience in restructuring and downsizing troubled firms (about one-fourth of the total). The plan to conduct a public offering of shares in Tai-chi, for example, was a costly mistake. Nearly all areas of its operations had been overtaken by private firms, and its debt load exceeded the value of its assets. Lack of investor interest in Tai-chi ought to have been foreseen.

Another aspect of faulty planning concerned the pricing mechanism. The government encouraged formation of large committees representing supervisory agencies and SOEs but failed to select businessmen familiar with market conditions. Committee members tended to be most interested in obtaining the highest price for government assets. Lacking experience of the private sector, however, the committee set unreasonably high appraisals, which deterred investor interest.

The nature of the financial market in Taiwan also posed obstacles to expeditious privatization. Taiwan's market is small and volatile, with a history of little over three decades. The market lacked the capacity to absorb billions of shares in public enterprises, especially when the sales were timed closely together. Moreover, MOF's estimate that the government would have to sell at least 30 billion shares of its holdings in nine SOEs to meet NDC objectives troubled stock market experts in 1997. The release of such a large number of shares over a period of one year would reduce stock prices, in the opinion of analysts, and make it more difficult for private companies to raise funds from the domestic market to finance business expansion. The underwriting system in the Taipei market is also poorly developed to handle large stock offerings.

The government's decision to sell shares of enterprises to individual investors in public offerings reflected its concern for equity. Selling to institutional investors would have exposed the KMT regime to charges of facilitating conglomerate control and developing private monopolies, thereby violating the public trust. However, the sale system conceived originally allowed an underwriter to gain majority control of the first two enterprises, and conglomerates have purchased public enterprise shares on the secondary market. In addition, conglomerates and KMT enterprises have purchased individual factories of state enterprises.[57]

In 1997, the CEPD developed a blueprint to democratize stock holdings in the three largest SOEs scheduled for privatization—Taipower, Chinese Petroleum, and ChungHua Telecommunications Corp. (a public corporation formed in 1996 from the profit-making enterprises in the old Directorate General of Telecommunications). The plan would open 30 percent of each company's total equity to public subscription and allow citizens over 20 to purchase up to 3,000 shares at a discounted rate, requiring them to hold the shares for one year. This plan, too, met criticism because initially it might affect operational stability and efficiency and over the longer term might facilitate consumption of larger portions of stock by conglomerates at cheaper prices via the public.

The most pronounced difference between Taiwan and other privatizing states has been the iron curtain lowered on investment from foreign investors. Overseas investors purchased only a handful of shares of China Steel and no shares of other SOEs. This is a tiny rate of overseas participation for a country with such a small domestic market. Other small countries undergoing privatization have issued large numbers of shares overseas. For example, the New Zealand rate was 67 percent and that of Mexico exceeded 80 percent.[58]

Employee resistance to privatization and the huge cost of allaying employee concerns pose significant obstacles to the continued transformation of Taiwan's public enterprises. The 122 public enterprises in 1989 employed nearly 280,000 people, about 3.1 percent of Taiwan's labor force. As government employees, their salaries and benefits were higher than those of most private sector workers; their workload was lighter and their jobs more secure. Privatization threatened all of these favorable conditions and has met uniform opposition from employees.

To respond to employee concerns, the government wrote very liberal transfer and pension protection provisions into the enabling legislation. The regulations guaranteed employees of public enterprises compensation whether or not they were transferred within the enterprises and irrespective of their seniority. In addition to vast sums in compensation to be paid by enterprises (several would be bankrupt on privatization), the government obligated itself to compensate each worker who was laid off. For the MOEA enterprises on the priority list, the total enterprise payments would amount to US $1.38 billion (NT$ 34.39 billion), and the government's payments would be US $15.7 billion (NT$ 15.7 billion), as seen in Table 11.

The government met additional employee demands for participation in the transfer to private ownership by allocating priority shares to workers. They also gained rights to representation on the board of directors if they accumulated sufficient voting shares.

The final obstacle to privatization is wholly political: institutional conflict between the Legislative and Executive Yuans as well as partisan and personal political conflict over the implementation of transfer to private ownership. Had Taiwan's major privatization effort occurred 10 years earlier, little legislative and no partisan resistance would have been encountered. But the legislatures of the 1990s are popularly elected, and they celebrate their ability to criticize and delay executive action. The KMT's majority was reduced to a two-vote margin by 1996, and the populist impulses now driving election campaigns have feasted on the privatization issue.

Table 11. Estimated Employee Compensation upon Privatization

Enterprise	Paid by Enterprise* *(NT$ 1 mil.)*	Paid by Government *(NT$ 1 mil.)*
Chinese Petroleum Development Corp.	2,623	631
China Steel Corporation	8,209	2,154
Tai-chi	2,497	1,007
China Shipbuilding Corporation	13, 166	9,652
Taiwan Fertilizer	4,887	861
BES Engineering	3,112	1,395
Total	34,494	15,700

*excluding the existing retirement funds of the SOEs

Source: Carl D. H. Chang, "Present Phase of Privatization in Taiwan, R.O.C." , April, 1995, 10.

Most privatization plans have required the legislature to adopt authorizing statutes, and legislators have taken ample time to review these, a process that in two cases delayed timing of public offerings. Too, in 1992, the legislature required that all proposals to reduce government shares in enterprises to less than 50 percent receive its prior approval.

Notwithstanding nearly unanimous support for the concept of privatization, legislators are loathe to give up the oversight role they play in public enterprises. The legislature reviews each enterprise's annual budget, including proposed capital expenditures, disposal of assets, issuance of debt obligations and equity. Moreover, the enterprises' purchasing system, personnel, accounting and finance operations fall under government scrutiny. Altogether, more than 100 regulations govern public enterprises. The legislature's oversight role provides an avenue for intervention from politicians as well as from interest groups.

The issue of most concern to legislators in the 1990s has been employee welfare. Unions of employees in public enterprises have demonstrated regularly before the Legislative Yuan, and most of the 17 legislators on the budget and economics committees interviewed on this topic reported being contacted by SOE employees. Some partisan differences cloud the privatization campaign. Although the ruling KMT inaugurated privatization, it is suspect because of alliances forged between many KMT leaders and the conglomerate groups (or KMT enterprises themselves) who stand to benefit greatly from it. The DPP has strongly supported privatization, a logical extension of its role as champion of

Taiwan's SMEs and chief opposition to combined conglomerate and KMT power.

One critical observer of the government's privatization program disputed whether much had been done to achieve its goals:

> What we've seen so far isn't privatization—it is false, phony privatization. That is, the conglomerates are expanding their grasp by seizing ownership of government enterprises. The KMT also is gaining control of more enterprises. This is privatization only in form. Does it remove government from the picture? Not with the government retaining 49 percent ownership. We want genuine privatization, but the government still is in control, the Executive Yuan is in charge. Moreover, now it is even more corrupt because we don't see the SOE figures in the budget.[59]

The details of implementation have occasioned heated debate. The DPP and, lately, New Party representatives have criticized government plans as favorable to conglomerate interests and insufficiently attentive to workers' rights. The issue of conglomerate control is less bothersome to the KMT. One legislator with a big business background was satisfied with the privatization process and expected it to lead to increases in the size of business enterprises:

> I suspect that after privatization begins a small number of people will control the industries, and there will be minority control. But in an open market, gradually over time, ownership will spread out. People oppose control of privatizing SOEs by the conglomerates, but in fact this is very hard to avoid.[60]

The details of implementing privatization provide fodder for political entrepreneurs in a democratic political market that emphasizes popular appeals. Even KMT legislators have taken advantage of opportunities to criticize the government's privatization planning.

Implications

Although Taiwan's government has several experiences with privatizing SOEs, the campaign launched in 1989 was more comprehensive and vaster in scale than all of the previous efforts combined. The campaign has produced some successful transfers of ownership, moderately increasing the competitiveness of Taiwan's enterprises. It has not, however, come close to fulfilling the expectations of planners or matching the successes of privatizations in Singapore and Japan.[61]

Several impediments to privatization could have been anticipated based on the experience of other countries. For example, employee resistance is a generic response to changes in working conditions and uncertain futures. Collectively, employees are the clients of SOE enterprises, and now in democratizing Taiwan, they have the influence to retard the process of privatization. Also, complex planning processes tend to crash under the pressure of elaborate timelines and interest group protests.

The unique aspects of Taiwan's privatization process concern the structure of its political economy: dominance of SMEs in the export sector, a wealthy ruling party with its own business sector, and conglomerates once operating primarily in the domestic marketplace but now moving overseas. Public enterprises in Taiwan historically have been a bulwark against control by foreign multinationals and domestic conglomerates. Avoiding foreign or private monopoly ownership, given Taiwan's small domestic market, will be increasingly difficult as privatization proceeds.

The timing of Taiwan's major privatization has not been fortuitous. The combination of intensive economic liberalization and democratization has made the privatization process more conflict ridden than would otherwise have been the case. This has slowed the pace and greatly increased the cost of Taiwan's privatization. By stalling the process, however, critics of conglomerate control have bought time that can be used to enhance equity.

Conclusions

At the start of this chapter we asked whether and, to what extent Taiwan's democratization process has influenced economic and regulatory policy-making. Specifically, we directed attention to the concentration of elite power and the closed nature of decision-making processes before democratization began.

Of the policy areas under review, monetary policy-making showed the least influence of democratic forces. It is typically the case in industrial democracies, however, that central banks operate behind a curtain and make decisions independently; the lack of significant change in this area is not an indictment of the democratic process. Moreover, in several small ways, the Central Bank of China has become more responsive. Legislators have resisted its drive for autonomous budgetary powers, and the bank now publicizes its decisions (and promises to release the decision-making record in the future).

In fiscal policy, the bottom line proposed by the executive is little affected by the legislature, but this is attributable to Taiwan's constitutional arrangements. However, the composition of the budget has changed. Defense spending now takes a smaller slice out of central government spending than at any time in Taiwan's post-war history. Conversely, social welfare spending comprises a higher share of government dollars than at any time in Taiwan's history. Legislators are partly responsible for these changes (although the trends were evident before the legislature became influential). A quickly aroused and attentive mass public, which is no longer hesitant to place demands on the state, is a factor, too.

Detractors complain that the Legislative Yuan is a collection of grandstanding, credit-claiming, frivolous politicians who compromise the public interest when they delay or deny executive requests for action. The deliberative function, however, is time consuming and messy, and legislators have used it to expand public protections and benefits. Most legislators are responsive to clear constituent demands, and they show this when pressures heat up. One area reflecting responsiveness is tax policy, and most legislators are reluctant to increase taxes without producing clear benefits.

Regulatory policy-making shows the impact of democratic forces very clearly. Popular concerns now are translated into law within a relatively short period of time. Although social regulatory movements got off to a slow start, if they developed a groundswell of support, both legislators and executives responded to them. The series of 1990s laws protecting workers' rights, improving consumer product safety, and tightening pollution standards are evidence of this.

It is the case that the public will is sometimes frustrated by economic interests. Some of the economic interests speak in the voice of Taiwan's richest and most powerful, who are able to convert public resources to private benefits (as, for example, in public construction). However, CEOs of conglomerates are not the sole clients of the state. Established economic interests such as farmers, laborers, and professionals have access to economic and social regulatory policy-making, too, and newer public interest groups that have organized well and mobilized many followers also have been able to gain access and some influence. The analysis of regulatory policy in terms of four quite different political processes allows us to focus on the kinds of issues likely to be subject to the influence of economic groups.

Our fullest example of the impact of democratic processes on policy-making was the privatization case. Although Taiwan's central economic policy-makers uniformly supported the expeditious sale of state enterprises, this has not transpired because of popular and democratic obstacles to the plan. Such an outcome could not have been predicted in the mid-1980s, when democratization was just under way.

We cannot say that Taiwan has become a state with freely competing and relatively well-balanced economic interests sharing influence over policy-making. No state satisfies this idealistic conception. Taiwan does demonstrate signs of decentralization in economic policy-making, however, and the decisional system has become more open to public view.

In chapter 7, we will see whether these characteristics apply to foreign trade policy-making as well.

Notes

[1] See, for example, Robert Wade's discussion of the economic policy elite in *Governing the Market* (Princeton, NJ: Princeton University Press, 1990), 195.

[2] Hsin-huang Michael Hsiao, 'The Labor Movement in Taiwan', in Denis Fred Simon and Michael Y. M. Kau, *Taiwan: Beyond the Economic Miracle* (Armonk, NY: M. E. Sharpe, 1992), 153-54.

[3] 'The Central Bank of China', *Central Banking*, vol. VII, no. 4 (1997), 3.

[4] Central Bank of China, *The Central Bank of China: Purposes and Functions (1961-1991)* (Taipei: 1996), 11; see also *The Financial System in the R.O.C* and *The Financial Market Integration in Chinese Taipei* (Taipei: Ministry of Finance, Bureau of Monetary Affairs, 1996).

[5] Personal interview with Ty Lin, Assistant Director-General, Central Bank of China, May 27, 1997.

[6] 'The Central Bank of China', 1997, 17-18; see also Fa-Chin Liang, 'Monetary Policy in Taiwan', in Joel D. Aberbach, David Dollar, and Kenneth L. Sokoloff, eds., *The Role of the State in Taiwan's Development* (Armonk, NY: M. E. Sharpe, 1994), 233-236.

[7] 'The Central Bank of China', 1997, 18.

[8] 'The Central Bank of China', 1997, 19.

[9] 'The Central Bank of China', 1997, 21.

[10] 'The Central Bank of China', 1997, 11.

[11] Personal interview with Ty Lin, May 27, 1997.

[12] Jia-dong Shea, 'Taiwan: Development and Structural Change of its Financial System', in Hugh T. Patrick and Yung Chul Park, *The Financial Development of Japan, Korea, and Taiwan* (London: Oxford University Press, 1994), 226.

[13] 'The Central Bank of China', 1997, 25-27.

[14] 'The Central Bank of China', 1997, 28-30.

[15] 'The Central Bank of China', 1997, 14.

[16] Personal interview with Yang Ou, Director, Treasury Department, Central Bank of China, May 15, 1996.

[17] See Chih-heng Yang, *The Structure of Fiscal Policy* (in Chinese) (Taipei: Institute for National Policy Research, 1991), 115-21; and Wade, 1990, 210.

[18] Personal interview with Yaw-hsing Lin, chair, Legislative Yuan budget committee, May 23, 1997.

[19] See Directorate-General of Budget, Accounts, and Statistics, 'A Brief Introduction to the Central Government's Budget Act', and 'Outline of the Fiscal Year 1998 Central Government Budget' (Taipei: Executive Yuan, 1997).

[20] Personal interview with Tien-tsai Hsu, independent legislator, May 21, 1997.

[21] Taxation and Tariff Commission, *Government Finance of the Republic of China* (Taipei: Ministry of Finance, 1995), 14.

[22] Peter Ching-yung Lee, 'Social Welfare of Hong Kong, Singapore, and Taiwan', *American Journal of Chinese Studies*, vol. 3, no. 2 (October 1996), 229.

[23] Taxation and Tariff Commission, 1995, 18.

[24] *United Daily News*, June 29, 1996.

[25] See Taxation and Tariff Commission, *Guide to ROC Taxes 1995* (Taipei:　Ministry of Finance, 1995), 104-120, for a description of the modernization of this traditional Chinese tax.

[26] Chi-wei Tseng and Wei-lin Mao, 'Fiscal Policy and Economic Development in Taiwan', in Aberbach, Dollar, and Sokoloff, 1994, 269.

[27] Taxation and Tariff Commission, 1995, 32.

[28] James Q. Wilson, 'The Politics of Regulation', in James Q. Wilson, ed., *The Politics of Regulation* (New York:　Basic Books, 1980), 357-394.

[29] Shiow-duan Hwang, 'Interest Groups and Legislative Politics' (Paper presented at the International Conference on Political Development in Taiwan and Hong Kong, Center of Asian Studies, University of Hong Kong, February 8, 1996), 11-12.

[30] For a review of the movement in the 1980s, see Jack F. Williams and Ch'ang-yi Chang, 'Paying the Price of Economic Development in Taiwan:　Environmental Degradation', in Murray A. Rubinstein, ed., *The Other Taiwan:　1945 to the Present* (Armonk, NY:　M. E. Sharpe, 1994), 237-56.

[31] Hwang, 1996, 15-16.

[32] Jenn-hwan Wang and Zong-rong Lee, 'The State and Financial Capital:　The Transformation of Taiwan's Banking Policy' (Paper presented at the American Sociological Association Conference, Miami Beach, FL, August 13, 1993).

[33] Hwang, 1996, 13-14.

[34] This case study is based on the author's article 'Taiwan Privatizes by Fits and Starts' in *Asian Survey* (forthcoming).

[35] Robert W. Poole, Jr., 'Privatization for Economic Development', in Terry L. Anderson and Peter J. Hill, eds., *The Privatization Process:　A Worldwide Perspective* (Lanham, MD:　Rowman & Littlefield, 1996), 1.

[36] Wade calls Taiwan's public enterprise sector one of the largest outside of the communist bloc and Sub-Saharan Africa. See Wade, 1990, 176.

[37] Jose Edgardo Campos and Hilton L. Root, *The Key to the Asian Miracle:　Making Shared Growth Credible* (Washington, DC:　The Brookings Institution, 1996), 112.

[38] Chi Schive, 'Experiences and Issues of Privatization in Taiwan', *Industry of Free China* (January 1995), 20-21, and Council for Economic Planning and Development, Executive Yuan, *Taiwan Statistics Data Book 1996*.

[39] China Credit Information Service, Ltd., *Top 500:　The Largest Corporations in Taiwan 1996* (Taipei:　1996), 310, 312.

[40] See Tun-jen Cheng and Stephan Haggard, 'Regime Transformation in Taiwan: Theoretical and Comparative Perspectives', in Tun-jen Cheng and Stephan Haggard, *Political Change in Taiwan* (Boulder, CO:　Lynne Rienner Publishers, 1992), 8-11, and Yun-han Chu, 'The Realignment of Business-Government Relations and Regime Transition in Taiwan', in Andrew MacIntyre, ed., *Business and Government in Industrializing Asia* (Ithaca, NY:　Cornell University Press, 1994), 118.

[41] Schive, 1995, 14; K. T. Li, 'Taiwan's Economic Development:　Experiences and Strategies', *Industry of Free China*, vol. LXXXI, no. 2 (February 1994), 28.

[42] Carl D. H. Chang, 'Present Phase of Privatization in Taiwan, R.O.C.' (Unpublished manuscript, Taipei, 1995), 1, 5.

[43] See Ministry of Economic Affairs, 'Summary of Recommendations on Privatization Policy (in Chinese) (Taipei: 1996).

[44] Chang, 1995, 5.

[45] Agnes Syu, *From Economic Miracle to Privatization Success* (Lanham, MD: University Press of America, 1995), 125.

[46] Council for Economic Planning and Development, Executive Yuan, 'Administrative Review of the Situation Concerning the Effort to Privatize Public Enterprises', (in Chinese), staff memorandum, April 25, 1996.

[47] Chang, 1995, 6; see also, Elizabeth M. Freund, 'States, Markets and Industry: State Enterprise Reform in Taiwan and China' (Paper presented at annual meeting of the Association for Asian Studies, Honolulu, HI, April 14, 1996).

[48] Personal interview with H. Lee, General Manager, Human Resource Department, China Steel Corporation, Kaohsiung, June 19, 1996.

[49] P. K. Chiang, 'Discussion of the Implementation of Privatization of State-owned Enterprises' (in Chinese) (Taipei: Council for Economic Planning and Development, Executive Yuan, 1997).

[50] Personal interview with Kuang-nan Lu, Manager, Business Department, Taiwan Machinery Manufacturing Corp., Kaohsiung, June 20, 1996.

[51] Chang, 1995, 7.

[52] Christopher Ruhr, 'Privatization: The Sun Sets on an Era of Government Ownership', *TOPICS*, vol. 15, no. 4 (May 1995), 21.

[53] Personal interview with Wayne Y. Dai, Director, Corporate Planning Division, May 13, 1996.

[54] Ruhr, 1995, 17.

[55] Vocational Assistance Commission for Retired Servicemen, Executive Yuan, 'Investigation of the Privatization of VARS Enterprises', Executive Yuan (in Chinese), staff memorandum, April 15, 1996.

[56] Personal interview with David W. Y. Tai, Industry, Mining and Engineering Department, VARS, May 17, 1996.

[57] For discussion of KMT enterprises in Taiwan's evolving political economy, see Laurie Underwood, 'Inside the Ruling Party's Moneymaking Machine—KMT, Inc.', *TOPICS*, vol. 27. no. 4 (April 1997), and Shih-meng S. Chen, Chung-cheng Lin, C. Y. Cyrus Chu, Ching-hsi Chang, Jan-ji Shih, and Jin-tan Liu, *Disintegrating KMT-State Capitalism: A Closer Look at Privatizing Taiwan's State- and Party-Owned Enterprises* (in Chinese) (Taipei: Taipei Society, 1991).

[58] Poole, 1996, 7.

[59] Personal interview with Tien-tsai Hsu, then DPP legislator, February 16, 1996.

[60] Personal interview with Robert Hsu, KMT legislator, April 23, 1996.

[61] Research, Development, and Evaluation Commission, Executive Yuan, *Research on the Problems of Privatization of Public Enterprises and Their Resolutions* (in Chinese) (Taipei: 1995), 89-96.

7 Taiwan's Internationalization Campaigns

Introduction

The loss of her United Nations seat in 1971 and derecognition by most powers left Taiwan diplomatically isolated. China vigorously opposed Taiwan's attempts to maintain official relations with foreign countries, arguing that the PRC was the sole representative of China and that Taiwan was a province of China. At the nadir in 1978, only 21 states recognized the Republic of China; in 1997, 29 countries have diplomatic relations with Taiwan. As South Africa prepared to transfer its diplomatic ties to mainland China, the remaining countries with embassies in Taiwan were mini-states of the South Pacific, Caribbean, and Central America.

Taiwan depended heavily on international trade to maintain its high growth rate; in 1978, exports were 52.5 percent and imports 46 percent of Taiwan's GNP.[1] Therefore, the state moved quickly to establish informal and non-official ties with other nations. More than 30 states with which Taiwan has no diplomatic relations have now established informal offices in Taipei to promote trade. The largest of these are the American and Japanese representative offices, which function as quasi-embassies. Taiwan maintains trade promotion offices in more than 50 nations.

When Lee Teng-hui assumed the presidency after Chiang Ching-kuo's death in 1988, he spurred efforts to enhance Taiwan's international status. He made several high profile visits abroad, and said he would travel anywhere and meet with any national leader if it would advance Taiwan's international position. Lee's flexible attitude also removed stuffiness over titles as a stumbling block in Taiwan's diplomacy. Returning from a trip to Singapore, Lee remarked that he had been called the "president from Taiwan", and that while he did not appreciate this form of address, it was acceptable.[2]

186

Following this pragmatic direction, Taiwan aggressively sought to join international organizations. It joined almost 800 non-governmental organizations, such as the Olympics, using the title "Chinese Taipei". Taiwan also campaigned successfully to retain its seat in the Asian Development Bank, by agreeing to the name "Taipei, China" when the PRC applied to join. President Lee even dispatched a delegation, headed by the finance minister, to attend the bank's meeting in Beijing in 1989. This was the first visit of Taiwan's officials to the Chinese mainland in 40 years. Taiwan also succeeded in joining the Asia-Pacific Economic Cooperation (APEC) meetings under the name "Chinese Taipei" in 1991. However, Taiwan was not successful in regaining membership in the World Bank or the International Monetary Fund (IMF), and few of the international organizations it belonged to were prestigious or carried much weight in the East Asian power balance. Many of Taiwan's residents found it deeply humiliating that the world's 14th largest trading state was not represented in important international governing bodies.

The DPP made Taiwan's readmission to the United Nations a campaign issue in 1992 elections, and it was a popular appeal. For four years in the mid-1990s Taiwan's government sent missions to the UN to seek membership; each time the request was spurned because the PRC claimed it was another attempt to compromise her sovereignty by recognizing two Chinas.[3]

This chapter examines one internationalization campaign of the 1990s that likely will succeed: accession to the World Trade Organization (WTO). It looks briefly at the trade rules of the WTO and then examines the obstacles Taiwan has had to overcome to gain acceptance. The chapter also analyzes a less realistic campaign, to transform Taiwan into an Asia-Pacific Regional Operations Center. The chapter concludes by considering the roles that America and China have played in Taiwan's internationalization campaigns.

Preparation to Enter WTO

The Republic of China was a founding member of WTO's predecessor, the General Agreement on Tariffs and Trade (GATT) but left in 1950. As noted in chapter 2, during the import substitution stage of development, Taiwan erected high walls of protection around its fledgling industries. The United States gave Taiwan improved access to its markets without requiring that Taiwan reciprocate, as part of the overall US policy of assisting economic growth of anti-communist, developing nations.

In 1976, the United States introduced tariff preferences for developing countries in a program called the Generalized System of Preferences (GSP), and Taiwan was a major beneficiary. Between 1976 and

1978, Taiwan's exports to the United States increased by 64.9 percent.[4] Taiwan did not graduate from the list of GSP countries until 1989 (along with Korea, Hong Kong, and Singapore).

The United States used its market leverage to encourage Taiwan to engage in trade consultations annually, beginning in 1978.[5] The purpose of these meetings was to make Taiwan's trading regime more compatible with the rules of the international trading system, even though Taiwan was not a member of GATT. Meeting on an annual basis since 1984, under heavy American prodding, Taiwan lowered its tariff barriers. During the period from 1980 to 1989, Taiwan cut its tariff levels from 32 percent to 13 percent.

Taiwan's interest in joining GATT developed in the context of growing domestic pressure for economic liberalization. As noted in the discussion of privatization in chapter 6, sluggish growth in the mid-1980s stimulated a search for ways to improve economic efficiency and productivity. A central recommendation from scholars and business leaders was that the domestic economy be opened to competition, including competition from imports.[6] Application for membership in GATT would require modernization of Taiwan's economic structures and policies, enabling it to compete better in the world of the 21st century.[7] A Board of Foreign Trade report on WTO accession in 1997 reiterated this point, remarking that economic liberalization was essential for Taiwan's economic future, even if it were unsuccessful in entering the global economic organization.[8]

In 1986, the PRC applied for membership in GATT, a strong stimulus for Taiwan to apply, too. China faced many obstacles to entry, and critics pointed out that it would have to make significant economic reforms in order to enter. Taiwan was closer to meeting GATT requirements, and by becoming a member it would gain status in the international community.

A third factor influencing policy-makers was the discriminatory treatment that many of Taiwan's products faced in foreign markets. Formation of regional trading blocs in Europe and North America were particularly threatening.[9] GATT members had most-favored-nation (MFN) treatment in the markets of all other members, meaning their trade products could not be discriminated against; Taiwan's products could be assessed higher tariffs because it was not a member of GATT.[10] Membership in GATT would link Taiwan to the most progressive global states, assuring market access that would lead to increases in Taiwan's own development at a projected increased GDP growth rate of 10 percent annually.[11]

For these reasons, then, Taiwan applied for membership in GATT in early 1990, as the "customs territory of Taiwan, Penghu, Chinmen, and Matsu", and not for the China seat. GATT's charter provided that a country that acted "on behalf of a separate customs territory possessing full autonomy in the conduct of its external commercial relations" could join GATT.[12]

Taiwan applied to GATT during the middle of the Eighth or Uruguay Round of GATT negotiations. These were the most prolonged GATT negotiations, and they focused less on lowering tariffs (which had been progressively reduced to the lowest levels in the 20th century) than on changing the application of GATT rules. For the first time, global trade rules were to include trade in services and copyright protections. Agricultural subsidies were to be phased out, and a separate protocol covered government procurement. Also, this round attacked the problem of the weak enforcement structure in international trade by forming a new organization to monitor and resolve issues in global trade, the World Trade Organization. Taiwan sent observers to the Uruguay Round, which concluded in 1993 (and the WTO was inaugurated in January 1995).

For countries to join GATT, their trade laws and regulations must conform to GATT rules. The entry process has two stages. First, all of the applicant's trading partners have the opportunity to conduct bilateral negotiations with it and resolve differences. When the bilateral negotiations are complete, GATT members vote on the application, which by then is a formality.

Twenty-eight nations asked for bilateral talks, and by mid-1997, 20 had reached agreement with Taiwan. The United States is the primary nation with which Taiwan has not reached concurrence. Taiwan's trade talks with the United States began in 1991, and usually two to three sessions have been held annually. The United States has been Taiwan's major trading partner for most of the post-war period, and it has been most insistent on bringing Taiwan into compliance with GATT rules (which, in general terms, reflect American interests). Meeting conditions of eligibility for membership in GATT has been the primary vehicle for liberalization of the Taiwan economy.

Obstacles to Taiwan's Accession to the WTO

The new and more liberalized rules emanating from the Uruguay Round present challenges to all trading nations with protectionist policies[13] and particularly to Taiwan because of her relative diplomatic isolation and military vulnerability. We trace six areas of obstacles: agriculture, industrial trade, services, intellectual property rights (IPR), tobacco/spirits trade, and related protocols.[14] In each we illustrate the nature of the trade problem, the political problem this raised for the state, and the impact of new social forces and strengthened institutions (especially the Legislative Yuan) on the state's attempts to overcome trade obstacles.[15]

Agricultural Obstacles

In earlier rounds of GATT negotiations, agricultural products were mostly excluded from tariff reductions. Numerous exceptions were made to GATT prohibitions on quantitative restrictions, and issues concerning export subsidies went unresolved. Negotiators in the Uruguay Round reached agreement on a comprehensive package of measures to initiate a process of reform over a six-year implementation period (1995-2000). The agreement specifies new international trading rules for market access, domestic support, and export competition in agricultural products.[16]

Trade in agricultural products has been the major stumbling block to Taiwan's entry into the WTO. Agriculture in Taiwan, as in most other industrial states, is highly protected against foreign competition. The state provides subsidies to domestic producers and restrictions, both tariff and non-tariff barriers (such as sanitary and phytosanitary measures), to the importation of foreign agricultural commodities. (In fact, the average rate of tariffs on agricultural products is about 21 percent, compared to 7 percent for industrial products in 1996.) Some 100 agricultural products are still banned. Phasing out subsidies will present problems for Taiwan, as will the removal of import restrictions; tariffs and non-tariff barriers will receive far stricter scrutiny.[17]

Agriculture is a declining economic sector in Taiwan, today comprising less than 4 percent of GDP. Far fewer people work in agricultural pursuits, and a frequently heard comment is that "only the old are farmers in today's Taiwan, and all they do is irrigate and fertilize; the rest is done by specialists". Taiwan's agriculture is not cost efficient, as indicated by the high prices for some commodities, such as rice and vegetables, as compared to the global market price. Further specialization and investment in more efficient agricultural technologies are needed to make Taiwan's agricultural products competitive. Moreover, the strictures on land use protecting agriculture impede the conversion of agricultural land to commercial and industrial uses as land prices accelerate.

For these reasons, the state has supported agricultural modernization and liberalization.[18] One wonders, then, why the rate of progress has not been more rapid. A possible explanation is electoral. Some 807,000 households were considered farming in 1995, and they comprised 10.6 percent of the work force; only one in seven households is engaged in farming most of the time. As is the case in Japan, many residents of rural, farming areas do not derive all or even most of their income from agriculture, yet someone in the family may. Thus the electoral support for farmers' interests is larger than one would expect if one defined farmers as those who derived most of their income from working on the land. Second, farmers historically have been co-opted by the KMT. Farmers' associations, controlled by the KMT, are a cementing force in rural local factions. Farmers even had a caucus in the Second Legislative Yuan—the *Lao-nung-bang* (or Farmers' Group)—composed of six members. (Electoral defeats and retirements reduced this group to one, but the KMT continues to support the farming interest.)

Third, and perhaps most compelling, farmers are an identifiable group, distributed widely throughout Taiwan, who have organized themselves effectively to take advantage of new democratic rules. They also have an ability to connect with traditional beliefs at the agricultural roots of Chinese society and culture, denied virtually every other occupational group in modern Taiwan. They have held large and effective protest demonstrations in opposition to government attempts to acquiesce to foreign demands for market access.[19] In product areas in which Taiwan has few producers, the state has been able to reduce or eliminate barriers to market entry. However, in areas in which farmers have traditionally produced, such as rice, or areas in which farmers are protected by arrangements with conglomerates, such as the chicken and pork industry, opposition to change has been strong.

The government has sought to move farmers out of rice production[20] as local production exceeds domestic needs (making it necessary for the government to purchase and store or export excess production to support domestic rice prices). The government has attempted to use the Japanese and Korean formula to restrict rice imports to a manageable level.[21] American negotiators, however, in 1997 found unacceptable the figures on rice consumption provided by Taiwan's government; they suspected the government was understating rice consumption, which reduces the base for determining the level of imports.[22]

Both the chicken and pork raising businesses are vertically integrated industries in Taiwan that have imported grain to feed chickens and pigs then sold them on the local market. Pork, of course, is the major meat product consumed in Taiwan. The market for chicken is large and increasing, as hundreds of franchises of Kentucky Fried Chicken, Church's Chicken, and other outlets sprout throughout the island. Both industries receive state protection through tariffs and import restrictions. Conglomerates such as President Industries, whose CEOs have direct access to President Lee, dominate production and distribution, and they want to exclude foreign producers, such as Tyson (with joint ventures in mainland China). Taiwan objected to the introduction of pork and chicken (also offal of both) to the agenda of the talks in 1996. US negotiators believed these items were only fair game. Two years previously, the US had made a concrete offer on agricultural products that moved the American position substantially closer to Taiwan's. Taiwan neither accepted the offer nor countered it, so the US reformulated its approach.

An additional dimension of the agricultural problem concerns government benefits for elderly farmers (called *Fu-li Ching-tieh*), which are a form of subsidy to Taiwan's agricultural production. Despite the diminished influence of agriculture, it has been exceedingly difficult for the state to reduce or eliminate these increasingly costly benefits. The reason is that the party in power pays the benefit, but the credit under new democratic rules is subject to a bidding war between parties. The DPP has been in the forefront of calling for an increase in support of farmers' benefits and has used this issue to gain electoral support.

Industrial Products

During the Uruguay Round, negotiators agreed to reduce tariffs on industrial products by 38 percent. Industrial tariff rates were already relatively low, however, and what this meant was that trade-weighted tariffs would be reduced from 6.3 percent to 3.9 percent.[23] Taiwan today has relatively few compliance problems in its trade of industrial products. It has freed hundreds of product areas for importation, and its average *ad valorem* rate of tariffs has dropped to within a few percentage points of the WTO rate. Most recently, in 1997, the government signed an information technology agreement (ITA) that lowered high tech tariffs, and not all WTO members states have done this.[24] There are some sensitive products, however, such as automobiles, which presented problems for Taiwan's entry into the WTO.

Taiwan has only 11 automobile producing plants, and they are joint ventures with foreign firms (mostly Japanese). The market was closed to imports until, under American pressures in the 1980s, US and European cars were given preferential access; Japanese cars were excluded to protect the domestic car manufacturers who produced Japanese-designed small vehicles. (Taiwan became the largest import market for US automobiles in Asia; ironically, about 70 percent of the content of the American vehicles was supplied by Japanese companies.) Then, when South Korea broke off relations with Taiwan in 1992, Korean vehicles were excluded, too. These practices clearly violated WTO rules, and, reluctantly, Taiwan agreed to drop restrictions on Japanese and Korean vehicles, which will probably cause several of the least efficient joint venture firms to fail. This serves nicely the interest of Japan, however, which prefers to use extra capacity in Japan to make cars instead of maintaining a far-flung network of joint ventures in Taiwan. Taiwan's interests have always been to keep the auto industry for its strategic importance and for its symbolic role—as the sign of a mature, diversified economy.[25]

The industrial products area also presented a problem of tariff staging. When negotiations reached closure on most industrial products in 1993, Taiwan asked for phase-in agreements over eight or nine years, as received by countries participating in the Uruguay Round. The United

States agreed, assuming that Taiwan's entry was likely to be immediate. Four years later, Taiwan insisted on the same phase-in period, when most countries signing the WTO treaty had already completed theirs. The United States found this request unfair to other members, as Taiwan had benefited from lower tariff rates, and asked Taiwan to follow the schedule on more than 1,000 items.

Trade in Services

The establishment of the General Agreement on Trade in Services (GATS) was a major achievement of the Uruguay Round, given the wide range of services to be covered. International trade in services is growing at the rate of about 12 percent a year, much faster than the rate of growth in merchandise trade. The framework agreement in services established two important GATT principles as applied to services—most-favored-nation (MFN) and national treatment—but required commitments to specific areas of services.

Taiwan trade talks focus on the service areas of insurance, banking, and law. (Telecommunications figures in the APROC discussion in the next section.) In these areas, foreign firms, representatives of American and European chambers of commerce in Taiwan, and foreign governments consistently protested lack of market access and fairness. Lawyers, for example, could not practice law independently in Taiwan unless they had passed the local bar examination, which formerly had a passage rate of under 5 percent. (This led to a very small number of lawyers in Taiwan, insufficient to handle the burgeoning legal business associated with democratization.) Those with foreign law degrees who had passed bar examinations did not have reciprocal rights (or national treatment) customarily granted in Western societies; to practice they needed to be retained as consultants to Chinese firms.[26] Parts of this problem of market access were resolved in 1997.

American multinational corporations also protested Taiwan's insurance laws, which fail to acknowledge the complex, globally comprehensive insurance policies issued by firms in headquarters states for the MNCs' global operations.[27] Taiwan's insurance laws restrict mutual insurance, and the supervising agencies are very cautious. The largest fear is that if American and other firms entered the market, they would overwhelm local agencies, and for this reason the government intends to await the conclusion of talks before making major revisions to the law.[28] Also, recent legislation spelling out criteria for establishment of insurance companies is discriminatory and violates WTO rules because it does not allow foreign insurance companies with branch offices in Taiwan to establish new insurance companies (but does allow local companies to do so).[29]

In the field of banking, reform of the services trade intersects with ongoing privatization efforts, for a major bulwark against foreign banks has been national, provincial, and local government monopoly banks. These have had freedom to establish branches while foreign countries were limited to one bank per country. In 1989 a new banking law passed the Legislative Yuan, and it permitted the establishment of private banks. One unintended consequence of the new legislation was to enable conglomerates to establish a bank among their other business operations, following the model of Japanese business groups.

Restrictions still inhibit the ability of foreign banks to offer financial services in Taiwan's market. Bank branching is restrained by the way the law treats the capitalization needed to expand. In most nations, the foreign bank can include the capital of its parent bank to meet criteria for branching, but Taiwan looks at the ratio of bank assets in Taiwan. Also, restrictions on capital flow limit banks from offering offshore banking services to customers, which would enable them to participate in overseas stock markets. Banks licensed in Taiwan cannot offer intermediate services to customers, who must go abroad themselves (and are limited to transferring US $5 million). Moreover, it is illegal for foreign banks to open accounts for customers in their headquarters offices or branches abroad. These measures are designed to curtail capital flight, but foreign bankers argue that such flight has already occurred and is beyond the power of the government to prevent.[30]

Intellectual Property Rights (IPR)

The agreement on trade-related aspects of intellectual property rights (TRIPs) was another major achievement of the Uruguay Round. It integrated the substance of existing international property rights conventions into the WTO, and it carried legally enforceable obligations under the uniform dispute settlement procedures. Thus, national treatment and non-discrimination are now applied to IPR, with minimum standards including copyrights, trademarks, patents, industrial design, layout designs for integrated circuits, and company secrets.[31]

IPR long has been an area of concern between East Asian nations and European trading states. The issue in the 1960s and 1970s was adherence to international copyright prohibitions concerning pirating of books, audio and video cassettes, and films. Back then Taiwan was a haven for book, film, and tape pirating. Increasingly in the 1980s, however, pirating of patents and industrial designs became a serious issue in Taiwan's relations with the United States.

The United States during this period took unilateral actions to achieve its policy goals. It employed threats of retaliation under Section 301 of the 1974 Trade Act and "Super 301" of the 1988 Omnibus Trade and Competitiveness Act. These required the US administration to identify priority countries (often referred to as the "hit list") whose policies erected major barriers to US exports and undertake negotiations with them to eliminate or reduce the barriers.[32]

Placing Taiwan on the hit or "watch" list (for countries close to the priority) stimulated government response, including widely publicized roundups of pirated books, tapes, and other materials for public bonfires. Finally, in 1994, Taiwan's legislature enacted intellectual property rights legislation. This was the subject of some protest, for terminating the pirating of foreign printed and visual media not only put firms out of business but also increased the cost of these products in the market. A DPP legislator commented about that debate: "Too many of us were parochial, nationalistic, speaking for the interest of our local constituents who pirated things. We were not interested in the cosmopolitan dimensions".[33] The United States removed Taiwan from the "watch" list in 1996.

The issue was more serious by the 1990s in mainland China, where pirating flourished in companies operated by the People's Liberation Army. Some Taiwanese entrepreneurs were involved, too. However, the American annual process of the "Special 301 review," under which the administration asked the industry to comment on the practices of their trading partners, producing the hit list, worked effectively with Taiwan. Taiwan was removed from the list in 1996 after demonstrating a commitment schedule for IPR compliance, and it was not included on the list in 1997.

Tobacco and Wine

Initially a very large obstacle in Taiwan's trade talks with the United States and in its accession to WTO was market access for foreign tobacco and spirits. Since the Japanese colonial period, production and distribution of tobacco and spirits were monopolized by the state in the *Yen-chiu Kung-mai-chu* (Taiwan Tobacco and Wine Monopoly Bureau). This branch of the provincial government also held a monopoly over the importation of these products. Through high import duties and domestic prices, TTWMB garnered for the national and provincial government a major portion of their revenue.[34]

Beginning in the early 1980s, the United States pressured Taiwan to liberalize the importation of foreign tobacco and spirits products. It took several years of negotiating, including threats and finally imposition of retaliatory sanctions under the Special 301 powers before Taiwan agreed on liberalizing and setting reasonable tariff levels.[35] The amount of advertising permitted for foreign cigarettes and alcohol also was an issue. US producers, especially the powerful tobacco lobby, sought print and electronic media broadcasting of advertisements, contending that years of protection under the government monopoly made it difficult for the new foreign products to gain market share, while Taiwan's authorities wanted to restrict advertising to limit increased sales and their negative social consequences.

Both advertising and sales increased on market liberalization, with the greatest rates of increase among teens. This sparked protests from anti-smoking groups in Taiwan, another new social protest movement relatively successful in raising consciousness about the perils of smoking and with sufficient clout in the Legislative Yuan to pass laws against smoking in public places.

In 1997, the likelihood of privatizing TTWMB increased, as plans were made for the first stage of the process, transforming the large monopoly into several public corporations. This raised concerns from foreign tobacco and spirits producers who believed that product distribution in the future would involve more agencies, such as the MOF, BOFT, and the Health Department, creating a greater bureaucratic roadblock.

A final issue concerns the trading classification of Taiwan's rice wine (*Mi-chiu*). WTO rules include rice wines in the classification of spirits because of their alcohol content (Taiwan's rice wines range from 6 to 40 percent alcohol). Both Japan and South Korea sought treatment of their rice wines as non-alcoholic products, for which a low tariff rate applies. The United States contested this. Taiwan has followed Japan and Korea, arguing that most of the rice wines are used in cooking, as a daily necessity. Moreover, only aboriginal and low income people drink rice wine directly. If it were classified as a spirit, prices would rise two to three times, and this would have a deleterious social effect.[36] The United States has taken the position that recent figures show consumption of seven million litres of rice wine, and it is the second most popular beverage on the island (after beer). As a "substantially consumable drink" it should be taxed at a higher rate; alternatively, producers could make it non-drinkable, for example by adding salt.[37]

Government Procurement

Two other trade areas have influenced Taiwan's WTO accession drive, government procurements and civil aircraft. Not all WTO members are required to accept agreements in these areas, but the United States made its support for Taiwan's accession bid contingent on signing them. The civil aircraft issue is less important in the context of US-Taiwan trade talks than government procurement. Taiwan has attempted to enter the manufacturing market for aircraft, while the US believes there is over-capacity in this market and that Taiwan should commit itself to the same level of production.

Non-discrimination is the chief concern related to government procurement, as governments prefer to award contracts to domestic suppliers when making non-military purchases of goods and services, and government discrimination has a large trade-distorting effect. Discussions at the Uruguay Round resulted in adding a pluri-lateral agreement to WTO that would include procurements by central governments, by sub-national governments (such as provinces and cities) and procurements by public utilities.[38] Government procurement codes will receive scrutiny, and challenges to codes will engage the dispute-settlement procedures.

Foreign firms consistently complain that the criteria Taiwan uses in the bidding process are unclear,[39] and the government has too much discretion in the award of contracts. Also, the contractual damage provisions do not accord with Western law on torts. This is an issue in the dispute between the European firm that built the high speed rail system in Taipei and the city government, an issue that has languished in local courts for more than three years. This particular issue, and the prevalence of corruption and gangsters in public construction projects (such as the April 1996 imbroglio over improvements to the Chiang Kai-shek International Airport), caused several European and Japanese construction firms to leave the Taiwan market in 1997.

Strategic Calculations

It is apparent from this discussion that Taiwan has made great progress in meeting the changing demands of the international trading regime. Said one foreign observer: "Taiwan has used the lens of WTO accession judiciously. It has gotten a lot of mileage out of this".[40] The obstacles that remain are difficult but not insurmountable. On the one hand, in the words of an American trade official, Taiwan has done the "easy stuff", and remaining steps would produce economic dislocations with serious political repercussions.

Public support for Taiwan's entry into the WTO is strong, as is support among Taiwan's leaders. Most economic organizations support it as well: only those trade associations anticipating a flood of foreign competition oppose entry. The prevalent response from business association presidents and secretaries-general is that "globalization is the trend of the times, and we must go along with it". Nonetheless, those who would lose jobs and enterprises will continue to focus attention on their plight, and they will march on the Legislative Yuan as it revises laws in order to make them compatible with WTO rules. A prominent legislator (who previously held three different cabinet positions) put Taiwan's accession to the WTO in context:

> Most want it to happen. They want Taiwan to relate to international organizations. Few oppose it. Even the farmers don't oppose it. They just want to protect their interests effectively; they don't want to lose too much.[41]

All three of Taiwan's political parties support Taiwan's accession campaign, and the initial raft of legislation on the WTO sailed through the legislature in 1997 (more than half the legislative work remains to be done). Yet the process is sufficiently complex that maverick politicians of any party can make capital out of implementation issues, particularly in the context of election campaigns. This has already occurred with respect to annuities for elderly farmers. Thus, the government can be criticized for not moving with sufficient speed to enter the WTO, while it is criticized for failing to take into account those displaced by change. For this reason, government officials are reluctant to complete the necessary adjustments until they are assured that meeting the WTO's terms will bring about entry.[42]

That is the "other hand" of the issue of Taiwan's accession to WTO. China is also a candidate member of WTO, and until it does enter, the secretariat is unlikely to approve Taiwan's accession. As another American observer remarked, "China has lots of friends in the WTO, and can block Taiwan's entry". The WTO process for membership up to the present has relied on consensus, and thus Taiwan's entry campaign is stalled.

Taiwan is not likely to complete its bilateral negotiations with the United States and Europe until the whole strategic process is moving. To finish talks with all relevant parties and not be admitted would result in great loss of face for the government, and this explains its slow, foot-dragging pace in negotiations over the last two years with the United States. To move the strategic process also seems likely to require high level political attention from China's leader Jiang Zemin and President Clinton, and for an agreement to be struck on China's entry, which could transpire as early as 1998.

The Asia-Pacific Regional Operations Center (APROC)

The second campaign to internationalize Taiwan is embodied in the slogan "Making Taiwan the Asia-Pacific Regional Operations Center". Its current popularity is attributable to at least four factors: a response to regionalism in global trade, an attempt to increase the presence of multinational corporations in Taiwan, a hope to replace Hong Kong as the staging center for world trade with China, and an interest in continued economic liberalization.

Factors Motivating APROC Development

First, global trade has become increasingly regionalized in recent years, and regional trading blocs are among the most prominent global trading forces. If the European Union achieves the development of a single currency by the start of the 21st century, it will have overpowering unity and integration in its trading practices. The formation of the North American Free Trade Area (NAFTA) in 1993 among the United States, Canada, and Mexico gives that region greater internal integration and external clout. APROC is a response to the development of regionalism in global trade, both because it offers Taiwan as a link to the huge Chinese market and because it is dedicated to keeping a strong presence for the European and North American trading blocs in East Asia.

The second and related factor pertains to the agents of international trade and specifically the role of multinational corporations (MNCs) A growing pattern in international trade is control by MNCs. One expert argues that corporations have developed the capacity to "minimize taxes, skirt trade barriers, and take advantage of global shifts in comparative advantage".[43] Increasingly, intra-firm trade captures a larger portion of international trade, as much as an estimated one-fourth to one-third of all trade. Global firms have been able to integrate production across national borders. A motivating factor in the development of the APROC is the desire to localize in Taiwan the operation of European, American, and Asian MNCs, which would redound to the benefit of the domestic economy.[44]

A third and also recent stimulus to the APROC is the transfer of Hong Kong from colonial British rule to the sovereignty of the PRC on July 1, 1997. Assuming that Hong Kong would lose both political and economic freedom, and thereby would become less attractive as corporate headquarters for MNCs, Taiwan's leaders pointed to Taiwan's advantages as a headquarters for Western corporations: its capitalist economy and democratic polity. While aware that the government's mainland policy and APROC are in conflict (the latter requires direct links with China while the former precludes direct links until the second stage of normalization), leaders nevertheless argue that Taiwan has the skills and services necessary for exploitation of the mainland market.

The fourth and most compelling stimulus to the APROC is its use as a vehicle to continue progressive political-economic reforms in Taiwan. Small states in international affairs are entrepreneurial, seeking to turn foreign events to domestic advantage, and that is what APROC promises. Now that Taiwan's accession to WTO is stalled, only through APROC or another similar vehicle can economic liberalization so critical to Taiwan's continued prosperity thrive.

That Taiwan's economic liberalization program needed a jump start was painfully evident in 1996 and 1997, as poor economic reports flooded the island. The military exercises conducted by mainland China off Taiwan's shores in late July-August 1995 and March 1996 caused nearly US $20 billion in capital to flee, and emigration from Taiwan to other countries reached an all-time high. Then came two "competitiveness" bombshells.

In May 1996, the Swiss-based International Institute of Management and Development released its annual competitiveness survey. The institute began publishing an annual *World Competitiveness Yearbook* in 1987. The yearbook compares the competitiveness of 46 selected economies using 244 criteria in eight major economic categories. Taiwan's global ranking dropped from 14th to 18th, to the same position it held in 1994.[45] The institute explained Taiwan's decline in rankings as attributable to the use of so many government resources over the previous year in presidential and legislative elections, as well as growing tensions with China. This survey of corporate investors also showed Taiwan as ranking eighth among countries with rampant insider trading (from 1993 to 1995, more than 500 investors involved in insider trading were detained by Taiwan's prosecutors).[46]

The next year, Taiwan ranked 23rd in international competitiveness, a drop of five notches from 1996. After the institute publicized preliminary results of its survey in March, showing Taiwan in 24th place, the Council for Economic Planning and Development dispatched two officials to the institute's headquarters in an attempt to "inform researchers about the situation on Taiwan".[47]

Taiwan lagged behind other regional economies such as Singapore, Hong Kong, Japan and Malaysia in the 1997 survey. The report listed six problem areas explaining Taiwan's five-notch drop from the 1996 rating: worsening government efficiency as well as lackluster scores for domestic economic performance, internationalization, manpower, quality of life, and financial performance. The steepest fall was in the government efficiency score, which plummeted from 6th place to 20th. The domestic economic performance rating slid from 11th to 17th place, and was lower than both China and the Philippines. In internationalization, Taiwan's ranking fell from 26th to 30th place. The financial performance rating dropped from 21st to 23rd place, and both manpower and living quality rankings plunged to 21st place from the 1996 ranking of 16th place.[48] The only bit of good news was that China's rating also dropped, but just one notch, from 26th to 27th place, because of slower domestic economic growth and lagging infrastructure development.

This survey caused considerable embarrassment to the government, which had boasted that Taiwan would join the top five most competitive countries in the world by the year 2000. It was evidence of the need for a clear strategy to rapidly improve Taiwan's economic liberalization process.

Implementation Difficulties in the APROC Campaign

The concept of a regional operations center is imprecise, and what it requires depends on its proponents.[49] Economic officials in Taiwan have described it as composed of six operations centers: manufacturing, sea transportation, air transportation, finance, telecommunications, and media.[50] The idea is variously credited to Hsu Li-teh, mainlander vice premier, as one means to pre-empt pro-independence forces, and to premier Lien Chan, as a symbolic vision for his disjointed administration, among others. We consider the overlapping financial, transportation, and telecommunications centers briefly along with the attendant pressures for democratic change.

The financial requirements for the APROC are large. Flexible banking services, as noted above, are necessary, but more important are legal and procedural changes to ensure the rapid flow of capital. Further loosening of foreign exchange and capital movement controls is required, as well as making the NT dollar readily convertible to foreign currencies. And modernization of the stock and bond markets, so they are fully accessible to foreign corporations, is a necessary step.

Although strides have been made recently in financial and banking services, most foreign observers believe Taiwan has some distance to go before its financial services aspirations are credible. In their opinion, Taiwan needs the untrammeled flow of capital, both in and out, to become an attractive operations center, and currently capital movements are restricted. Even the CEPD, when comparing Taiwan with two major regional hubs, Hong Kong and Singapore, found that it had the most restrictions on foreign investment in securities.[51]

Taiwan already has an adequate transportation infrastructure for trading purposes, as indicated by the port of Kaohsiung, the world's third largest container port, and the Chiang Kai-shek International Airport. What is needed most is increased capacity to process people and goods. For example, Taiwan's international airport lacks adequate transfer facilities, and the immigration control system for foreigners, with its requirement of visas for most visiting foreign nationals, is inefficient and inhibits an increase in Taiwan's role as a transfer point. The CEPD report found that Taiwan's customs services for commodities fared far worse than Hong Kong's and Singapore's. It took three days to pass airport customs in Taiwan, but two to six hours in Hong Kong and only two to four hours in Singapore.[52] Both air and sea transportation systems lack processing facilities to repackage, consolidate cargo, and add value through other means.[53] Expansion of ports at Keelung and Taichung is necessary to increase their use as hubs for intra-regional trade.

There are also requirements with respect to the management of transportation services. Monopolies and private/public corporations tend to dominate in the provision of transportation services. For example, catering and baggage handling at airports are monopolistic or quasi-monopolistic functions. And, longshoreman labor at ports is unionized. Privatization of monopoly and private/public corporations would cause some employee distress, and worker protests would increase popular pressures.

Developments in the establishment of air courier services demonstrated the potential for the APROC concept. In April 1997, United Parcel Service opened a hub at the international airport, with a dimensional weight system and computerized lasers to record packages' exact measurements. This enabled it to offer 24-hour customs clearance.[54] However, government foot dragging caused FedEx temporarily to halt its plans to develop a regional air hub in Taiwan. FedEx needed to threaten to move its operations to Subic Bay in the Philippines to gain government support for establishing its own container center.

The third and most interesting area is communications: providing rapid telephone, cable, video, and computer transmission services is essential to attract foreign MNCs to use Taiwan as a local and regional base. One obstacle in this area is technological: to make the large investments in equipment would drain resources from other infrastructural needs, such as domestic rapid transit. A larger obstacle is structural, that of reorganizing the state-owned telecommunications operation into a corporate structure that is competitive and market driven.

In the APROC planning process, democratic impacts have been most noteworthy in the field of telecommunications. The state used the APROC to justify modernization, and in 1994, it proposed that the Legislative Yuan enact three privatization and liberalization laws, the *Dian-hsin San-fa*. These measures, although declared high priority by the Executive Yuan and the Ministry of Transportation and Communications, languished in the Legislative Yuan, and then, as the January 1996 end of session approached, became highly controversial.

Lack of unity, attention, and perhaps skill in the majority party contributed to the controversy. In fact, votes had to be postponed in order to round up errant KMT lawmakers, and the act took three attempts to pass. Most surprising was the degree of organization of those who protested enactment of the legislation and their support by opposition legislators from both the DPP and the New Party.

As with the other government monopolies discussed in chapter 6, in the area of communications the most affected group was composed of employees. The Directorate General of Telecommunications (DGT) has a large work force of more than 35,000 employees who resented the abrupt privatization of the industry and were trepidatious about their fate. They held 50 demonstrations during the readings of the legislation, many outside the Legislative Yuan (which, on at least two occasions, drew 1,000 supporters) and found a large audience sympathetic to their complaints. What they sought among other things was one-third of the seats on the board of directors of the new corporation. Such a request is not considered unusual in states with well-defined co-determination systems, but if enacted, it would have been precedent-setting in Taiwan; for this reason, the government objected strongly.

Supporting the communication workers were DPP legislators who may have seen the logic of co-determination but who definitely saw votes in representing workers fearful of the future. The lawmakers took up the cause of the protesters and drafted a compromise: one-fifth of the directors of the new corporation (ChungHwa Telecommunications, Ltd.) were to be private sector telecommunication experts, including employee representatives. To further protect the interests of DGT employees, clauses were added to the legislation prohibiting employee layoffs as a result of restructuring and assuring equal labor conditions in the new corporation.[55] This is a pattern that we can expect to see repeated at each and every privatization and liberalization attempt that makes jobs in Taiwan less secure.

Critical Reactions and Prospects

The proposal of the APROC has met with, at best, a skeptical response from government research offices, critical academics, business organizations, both foreign as well as domestic leaders, and opposition political parties.

Vice chair of the CEPD Schive Chi remarked in response to Taiwan's low competitiveness ratings that Taiwan has much work to do, especially in the areas of government debt, government expenditures, and judicial and legislative inefficiency.[56] A department head in the CEPD charged with drafting plans for APROC noted that Taiwan lagged far behind Hong Kong and Singapore in government efficiency and market liberalization and that these obstacles jeopardized the APROC goals.[57]

A research report prepared for the Taipei city government compared Taipei's status as an international city to that of other Asian capitals. The results were unflattering. The report found Taipei to rank 25th in the world in terms of population, number of multinational corporations, international airlines, air mail and bank service. In Asia, Taipei fell far behind Tokyo, Singapore and Hong Kong. Other Asian cities, such as Shanghai, Bangkok, Kuala Lumpur and Seoul, were rapidly catching up to Taipei.[58]

As the most internationalized city in Asia, Tokyo hosted 321 MNCs. Hong Kong had 253, Singapore 251, and Taipei only 166. The report assessed Taipei's prospects at becoming an international city as quite poor because of its limited political, economic, and cultural currency worldwide and the remote chance of improvement.   Further reducing Taiwan's competitiveness were such diverse factors as Beijing's pressuring groups not to meet in Taipei and the speculatively transient nature of the money market.   Poor air and water quality standards and inadequate transportation facilities detracted from Taipei's competitiveness, too.[59]

Academic reactions to APROC have ranged from the constructively critical to the sharply derisive. One stream of criticism reacts negatively to the hortatory rhetoric accompanying new government programs: according to it, boosting Taiwan's competitiveness to the world's top five before the end of this century is yet another unrealistic and empty slogan. A second stream of academics agrees that Taiwan's competitiveness has declined relative to that of other countries and that Taiwan has encountered economic bottlenecks. They see the financial market as fundamentally unhealthy with unclear cross-strait ties, difficulty in land acquisitions, and a deteriorating political environment. The plan to build the island into a regional financial hub, said a group of finance and banking scholars, was "pure fantasy".[60]

Both the European Council of Commerce and Trade (ECCT) and the American Chamber of Commerce—Taiwan's primary foreign business organizations—have criticized the development of APROC. Most critical has been the ECCT.   In 1996, it contracted with the accounting and consulting firm KPMG Peat Marwick to study the clarity of the government's rules and regulations as well as the time spent and costs incurred in setting up business operations in Taiwan.[61] To gain approval for the establishment of a bank branch in Taiwan took six to ten months as compared to two to four weeks in Singapore, three months in the Philippines, three to six months in Indonesia, and six months in Hong Kong. Taiwan also required more registrations and levels of approval.[62]

English-language laws and regulations were "generally" available in Taiwan, but rulings and court decisions were available only in Chinese. In Australia, Singapore, Hong Kong, Malaysia and the Philippines, laws, regulations, rulings, and court decisions were all available in English. More levels of approval were required in Taiwan in the application for work permits and visas for expatriates as compared to Australia, Hong Kong and Singapore. Finally, to establish a manufacturing branch, a company took from five to ten months to gain approvals in Taiwan compared to two to four weeks in Australia and Singapore, two months in Hong Kong, one to three months in the Philippines, and three to six months in Indonesia and Malaysia.   Taiwan also required the highest number of registrations and levels of approval.[63] This study lends some credence to the oft-repeated criticism of Taiwan's bureaucracy as obsessed with control and red tape.

The ECCT also led the charge of business organizations opposed to proposed changes in Taiwan's tax regime. Comparing Taiwan with Hong Kong, Malaysia, Singapore, and China, the organization found Taiwan's effective tax rates high. It was a relatively expensive country in which to operate, with significant regulatory barriers to setting up and maintaining investments. Also, its regulatory system was not easily understood by investors; moreover, it did not offer unrestricted access to the Chinese economy, a major drawing card for Hong Kong. The group charged the government with building inequities into the taxation system that discriminated against foreign investors "with a view to using this inequity as a basis for encouraging countries to negotiate and finalize tax treaties with Taiwan". Such a view, it believed, violated principles of openness, transparency, and fairness to all taxpayers.[64]

To dramatize its concern over Taiwan's slow pace of economic liberalization, the ECCT developed an "APROC Clock" to measure the effect that restrictions were having on the development of regional hub plans. The clock covered the 1995-2000 time frame established by the government and had a total of 60 minutes representing progress in the general infrastructure and various APROC centers. It advanced the clock two minutes after favorable developments in shipping, telecommunications, and banking, but still it showed movement only 17 minutes into the hour—a completion rate of 28 percent.[65]

The American Chamber in Taiwan has taken a back seat on APROC prospects, but its annual briefing statements are filled with critical commentary concerning the slowing pace of economic liberalization. A January 1997 survey of work permit laws noted: "Why does a place competing for regional operations center make it so difficult for foreigners to do business here"? Noting some progress in lifting exit visa requirements and providing multi-year terms for alien residency certificates, the report asked for greater clarifications, more de-regulation, and expeditious government work. Echoing the sentiments of many foreign businessmen with long term experience of the island, AmCham's president noted that the government was now more efficient than previously, but that most of Taiwan's competitors had moved much faster than it had. The American businessman defined the problem as one of leadership:

> There's an inability to articulate a realistic vision of Taiwan's role in the world. Discussion is always defined in terms of local agendas, keeping some party in power, or it is defined in terms of cross-strait relations. This makes APROC unrealistic . . . They're making it up as they go along.[66]

A highly successful Taiwan businessman, Acer Group chairman and CEO Stan Shih, in addressing members of the American Chamber and the

ECCT, called on the government to push for market-opening reforms, warning that protectionism would only stymie growth and undermine Taiwan's competitiveness. Shih, who led Acer to its place near the top of the worldwide computer industry, said the root of Taiwan's ills lay in its value system. In his opinion, government policies regulating trade and investment reflected the belief that "human nature is not good", and that was a problem:

> All companies, including the foreign companies that come to Taiwan, try to take advantage of Taiwan. So the government is in a position to make laws and regulations that protect the country's interests . . . (B)ut looking into the legal system in the United States or Europe, it is the opposite. Everyone is good unless you are proven to be wrong. You are free to do anything. But in Taiwan it is the reverse.[67]

Shih said the regional operations center concept was correct, but the government's controlling approach was mistaken. He suggested that the government set a timetable for the liberalization of the economy and develop an empowerment system much like the one he adopted at Acer, so that officials below the top would willingly take responsibility.

Finally, the APROC itself has entered partisan debate in Taiwan. The KMT sponsored the concept and the legislation intended to implement it. While vacillating initially, the DPP has announced opposition to the concept, for two reasons. First, Taiwan lacks current capability to serve as such a center. The pool of English-language technicians and secretaries, for example, is insufficient to support such a center. Second, the DPP questions why Taiwan could be an operations center more easily than Singapore, Hong Kong, or even Shanghai. For Taiwan to become an APROC, in the DPP view, would require the acquiescence of Beijing. That would come at a cost, and the cost might be greater than the people of Taiwan would be willing to pay. The DPP objection to the APROC is an interesting extension of its Taiwan independence campaign, making it relevant to domestic matters.

Taiwan's officials implementing the APROC strategy are not insensitive to these criticisms. A CEPD section chief, comparing the APROC plan with the privatization effort of the government, stated: "APROC is only a vehicle, and so is privatization. We do them for the sake of economic liberalization. They are like cars we drive to reach our objectives".[68] The concern about APROC is whether it has enough gas to take Taiwan to the 21st century.

The US Role in Taiwan's Internationalization Campaigns

The United States has been Taiwan's primary trading partner since the end of World War II to the present, the 1990s. The United States and Japan have accounted for a majority of both Taiwan's imports and exports. The United States was also the architect and effective leader of the post-war liberal trade regime. Although American economic power faced challenges from resurrected Japan and Germany beginning in the 1970s, and the American growth rate from the 1970s to the present has not rivaled many of its competitors, the American voice still rings the loudest within global economics and trade conferences.

The United States also has been the primary security shield for Taiwan from 1950 to the present. During the 1950s and 1960s, Taiwan was an American client state in Asia, reliant on the United States for military and economic aid that supported many of its expenditures. The Sino-American defense pact guaranteed Taiwan's protection until the United States recognized mainland China. Afterward, the Taiwan Relations Act elaborated an American concern for the peaceful resolution of differences between Taiwan and the PRC. In the only outbreak of tension since the expiration of the mutual security treaty—the Chinese military exercises off Taiwan's coast in 1995 and 1996—the United States sent two aircraft carrier groups to Taiwan.

Both economically and militarily, Taiwan is highly dependent on the United States, and the relationship between the two states is asymmetric. Has the United States used its enormous bargaining leverage to foist economic policies on Taiwan that it otherwise would not adopt?

In the first years of their relationship, Taiwan was at its most vulnerable, both economically and militarily. American economic and military assistance exceeding US $4 billion cushioned Taiwan's budget. American assistance supported the land reform campaign, import substitution program, and export-oriented industrialization. At times, American support of Taiwan's economic programs countered American interests, in that the United States opened its vast market to Taiwan's products on preferential terms. However, the advice the United States gave Taiwan during this period was consistent with its policies internationally: modernize agriculture, develop industry, become a liberal trading state. Other developing nations followed this pattern of modernization too. America supported Taiwan less out of interest in creating a wealthy, grateful Asian state than out of the motive to maintain a militarily strong state, a bastion of anti-communism in East Asia.

During this early period of Taiwan's relationship with the United States, there is little evidence of America's using its bargaining leverage to force economic change on Taiwan. US advisors made recommendations, conducted studies, evaluated programs, and gave incentives. There is ample evidence that Taiwan sometimes disregarded American advice and suggestions—for example, with respect to the role of state-owned enterprises in the economy.

The structure of the US-Taiwan relationship changed in the 1970s and 1980s. American global economic hegemony declined throughout the 1960s, and the requirements of fighting a war in Vietnam and expanding the welfare state at home sapped US vitality and lowered productivity. Stubborn refusal to increase taxes in the face of mounting expenditures produced budget deficits; equally stubborn refusal to depreciate the US dollar brought a flood of imports to the American market. American corporations closed plants at home and established offshore enterprises, hollowing out the core of US industrial power. Protests against foreign wars, particularly that in Vietnam, led to neo-isolationist foreign policies such as the Nixon Doctrine, one offshoot of which was the American rapprochement with China and derecognition of Taiwan.

A long period of slow growth and high interest rates—"stagflation" of the 1970s—increased economic pressures on the US government and realigned interest group and partisan forces in the electorate. They produced the pivotal 1980 election result. The Reagan supply-side revolution, in turn, reduced revenues through massive tax cuts and increased military spending, while holding social welfare spending relatively constant. The colossal fiscal deficits produced by these policies led to the highest interest rates in the world, attracting global capital and bidding up the value of the dollar by 55 percent between 1980 and 1985. The dollar's high value made US exports expensive and imports to the United States cheap, an imbalance that produced chronic trade deficits and gave the US, in 1985, the status of the world's largest debtor nation.

These changes in the American political economy directly affected US trading partners, including Taiwan. The policies of the Reagan administration became increasingly protectionist; support for the post-war free trade policies waned, and the slogans adopted by both political parties were "level the playing field" and "fair trade". The United States, hungry for nations to punish for what were largely self-inflicted economic wounds, looked for targets, and Taiwan was available.

Although Taiwan suffered from diplomatic isolation in the 1970s and 1980s, its economic growth did not abate. Its trade surpluses with trading partners mounted and with the United States became larger than with any other nation except Japan by the mid-1980s. Diplomatic isolation made Taiwan militarily vulnerable, and growing trade surpluses rendered Taiwan economically vulnerable to American pressure. In the 1980s, in contrast to the 1950s and 1960s, the United States took advantage of its asymmetric relationship with Taiwan to insist on changes in Taiwan's trade policy. The only factor reducing American leverage in the 1980s was the pluralistic nature of US rule and the monistic structure of power in the Republic of China before democratization began.

In bilateral negotiations beginning in 1978, the United States first pressured Taiwan to liberalize its trade rules to correspond to the requirements of GATT. Increasingly, however, the United States sought special privileges for its products in Taiwan's market and limitations on Taiwan's exports to the US market. Examples of the former were American sales of fruit, beef, rice, cereal, and automobiles. Examples of the latter were quantity restrictions on footware, textiles (as in the multi-fiber agreement), and apparel.

Taiwan had no choice but to participate in bilateral talks because of its dependent relationship; it also benefited from regular contacts with the United States, which reduced marginally its diplomatic isolation. In the negotiations, Taiwan regularly made concessions to unilateral American demands. These concessions resulted in the opening of Taiwan's protected markets, initially to the United States alone, but over time to other nations and to some domestic firms that otherwise would have been excluded. Overall, then, despite the unilateral character of American pressures, the result was an increasingly liberalized Taiwan economy. Without American pressure, the changes would have occurred much slower, with different effects.

Robert Baldwin, Tain-Jy Chen, and Douglas Nelson summarize the role that US pressure played in changing Taiwan's economy:

> U.S. pressure is the only force that can bring about liberalization in some domestic markets in countries such as the ROC. This is the case when the domestic market is dominated by interest groups that are unchallenged internally due to their political clout. Given that most protected markets are monopolized or oligopolistic in nature, the entry of U.S. firms or simply the prospect of such entry also makes the market more competitive. Furthermore, where state-erected entry barriers are in place, the entry of U.S. firms paves the way for local entrants. In this regard, U.S. pressure helps improve the efficiency of markets.[69]

China's Role

China's relations with Taiwan have affected the political economy in widely divergent ways from America's. After the communists took power in 1949, Taiwan lost traditional markets on the mainland, and this disrupted trade and, briefly, Taiwan's economic development. Until the economic reforms of the 1980s, Taiwan had no direct economic relations with China. Only a small amount of trade trickled through Hong Kong, and smuggling occurred along the coasts of the Taiwan Strait.

During most of the post-war period, the civil war between the communists and nationalists technically continued. Although the PRC often made overtures for talks, Taiwan's response for 40 years was to have "no contact, no negotiation, and no compromise" with the Chinese communists. Then, in 1987, President Chiang Ching-kuo lifted the ban on travel to mainland China, which resulted in new economic relationships.

The thawing in relations with the mainland occurred at the same time Taiwan became a capital-exporting nation (it is now the seventh largest overseas investor in the world). The new "westward" opportunity competed with the government's preferred "southward" strategy—exporting capital and increasing economic linkages with Southeast Asian nations. Initially, the government attempted to ban investments and imports, but by 1991 it was forced to modify policy to accommodate reality.[70] By 1997, the government did not prohibit capital investments in China unless they were quite large and in projects benefiting the development of China's infrastructure, such as the investment proposed by Formosa Plastics Group CEO Y. C. Wang.

By 1997, at least 30,000 enterprises had moved to southern China locales and more than 100,000 Taiwan nationals lived on a permanent basis in mainland China, with the majority in the homeland of most Taiwanese, Fujian province.[71] The total amount of Taiwan's investment in China by this year totaled over US $30 billion. Trade between mainland China and Taiwan increased year by year. In 1993, the total amount of two-way trade flows equaled US $13.7 billion (an increase of 32 percent over the previous year). By 1996, the total volume of trade had reached US $22.2 billion, nearly twice the amount of four years previously.[72] In May 1997, Hong Kong, the conduit for most of Taiwan's trade with mainland China, replaced the United States as Taiwan's largest export market; it was also the major source of Taiwan's trade surplus.[73]

It is noteworthy that trade between China and Taiwan is indirect: most of it moves from Taiwan's ports through Hong Kong to China, or through other states. Taiwan has resisted direct shipping, air, and telecommunications linkages during what it calls the first stage of its mainland policy.[74] The only crack in this policy by mid-1997 was to admit Hong Kong ships to Taiwan's ports, even though the ships clearly fell under Chinese jurisdiction.

A second noteworthy feature of Taiwan's trade with the mainland is that, although reduced during the military exercises China conducted in 1995 and 1996, it continued and rebounded to higher levels within four months of the hostilities. The growing importance of this trade is bothersome to Taiwan's policy-makers, who have tightened rules for mainland investments. As investment and trade continue to grow, Taiwan's economy becomes increasing integrated with the mainland. In the view of policy-makers, this integration will make Taiwan politically dependent, leading to a compromise of Taiwan's mainland policy.

In the view of many scholars, this is the clear intention of Beijing's policy-makers: to make the mainland attractive to Taiwan's traders and investors (the carrots), while occasionally brandishing sticks, such as displays of force and blockages of Taiwan's internationalization campaigns. This policy will bring Taiwan to the reunification table on terms acceptable to China.[75] On both sides, however, mutual misperceptions easily can lead to policy mistakes, and these were doubtless a factor in the 1995 and 1996 military exercises.[76]

Despite the transformation of economic relationships between Taiwan and China, political differences have not significantly narrowed. The PRC continues to regard Taiwan as a renegade province of China and declines to forswear violence to exercise its sovereignty as China's sole legitimate authority. The Republic of China acknowledges that the mainland is under communist control, but Taiwan upholds its claim to sovereignty in the territories it governs.

Both China and Taiwan maintain that there is one China and that Taiwan is a province of it; both support the unification of Taiwan with China. However, there are sharp differences between the proposed structure and timing of unification. China adheres to the "one country, two systems" approach. It offers Taiwan the continuation of its capitalist economy, its social freedoms, self-government under the authority of the Chinese state, even the retention of its own army. All it requests is that Taiwan rejoin the Chinese state system and accept diplomatic representation by China. Recent sweeteners have included offers for Taiwan's political leaders to serve in the PRC's central government. Taiwan does not want to unify with China until it becomes democratic and has a free enterprise economy. Also, it wants the mainland to abjure the use of force with respect to Taiwan and to discontinue attempts to isolate Taiwan internationally.

China refuses to accept Taiwan as an equal government for negotiating purposes; Taiwan, in turn, refuses to negotiate with China as a mere provincial government. Taiwan also refuses to conduct party-to-party negotiations, claiming that Taiwan now has a multi-party system, and the KMT cannot represent the DPP and NP. Because of these obstacles, negotiations, meetings, visits, and other exchanges employ the sponsorship of non-governmental organizations. The Straits Exchange Foundation (SEF), headed by C. F. Koo, represents Taiwan in negotiations; the PRC established the Association for Relations Across the Taiwan Strait (ARATS) as its non-governmental negotiating body. After President Lee Teng-hui visited Cornell University in 1995, these negotiations stalled.

The chief economic effect of relaxed relations with China has been to diversify Taiwan's external capital investment flow. The opening of China to Taiwan's enterprises has probably lengthened the lives of businesses that are low tech and labor intensive. Mainland China also has seriously complicated Taiwan's two internationalization campaigns. Taiwan cannot accede to the WTO without China's assent or prior entrance. Although China applied before Taiwan, it is much farther from conformance to WTO rules. It has large, state-owned monopolies that, in the view of China's competitors, distort the market and reduce competitiveness. Its legal structure is not compatible with WTO provisions for non-discrimination, and its enforcement authority in curbing trade violations is weak. Further, China has sought entrance to WTO as a developing nation, which would lengthen the transitional period during which it makes adjustments, and this is unacceptable to the United States.

Second, creating the APROC requires direct economic linkages between China and Taiwan. China does not object to direct transportation, communication, and postal ties, but, as noted, Taiwan's leaders are reticent to form them without a Chinese renunciation of force in its relations with Taiwan. Resolution of China's objections to Taiwan's first internationalization campaign is likely to be easier than the second.

Conclusion

An old maxim in the foreign policies of many states is that "politics stops at the water's edge", meaning that parties and interest groups mute their differences over security issues and alliance policy in common service to the national interest. This maxim once appeared to characterize attitudes in Taiwan toward its foreign trade policies, given Taiwan's highly vulnerable political and diplomatic position and its extreme dependence on the global market. Just as the maxim is now obsolete in describing American foreign policy, it can be argued that it is no longer germane to Taiwan's foreign trade and economic policy, certainly with respect to their implementation. The argument is based on evidence of increased political pluralism—growing partisan differences and interest group mobilization.

Partisan differences result from weakening integration within the KMT and political entrepreneurialism of the DPP and other opposition elements. The KMT has undergone a steady erosion of electoral support; the most serious loss was caused by the splintering off of the NP, its coalition with the DPP in the legislative Yuan, and its support for independent candidates in the presidential election.

It can be argued that there are political economic roots to the weakening of the KMT, and ironically, KMT leadership of the state is largely responsible for these changes (see chapter 3). Pursuing economic liberalization, Taiwan's leadership spearheaded economic reforms that will result over time in the privatization of large sectors of government employment, increased competition, and dislocation of current government employees and employees of formerly protected enterprises. The irony lies in the fact that a large and loyal support base for the KMT has been government employees and their dependents. Thus, the party in power's urging of economic reforms costs the party in terms of electoral fortunes.

The various casualties of economic liberalization are tempting for opposition parties, who make appeals to represent political interests in exchange for campaign support and votes. Economic issues usually are not at the top of the slate in political debate until they become social-welfare issues. Thus, protectionist policies thrive as much in democratic as in authoritarian systems. What supports their continuance is an elected legislature.

We have also seen increasing incidences of interest group mobilization in Taiwan over the last ten years. Changing the rules of political activity facilitated this mobilization; it was caused by perceived threats to livelihood and survival. Agricultural protests, like those of communication workers, are directed against the state's implementation of foreign trade policies. It seems likely that these complaints will increase and that an increasing number of groups will take advantage of the opening political system to vent demands for meliorative action.

Political pluralism in Taiwan has not challenged the necessity for retaining and in fact increasing economic competitiveness globally. Instead, the focus has been on the processes of liberalization and on cushioning the deleterious outcomes. And now these procedures are more public than at any time in Taiwan's history.

These developments also are occurring during a major transformation of the world economy and polity. The end of the Cold War has reoriented China's policies and those of the United States, the two players most influential to Taiwan's development since World War II. The outcome of Taiwan's internationalization campaigns ultimately depends on the way this tripartite relationship evolves.

Notes

[1] Ministry of Finance, *Monthly Statistics of Exports and Imports, Taiwan Area, R.O.C.*, February, 1979.

[2] See Samuel S. Kim, 'Taiwan and the International System: The Challenge of Legitimation', in Robert G. Sutter and William R. Robinson, eds., *Taiwan in World Affairs* (Boulder, CO: Westview Press, 1994), 170.

[3] See Michael Yahuda, 'The International Standing of the Republic of China on Taiwan', *China Quarterly* 148 (December 1996), 1337-38.

[4] Robert E. Baldwin, Tain-Jy Chen, and Douglas Nelson, *Political Economy of U.S.-Taiwan Trade* (Ann Arbor, MI: University of Michigan Press, 1995), 43.

[5] See Chien-pin Li, 'Trade Negotiations Between the United States and Taiwan', *Asian Survey*, vol. XXXIV, no. 8 (August 1994), 699.

[6] Baldwin, Chen, and Nelson, 1995, 44.

[7] Personal interview with Chia-sheng Wu, Director General, Department of Customs, Ministry of Finance, March 17, 1997.

[8] Board of Foreign Trade, *Taiwan's Accession to the World Trade Organization: Reference Materials* (in Chinese) (Taipei: BOFT, Ministry of Economic Affairs, 1997), 30-31.

[9] See Yun-han Chu, 'The East Asian NICs: A State-led Path to the Developed World', in Barbara Stallings, ed., *Global Change, Regional Response* (Cambridge: Cambridge University Press, 1995), 208-09.

[10] Over one-third of the business association leaders surveyed by the author in 1996 mentioned that their commodities were taxed at higher rates abroad than the customs rates charged by Taiwan on comparable products.

[11] Chi Schive, 'Taiwan's Economic Policy Reforms in the 1990s: A Supply-Side Approach', *Joint U.S.-Korea Academic Studies*, vol. 6 (1996), 220. One recent study argues that if China and Taiwan entered the WTO, world trade would increase by about US $38 billion (imports plus exports). Their entry would improve industrial countries' terms of trade, but worsen developing countries' external trade environment because their participation in WTO would induce more competition in labor-intensive products. See Zhi Wang and Francis C. Tuan, 'The Impact of China's and Taiwan's WTO Membership on World Trade—A Computable General Equilibrium Analysis', *American Journal of Chinese Studies*, vol. 3, no. 2 (October 1996), 195, 201.

[12] *Far Eastern Economic Review*, March 8, 1990, 48.

[13] See Michael P. Ryan, 'East Asian Political Economies and the GATT Regime', *Asian Survey*, vol. XXXIV, no. 6 (June 1994), 556-571.

[14] See Ministry of Economic Affairs, *A Report on the Conditions of ROC's Accession to the World Trade Organization* (in Chinese) (Taipei: January, 1997).

[15] This and the following section use materials from the author's article 'Political Pluralism and the Implementation of Foreign Trade Policy', in *Taiwan on the Move* (Chungli, Taiwan: National Central University, 1997).

[16] Gary P. Sampson, 'What the Uruguay Round Means for East Asia', in David Robertson, ed., *East Asian Trade after the Uruguay Round* (Cambridge: Cambridge University Press, 1997), 169-70.

[17] For a review of the obstacles and responses in the area of agriculture, see Chang-fa Luo, An-ting Liao, Hsi-hung Chen, Tso-kuei Peng, Yun-han Chu, Ying-wen Tsai, Yi Chu, Wu-hsing Chen, Hung-yu Hu, Chin-rong Kuan, Kuo-ching Lin, Hung-jin Tsai, Kun-hsing Hsiao, and Hsin-you Chen, *The Impact on Agriculture of Taiwan's Accession to GATT and Policy Responses* (in Chinese) (Taipei: Institute for National Policy Research, 1994).

[18] Personal interview with Wu-hsiung Chen, Director, Economics and Planning Department, Council of Agriculture, March 19, 1996. See also Luther Tweeten and Hsiai-hui Hsu, *Changing Trade Environment after GATT: A Case Study of Taiwan* (Taipei: Council of Agriculture, 1994).

[19] The first protests occurred in 1987, when 3,000 fruit growers protested before the Legislative Yuan over entrance of American fruit into the Taiwan market, which reduced prices of local fruits. A second protest the following year resulted in violence when southern rice growers protested imports. See Hsin-huang Michael Hsiao, 'The Rise of Social Movement and Civil Protests', in Tun-jen Cheng and Stephan Haggard, *Political Change in Taiwan* (Boulder, CO: Lynne Rienner Publishers, 1992), 64-65.

[20] State agricultural policy emphasizes specialization in areas that are less competitive in world trade. When US fruits entered Taiwan's market in the late 1980s, the

government asked farmers to specialize in mangoes and *li-chih* (lichee). Government agricultural policy was less successful in livestock. When US beef entered the market, the government urged farmers to raise pigs instead. Then the farmers produced too many, flooding the market. A beneficent disaster—the British mad cow disease in 1996—spurred pork sales, but it was followed by a maleficent disaster, the outbreak of hoof-and-mouth disease in 1997, which nearly destroyed the pig raising industry.

[21] Declaring rice a primary agricultural product that is the predominant staple in the traditional diet, both Japan and Korea were able to reduce the importation of foreign rice to less than 4 and 8 percent, respectively, of domestic consumption; see Sampson, 1997, 171.

[22] Personal interview with Ray Sander, Director of Trade and Commercial Relations, American Institute in Taiwan, July 1, 1997.

[23] Sampson, 1997, 163-64.

[24] The treaty helps Taiwan, too, as computer peripherals are an expanding part of Taiwan's exports.

[25] Personal interview with Francis F. Ruzica, Deputy Assistant, US Trade Representative for Asia and the Pacific, November 8, 1996.

[26] Personal interview with Paul Cassingham, Perkins Coie, Taipei, May 22, 1996.

[27] Personal interview with Chris Murck, President, American Chamber of Commerce, Taipei, February 5, 1996.

[28] Personal interview with Ying-wen Tsai, Fair Trade Commission, May 26, 1997.

[29] American Chamber of Commerce, "Insurance Company Brief" (Taipei: Issues Papers, 1997).

[30] Personal interview with Jeffrey Williams, President, American Chamber of Commerce, Taipei, May 29, 1997. See also United States Trade Representative, *1996 National Trade Estimate Report on Foreign Trade Barriers* (Washington, DC: 1996), 323.

[31] Geoff Raby, 'The New World Trade Order and OECD', in Robertson, 1997, 55.

[32] Baldwin, Chen, and Nelson, 1995, 64, 128.

[33] Personal interview with Parris Chang, DPP legislator, February 6, 1996.

[34] Personal interview with Martin M. L. Tsai, Secretary General and Director, Taiwan Tobacco and Wine Monopoly Bureau, April 10, 1996 and May 26, 1997.

[35] Baldwin, Chen, and Nelson, 1995, 106-07.

[36] Personal interview with Ying-wen Tsai, Federal Trade Commission, May 27, 1997.

[37] Personal interview with Ray Sander, AIT, July 1, 1997.

[38] Baldwin, Chen, and Nelson, 1995, 77.

[39] Personal interview with Chris Murck, Managing Director, Chemical Bank, and President, American Chamber of Commerce, Taipei, April 23, 1997.

[40] Personal interview with Scot Godin, Head, Chinese Economic Area, US Department of Commerce, March 5, 1996.

[41] Personal interview with Vincent Siew, KMT legislator, April 22, 1996.

[42] Personal interview with Yi-fu Lin, Director General, Board of Foreign Trade, Ministry of Economic Affairs, April 5, 1996.

[43] Robert Gilpin, *The Political Economy of International Relations* (Princeton, NJ: Princeton University Press, 1987), 218.

[44] See Chi Schive, *The Foreign Factor: The Multinational Corporation's Contribution to the Economic Modernization of the Republic of China* (Stanford, CA: Hoover Institution, 1990).

[45] *United Daily News*, July 10, 1996.

[46] *United Daily News*, May 20, 1997.

[47] *Central Daily News*, July 10, 1996.

[48] *United Daily News*, May 19, 1997.

[49] Chi Schive calls it a "supply-side approach" in his article 'Taiwan's Economic Policy Reforms in the 1990s', 1996, 225.

[50] See Council for Economic Planning and Development, *Plan for the Development of Taiwan as an Asia-Pacific Regional Operations Center* (in Chinese) (Taipei: Executive Yuan, 1996). See also related publications of the Coordination and Service Office for the Asia-Pacific Regional Operations Center, CEPD, such as 'APROC Plan' (1995) and 'An Initiative into the Next Century' (1996); and Chi Schive, *Taiwan's Economic Role in East Asia* (Washington, DC: Center for Strategic and International Studies, 1995), 43-53.

[51] *United Daily News*, December 17, 1996.

[52] Ibid.

[53] Schive, 1996, 224.

[54] *United Daily News*, April 30, 1997.

[55] *United Daily News*, January 17, 1996. Also see Legislative Yuan Reports, from the Executive Yuan Proposal (12/27/94, No. 2757, 61) through readings (No. 2828, 346-43), in Chinese.

[56] *Central Daily News*, May 19, 1997.

[57] *United Daily News*, December 17, 1996.

[58] *China Times Express*, September 20, 1996.

[59] Ibid.

[60] *United Daily News,* November 21, 1996.

[61] Including such factors as establishing and maintaining registrations for expatriate employees, ease of understanding rules and regulations, time and cost of making changes in registrations once a business had been established.

[62] *China News*, December 9, 1996.

[63] Ibid.

[64] *China News*, April 27, 1997.

[65] *China News,* February 27, 1997.

[66] Personal interview with Jeffrey Williams, President, American Chamber of Commerce, Taipei, May 29, 1997.

[67] *China News*, May 17, 1997.

[68] Personal interview with Chong-ying Hu, Council for Economic Planning and Development, May 22, 1997.

[69] Baldwin, Chen, and Nelson, 1995, 122.

[70] Yun-han Chu, 'Making Sense of Taiwan's Mainland Policy' (Paper presented at the Association for Asian Studies Conference, Chicago, IL, March 25, 1997).

[71] Jean-Pierre Cabestan, 'Taiwan's Mainland Policy: Normalization, Yes; Reunification, No', *China Quarterly* 148 (December 1996), 1272.

[72] International Trade Office, 'Analysis of the Cross-Strait Trade Situation' (in Chinese) (Taipei: Ministry of Economic Affairs, May, 1997).

[73] *United Daily News,* June 8, 1997.

[74] The National Unification Guidelines, adopted in 1991, stipulated three preconditions for lifting the ban on indirect trade, air, and sea links with mainland China: renunciation of the PRC's use of force against Taiwan, recognition of Taiwan as a political entity on an equal footing with the PRC, and allowance of Taiwan to have reasonable space for international participation. See Hung-mao Tien and Yun-han Chu, 'Building Democracy in Taiwan', *China Quarterly* 148 (December 1996), 1168.

[75] See, for example, Robert G. Sutter, *Shaping China's Future in World Affairs* (Boulder, CO: Westview Press, 1996), 41-43; and also Tse-kang Leng, *The Taiwan-China Connection* (Boulder, CO: Westview Press, 1996), 119-23.

[76] Edward Friedman, Chinese Nationalism, Taiwan Autonomy and the Prospects of a Larger War', *Journal of Contemporary China*, vol. 6, no. 4 (March 1997), 19; also see John W. Garver, *Face Off: China, the United States, and Taiwan's Democratization* (Seattle: University of Washington Press, 1997).

8 Comparative Perspectives on Taiwan's Political Economy

Introduction

Up to this point, we have considered Taiwan's political and economic development as largely *sui generis*, as a product of unique historical circumstances and environmental constraints and opportunities. In fact, several of Taiwan's institutions and processes resemble those of other nations, and its people share attitudes and values with many of their neighbors in East Asia. Only by comparing Taiwan's developments with those of other similar states can we determine what is unique and what is not.

In this chapter, we compare Taiwan's political economy with that of five other Asian nations: the People's Republic of China (PRC), Japan, South Korea, Hong Kong, and Singapore. All of these states were strongly influenced by Confucianism. Today, examination systems are still gatekeepers for schools and government jobs, and individual preferences are second to the needs of the group. Each state seems to express the work ethic that Ezra Vogel finds analogous to the ethic of self-cultivation in traditional Confucianism.[1] And governments of all the states except China are operated by bureaucrats selected following the principles of merit.

More relevant to our objective, each of the six is a high growth state. Japan was the world's second leading economy in 1997. China has had double digit growth rates in recent years and is expected to be the world's leading economy by the year 2020. The remaining four states have had extremely high rates of growth for most of the post-war period. For example, from 1980 to 1991, the real GDP annual growth rate for Korea was 9.6 percent, for Taiwan 7.7 percent, for Hong Kong 6.6 percent, and for Singapore 6.6 percent.[2] Much of this growth is attributable to export expansion, and all of the states but China are largely dependent on foreign trade. Again with the exception of China, all are resource poor states, meaning that one would not anticipate such a pattern of rapid economic development.

There are significant differences among the states, too. China's population of 1.2 billion is more than six times larger than the population of the other states combined. It is a continental state, while the others are densely populated islands (or, in the case of Korea, the southern part of a peninsula). China is the only communist state among the group; it has a "socialist market" economy, while the others are all capitalist market economies. Both Hong Kong and Singapore are small islands lacking extensive hinterlands (which tend to drag the pace of development), and each has a small population. They are city-states more than nation-states. Both also have histories as British colonies (Singapore until 1959, Hong Kong until July 1, 1997), which expedited their westernization and also left Singapore with a substantial non-Chinese population (Malays compose 15 percent and Indians 7 percent of its diverse population). Hong Kong has no history as an independent nation. From 1841 to 1997, it was a British colony, and thereafter it became an administrative region of China.

In the discussion that follows we will employ the "most similar" systems approach in comparative politics[3] and focus primarily on the similarities and differences of Taiwan, South Korea, and Japan. We look first at the amount of centralization of authority in the state and its degree of autonomy (including bureaucratic autonomy). Then we discuss the amount of competition in the economy by comparing state-owned enterprises, conglomerates, and small- and medium-size enterprises (SMEs). Third, we investigate the degree of openness in the society and compare electoral processes to determine whether leaders are competitively selected and what is the influence of money on politics. Next, we ask whether the state is accessible to business interests. Finally, we turn to the degree of intervention by the state in the economy, with special reference to industrial policies.

Centralization in the State

The Confucian states show a range of variation in centralization. Most centralist is the communist party-state system of the PRC. Although there are different institutions of the state—the National People's Congress, the state council, people's courts and procurates—the fountainhead and source of all political power remains the communist party. It controls and directs the machinery of the state through an interlocking system of party personnel and a party structure parallel to that of the state organs. Thus, Jiang Zemin, the party general-secretary, is also president of the PRC. Premier and vice premiers of the state council are also politburo members, other members of which (or of the party's central committee) direct government ministries. The party-state is autonomous and of great institutional strength; the state bureaucracy lacks autonomy.

Until the 1980s, Taiwan's state system most resembled that of the PRC. It, too, was a Leninist state, and a similar interlocking system of personnel wedded members of the KMT's central standing committee to the government and the military. The president of the Republic of China was, throughout most of the post-war period, also chairman of the KMT, and he appointed the premier, who headed the Executive Yuan. Other institutions of the state—Legislative, Control, Examination, and Judicial Yuans and the National Assembly—took their direction from the central standing committee, too. Important social interests, such as powerful business leaders, were co-opted into the party-state. In the 1970s, some signs of autonomy appeared in the bureaucracy as Chiang Ching-kuo fostered a technocratic elite. And under the younger Chiang's leadership, Taiwan's authoritarianism became "softer", but it remained authoritarian and autonomous.

In the 1980s, Taiwan's state system underwent systemic changes, as first the opposition Democratic Progressive Party (DPP) formed and challenged the ruling KMT in elections with increasing success; then KMT factional conflict gave rise to the New Party (NP) and further declines in KMT electoral fortunes. Throughout, the Legislative Yuan rose in influence and could thwart the executive and the party. While the KMT party-state has not yet withered and died, it is clearly unable to control all important outcomes. Thus, to amend the constitution to produce a more efficient and pliable system of power in Taiwan, the KMT has been forced to ally with the DPP and to make concessions that critics regard as advancing the cause of Taiwan independence.

In some respects, Singapore bears resemblance to Taiwan, for it, too, has been a one-party state. That party, however, is not Leninist but the mildly socialist People's Action Party (PAP). It has held the majority in Singapore's parliament from 1959 to the present. The sole leader of Singapore from 1959 until his resignation in 1990 (but not retirement from government service) was the charismatic Lee Kuan Yew. Although criticized as paternalistic, authoritarian, and arrogant, Lee operated as party leader and prime minister within a team of close advisors.[4] The bureaucracy and the courts have a reputation for autonomy; Lee Kuan Yew's broad base of support prompted Singapore's ambassador to the UN to say that "politics (had) disappeared" and Singapore had become an "administrative state".[5] In 1991, Singapore voters amended the constitution to allow for direct election of the president, which will further weaken centralization of power within the state. The other city-state, Hong Kong, has had centralized rule but under the aegis of the British and now the Chinese state.

From 1961 to 1987, power was highly centralized in South Korea and concentrated in the hands of Presidents Park Chung Hee and Chun Doo Hwan who operated military dictatorships. Since that time, and most notably since the election of Kim Young Sam (after which time both Chun and previous president Roh Tae Woo were arrested and sentenced to prison), South Korea's state system has expressed many of the tensions evident in Taiwan. The state combines aspects of both presidential and parliamentary systems, as does the Republic of China; and like Taiwan's polity, there is constitutional ambiguity as to which system it follows most closely. The president has broad powers, including the selection of the prime minister and oversight of the cabinet.[6] A fluid party system, however, reduces the president's lock hold on the unicameral National Assembly, which may remove the State Council (cabinet). The relationship between the president and National Assembly resembles that between president and Legislative Yuan in Taiwan. The Korean civil service, continues to be meritocratic in its recruitment and promotion systems, with positions protected against political influence; it is considered quite clean compared to other post-war developing countries.

Finally, the Japanese parliamentary system, in formal terms, is less centralized than the party-states, but some critics allege its power elite is one of the smallest and most unified in Asia.[7] Under the 1947 constitution, written for the Japanese by Americans during the occupation, the emperor lost his divinity and autonomous ceremonial and ritual roles; nevertheless, the emperor remains a figure of respect and an important symbol of national unity. The two-house Diet (parliament) is the fulcrum of state power and selects the prime minister, who names the cabinet. Yet the Liberal Democratic Party (LDP), which has ruled Japan for most of the post-war period, is a collection of factions, and their intense rivalry brings about frequent changes in prime ministers and cabinets. Then, in 1993, the LDP lost power for three years, returning as the leader of a coalition cabinet.

The Japanese bureaucracy is the most autonomous of the six Asian states. It has made major decisions on economic and industrial policies and is the heart of what Chalmers Johnson calls the "corporate developmental state". The bureaucracy "drafts virtually all legislation, controls the national budget, and is the source of all major policy innovations in the system".[8] The bureaucracy works hand in glove with LDP and corporate elites, a partnership that leads some to call Japan an authoritarian bureaucratic state.[9]

Competition in the Economy

Of the five approaches introduced at the beginning of chapter 2, the six nations present aspects of corporatism, *laissez-faire* (liberalism), and pluralism. We see this in the roles that state-owned enterprises (SOEs), conglomerates, small- and medium-size enterprises (SMEs), and multinational corporations (MNCs) play in the economic system.

China

The most monopolistic economy in East Asia is that of the PRC. By the end of 1993, China had about 130,000 SOEs under one of four different levels of government (central, provincial, prefecture, or county). They accounted for approximately half of industrial output (but received 90 percent of the government subsidies).[10] The most dynamic parts of the economy, however, are the Township-Village Enterprises (TVEs) and private enterprises. TVEs have an ambiguous legal status, as they are owned collectively by all rural residents of the township or village that runs the enterprise (but managers of many TVEs operate them as if they, the managers, were the actual owners). There were 1.5 million of them in 1993, and they produced about 30 percent of national industrial output yet received less than 10 percent of state subsidies. TVEs, which are small and generally productive, are considered part of China's non-state economic sector. The non-state sector has been the most dynamic part of the Chinese economy since the 1980s and accounts for half of Chinese GDP.

Hong Kong and Singapore

Most Hong Kong enterprises are medium and small, and nearly all are family owned; Hong Kong lacks SOEs. It is the Asian model of a capitalist economy, and even the public utilities always have been privately owned and operated (but regulated by the state). Hong Kong is Asia's primary headquarters for MNCs, imposing no special restrictions on them; nor does it accord preferential treatment to them. In this respect, it differs from the other Confucian systems.

In Singapore, on the other hand, MNCs are leaders in the economy. Although numbering less than 20 percent of the manufacturing establishments, they employ over 40 percent of the work force and produce well over half of Singapore's output.[11] When Singapore began its industrialization drive, most of the firms were SMEs and lacked technology and capital. Political leaders decided to invite MNCs to Singapore and to establish some SOEs under direct or indirect state control. (The state did own more than 400 business firms with a total capitalization of US $2 billion but privatized them in the late 1980s.) The state was careful in selecting stable MNCs, with advanced technology, which would make long-term investments in Singapore, and it retained regulatory powers over corporate behavior. The state also established a number of businesses and even assigned regular civil servants as their managers. One Singapore official, praising the managerial efficacy and talent of government bureaucrats (whose promotion depended on the profitability of the firms they ran), called his economy "capitalism with socialist characteristics".[12]

Japan and South Korea

Japan and South Korea are the paradigmatic corporate development states in East Asia, and Taiwan is often compared to them. Japan, of course, is the mother of Asian conglomerates, which developed before the war as groups of industries, integrated both horizontally and vertically, called the *zaibatsu* (financial groups). Although the largest were eliminated by the occupation authorities, they soon re-emerged as large firms, called *grupu* or *kigyo shudan* (business groups), which linked horizontally a number of unrelated businesses, connecting them with a bank and often a trading company. The firms within the groups invest in one another's stock, exchange information and personnel, meet in a guiding executive council, and engage in joint enterprises. These groups of firms sit at the top of the Japanese economy. A second type of grouping, the *kereitsu*, is a vertically integrated set of firms, headed by a major corporation joined to medium- and small-scale enterprises in the same industry. The smaller firms depend on the major corporation to supply materials or other business resources.[13]

The Japanese conglomerates dominate the economy, and their networks reach virtually all manufacturing (and most service) firms. Non-Japanese MNCs play a very limited role in the Japanese economy. The state-owned sector in both Japan and Korea has declined steadily over the years and today comprises less than 5 percent of the value added in production.

Korea followed the Japanese pattern of conglomerate control, especially during the period of military dictatorship. Meredith Woo-Cumings points to the importance of historical reasons:

> Because of Korea's mainland connection to Manchuria and north China, Japanese colonizers and *zaibatsu* corporations developed heavy industries and spent huge amounts on social overhead, especially in northern Korea but also in the south, thus to stitch together a large marketing, communications, and transportation infrastructure in Northeast Asia, tied into the mother country.[14]

The *zaibatsu* thereby formed the mold out of which the *chaebol* (Korean for *zaibatsu*, or finance groups) were cast. However, the Korean *chaebol* became different in many ways from the Japanese *zaibatsu*. As the form was adopted in Korea, report Nicole Biggart and Gary Hamilton, the organizational structure took on important characteristics of Korea's pre-industrial patriarchal clans: today, most *chaebol* are headed by a family patriarch whose heirs run most of the firms in the conglomerate.[15] A second difference is in financing. The Korean conglomerates do not have their own banks; instead, they rely on the government or state-controlled trading companies for their finance. It is primarily through this means that the state controls them.

During the 1970s, the Korean government used the *chaebol*[16] as a vehicle of the state for the purpose of rapid industrialization. Those businessmen with good connections to the regime but also with records of business success received state support as means to create economies of scale and advance technological development in industries. By the mid-1980s, the top ten *chaebol* had become directors of the production and distribution of goods throughout the economy; they produced a sales volume amounting to two-thirds of Korea's GDP.[17] The largest group then, Hyundai, had sales of US $8 billion from 30 different companies. The *chaebol* represented even greater concentration of economic power in the Korean economy than the *keiretsu* in Japan. The conglomerates exert a powerful oligopolistic influence over the economies of both nations.

Taiwan

For a number of reasons, Taiwan's KMT rulers did not immediately tolerate large business groups. When the nationalists began their rule of Taiwan, there were few large enterprises. Most of the larger economic organizations were light industry and agricultural processing plants (mainly for sugar). There were no conglomerates for the KMT to nurture, and for several reasons, the state determined to take over Japanese corporations after the war, create its own enterprises, and favor the development of small family firms. The second difference pertains to ethnic conflict. The mainlander KMT regime entered an island populated mostly by Taiwanese, who were the business sector. To encourage the development of large enterprises would have increased the power of Taiwanese and jeopardized mainlander rule. Also, KMT leaders were suspicious of concentrations of economic power that might threaten their power base.

Size of firms As a consequence, the state preferred SOEs under its direct control. These countered the development of Japanese- or Korean-like conglomerates and became, in some respects, their functional equivalents, although "much smaller in size and less multisectoral".[18] They were also a counter to MNCs, which have played a far smaller role in Taiwan's economy than Singapore's and usually have been involved in joint ventures with local entrepreneurs.

SOEs also provided jobs to loyal mainlander followers of the regime. They gave the state control over strategic materials and were an efficient vehicle for both counter-cyclical fiscal policies and monetary management. Most important, notes Chu Yun-han, SOEs gave the technocratic leaders "the economic resources to build an array of satellite suppliers and downstream firms around state enterprises, which in turn effectively served as extended arms of the bureaucracy".[19] Yet, as we noted in the case study of privatization (chapter 6), SOEs have declined in economic influence since the 1950s. In 1952, their share of industrial production was 56.6 percent, but by 1995 it had dropped to 15.7 percent.

The vast majority of enterprises in Taiwan are SMEs, and most political economists consider them the most dynamic and productive part of the economy. Clearly, their role in the export sector in the 1960s through the early 1980s was greater than Taiwan's conglomerates. If we define SMEs as firms having fewer than 300 workers, then they produced nearly two-thirds of Taiwan's exports.

Taiwan's conglomerates (called *Tsai-tuan* [the traditional Chinese characters for financial groups, rendered *zaibatsu* in Japanese], *Chih-yeh Chi-tuan* [enterprise groups], or *Kuan-hsi Chih-yeh* [related enterprises]) are collections of family-controlled firms that are legally independent. Mostly, they bring together unrelated suppliers of intermediate products and services, and until the 1980s, they operated domestically in an economy that was export oriented. Also, up to the 1980s, the conglomerates did not rival the size of the business groups in Japan and Korea. They contributed no more than 32 percent of GDP. Most had just a few large firms, and their interconnections were, like those of the Korean *Chaebol*, familial: usually fathers and sons, but in some cases brothers controlled the assets.

A fourth element of the Taiwan economy is the KMT enterprise. Of the five other Confucian states, only China has party enterprises; at this stage of China's economic evolution, many SOEs could be considered to fall into this classification. As Taiwan democratized, opposition politicians demanded that KMT-owned enterprises be registered as such (formerly, the enterprises were listed in the names of their CEOs), at which time the size and collective power of KMT enterprises became evident.

Coordination at the top Two additional factors of the Taiwan economy command attention. First, operations of SOEs, conglomerates, and KMT-enterprises are interconnected. Chu noted that this cooperation increased as a result of diplomatic pressures on Taiwan in the 1970s:

> In order to secure the allegiance of key business groups, the party leadership strategically allocated entry rights to lucrative oligopoly arrangements. At the national level, these rent-taking opportunities were allocated to state-owned enterprises . . . and other semi-public (parastatal) corporations which employed large numbers of loyalist mainlanders; to party-owned enterprises; to a few politically well-connected mainlander firms; and to prominent Taiwanese families.[20]

Until recently, Taiwan's conglomerates lacked independent financing (the banks were almost all government owned), but as large corporations they had preferred access to bank financing for business expansion, import credits, and loans. They could borrow money without collateral at interest rates considerably lower than the market. KMT enterprises had even better access to state financing. SMEs, however, lacked collateral because of their size. They were forced to seek financing in the informal market, and the interest rates they paid often reached 300 percent. Also, Taiwan's SOEs are mostly upstream producers of goods, and conglomerates are among their most preferred customers.

The second factor, or complex of factors, is of equal importance: conglomerates are increasing in number and size, KMT enterprises are proliferating, but SOEs are privatizing at a snail's pace (and when they do privatize, they are likely to be purchased by conglomerates or KMT enterprises). We have discussed the second and third elements in chapters 3 and 6; here we discuss the increase in conglomerate power in Taiwan—its causes and consequences.

Expansion of conglomerates Conglomerate expansion is a recent and evolving phenomenon in Taiwan. It dates from the late 1980s, and is thus not covered by the magisterial studies of the political economy, such as Robert Wade's *Governing the Market*. Four developments explain the new prominence of Taiwan's conglomerates. First, as party and state leadership indigenized, resistance to conglomerate power decreased. When political leaders were mainlanders and business magnates Taiwanese, ethnic apprehensions frosted relationships. Now, leaders of both politics and business are more likely to be of the same speech group; they may even have kinship linkages. The state no longer has reason to fear the rise of conglomerate power.

The other three causes are reactions to pressures on Taiwan by its major trading partner, the United States, and reflect increasing economic liberalization. Reacting to the huge buildup of deficits in its trade with Taiwan, and seeking to erase the cost advantages of Taiwan's exporters, the United States insisted that Taiwan allow appreciation of the value of the NT dollar. Between 1986 and 1988, the Central Bank of China relaxed its control over currency appreciation, which raised the value of the NT dollar nearly 50 percent against the US dollar, and this left businesses awash with cash. Some squandered this in land speculation, some gambled it on the Taipei stock market, but many used it for business expansion.

Then, in reaction to primarily US pressure to liberalize the banking sector, the government revised banking laws in 1989 to allow formation of private commercial banks. Instantly, 15 new banks were established, all owned by conglomerates determined to follow the Japanese practice of adding a corporate bank to business groups in order to secure their diversified enterprises.

The other pressure on Taiwan came from US-Taiwan bilateral trade talks, in which the United States insisted that Taiwan open its markets to foreign competition. Because in the 1980s most conglomerate business transpired on the Taiwan market, this trade pressure led to a response that fits into the product cycle theory of business expansion: movement offshore. To protect themselves against potential losses from competition in the domestic market, while also improving their competitive edge through cheaper labor and land, conglomerates moved production to mainland China and Southeast Asian sites.

What resulted from these changes was a significantly larger (by about 35 percent) conglomerate stake in Taiwan's economy. In 1996, the total sales of Taiwan's 500 largest manufacturing corporations (most of which were parts of business groups) reached US $115.6 billion, and they accounted for 44 percent of GDP, with a growth rate of 25 percent.[21] Too, conglomerates that had once operated only in the domestic market became multinational corporations with enterprises in China, Indonesia, the Philippines, Thailand, and Malaysia. Meanwhile, it became harder for SMEs to enter the market, and to profit while there. Bankruptcy rates for SMEs exceeded their normal high level.

In summary, Taiwan's economic structure changed in response to foreign pressures and domestic processes related to democratization. The large firms got even larger, with a greater controlling power over the market, thus squeezing the SMEs.

Openness in the Society and Polity

By openness we mean the absence of state controls over thought, speech, and most importantly action—whether the society is a "free market of ideas", and whether the leaders who make policies are selected through a competitive process in which all adults can participate. The six states in our comparison are diverse with respect to openness and political competition.

Most controlled is the communist state of China. Although the PRC may be evolving toward a softer form of authoritarianism, speech and action are still monitored, and dissidents who challenge the guiding role of the communist party are imprisoned and, less frequently, killed. The massacre on June 4, 1989 of 1,000 to 1,500 Beijing students who rallied for the democratization of China testifies to the consistent refusal of communist leaders to tolerate opposition. Nevertheless, the regime schedules local elections that, since 1981, have permitted competition among candidates (but obviously not among parties). No meaningful elections are held above the county and township levels.[22] One advantage of tight party control is that elections are not much influenced by concentrated wealth.

As a one-party state, Singapore is a more controlled social and political environment than all of the other states except China; with a population of only 3 million on one small island, Singapore is also easier to control. The People's Action Party has taken at least 60 percent of the votes in generally free elections since independence from Britain in 1959. The several parties in opposition face the daunting challenge of a unified ruling party that built an effective growth state under highly adverse conditions, a state with extremely successful social welfare policies. Money does not buy elections in Singapore because the government keeps them inexpensive: it prohibits TV advertising, restricts the display of printed materials, and limits the campaign period to ten days.[23]

Hong Kong is the subject of much speculative judgment concerning its social, economic, and political future under the Chinese flag. Until the transfer of sovereignty, Hong Kong was a vibrant society with a free press, academic freedom, open and fair elections, and market freedom.[24] The most noteworthy political reform introduced by Great Britain was to open seats in the Legislative Council (LegCo) to election. Political parties have contested seats in the LegCo since 1991 in elections that were limited in expense. On July 1, 1997, the elected LegCo was replaced by an appointed one, but new elections were promised for 1998.

Japan is East Asia's oldest democracy, and in many respects it is a model for both Korea and Taiwan. Japanese society has become relatively open in the post-war period, but freedoms of speech and press lack strong constitutional protection. A multi-party system makes elections competitive, notwithstanding the stranglehold the LDP maintained over the lower house of the Diet until it lost its majority in the 1993 elections. The electoral system of Japan is, in the opinion of most specialists, the primary reason the LDP held power so long; it is also used to explain the corruption of Japanese elections.

Japan's electoral system is called the single-non-transferable-vote (SNTV) system (described in detail in chapter 3). Japanese constituencies are multi-member, but each voter casts a vote for one candidate only. The effect of this system is to pit candidates from several different parties against one another. This system gives parties strength in determining whom to nominate, but during the election, it is each candidate for him or herself. Incumbents, with higher name recognition, tend to be re-elected, and the LDP has had a majority of incumbents. Because candidates run against all other candidates, they form their own political support groups, and these are expensive machines to feed.[25] Political parties distribute millions of dollars to candidates before elections, and often the source of the contributions to parties and candidates is corrupt.

Election campaigns in Japan are extensively regulated, with rules proscribing individual TV advertising, limiting the size of leaflets and flyers, prohibiting house-to-house canvassing, and limiting the amount of campaign donations. The last rule often is violated, and the most egregious example was the Recruit scandal. Former prime minister Toshiki Kaifu admitted he had received $100,000 in contributions from the Recruit Company. Following this admission, a series of illegal contributions were revealed involving former prime minister Noboru Takeshita, other ministers and leaders of the LDP and opposition socialists; the contributions were not only earmarked for campaigns but as balder attempts to buy influence.[26] The LDP raised over $200 million in campaign donations for candidates in the February 1990 elections for the lower house of the Diet, mostly from businesses, despite the Recruit scandal.[27] Because of the belief that the electoral system was the primary cause of corruption in politics, the Japanese established a new electoral system in January 1995, using a combination of single-member constituencies and proportional representation.

The long period of military dictatorship interrupted South Korea's progression toward a free society. Elections for the National Assembly were held under military rule, but it was not until 1992 that an open presidential election was held. Elections for local government posts were restored in 1996 after a generation without them. Korea uses a different electoral system than Japan but one that still confers benefits on incumbents. It is one factor behind the electoral success at the national level of the Democratic Justice Party, South Korea's ruling party. However, the party has often held less than a majority of seats in the parliament, and in 1996 elections lost more races than it won at the provincial and local levels. At least two other parties compete with the Democratic Justice Party in presidential and parliamentary elections.

Of greater significance, South Korean parties are divided into many factions; they merge and split often, which makes campaigns and voting behavior very fluid. Few Koreans have stable party identifications (a statement that applies less well to Japanese voters). Because the focus of attention has been on the presidency, it is that office which has attracted money. The 1992 presidential election, which marked the peaceful transfer from military to civilian rule, was reported to be "clean and smooth".[28]

However, four years later, Kim Dae Jung, a long-standing freedom fighter who had come out of self-imposed retirement to challenge Kim Young Sam in the election, admitted that he had received US $2.6 million from Roh Tae Woo during the campaign.[29] This paled in comparison to the direct business bribes and kickbacks to presidents discussed in the next section.

Although 1996 was not a good year for the Taiwan economy, it earned high rankings from evaluators for both political and economic freedom. Taiwan entered the ranks of free nations for the first time in 1996 after successful presidential elections, reported the Freedom House in its annual year-end survey of political rights and civil liberties.[30] The report favorably contrasted Taiwan's democratization with the situation of China, in Freedom House's "least free" category because of its near total absence of civil liberties and political rights.

Taiwan's economy also earned high marks from the Heritage Foundation and *The Wall Street Journal*, which jointly published the 1997 Index of Economic Freedoms. The index placed Taiwan seventh among 150 countries graded in economic freedom. Its ranking surpassed Japan's but was below Hong Kong's (first overall) and Singapore's (second). China fell near the bottom of the list at 125th.[31] Contributing to Taiwan's high ranking were reduced barriers to foreign investment, capital flows, banking, and generally low average tariff rates on industrial products.

Indeed, Taiwan has become a nearly open society after more than ten years of democratization. Remaining restrictions on civil and political liberties are few, and the press is uninhibited. Only government ownership of the three major TV networks blemishes the media's freedom record. Citizens have free rights to criticize government officials and policies. Since revision of the Sedition Law in 1992, it has been legal to advocate independence of Taiwan, but freedom of demonstration is somewhat restricted.[32] Judicial rights are still limited, too.

In Taiwan's multi-party system, there are free and open elections with high rates of participation. It stretches the point, however, to suggest that a candidate other than Lee Teng-hui could have won the 1996 presidential election given not only his incumbency and the military exercises that prompted voters to rally around the flag but the superior island-wide resources (including money) of the ruling party. Like the Chinese communist party and the PAP, the KMT has never lost a presidential election; unlike them, it faces an increasingly competitive opposition party, and the KMT candidate may not win the 2000 presidential election.

Taiwan's electoral system is modeled on the SNTV, which was borrowed from Japan. During the National Assembly's discussion of constitutional reform in 1997, several delegates proposed that Taiwan make the same kinds of reforms that both Korea and Japan had made in order to reduce the corruption of the electoral process. Because both the KMT and DPP see the status quo as benefiting their electoral chances, that proposal received insufficient support to pass.

Corruption is difficult to evaluate cross-culturally, even within Confucian states. Taiwan seems most to resemble Japan in the degree and amount of corruption in electoral politics. Local elections have been corrupt since their onset in Taiwan. The influence of local factions, which drain resources from governments and corporations to win races, has declined in some regions of Taiwan only to be replaced by an equally expensive network of less organized interests. Because the legislature is now an important political arena, elections for legislators have become extremely expensive. The business establishment foots the bill for most of these electoral costs.

Access to Government

Private sector interests can be communicated to state systems through a variety of mechanisms, and we investigate three in the six Confucian states. Business interests can be *incorporated* into the state, by absorption into party or state policy-making councils. Business interests can *purchase* access through bribes or payoffs, which is in contrast to purchase of access through campaign funding, as discussed above. Business interests can also *represent* themselves directly by running for office or indirectly through business association activity. We consider several different examples of these types of access.

Incorporation

Incorporation is a characteristic of corporate states, which seek to influence economic activity through control of the state's economic leadership. Incorporation is partly symbolic and partly functional. Symbolically, it allocates status to business leaders based on previous or potential contributions; functionally, it uses economic leaders to legitimize state plans and economic activities. All Confucian states including the PRC have practiced incorporation over the post-war period. However, this practice is relatively recent, dating from the 1980s, and has not become a formula; that is, seats in people's congresses and party committees are not allocated with a set percentage for economic leaders.

Hong Kong provides most examples of symbolic incorporation. During the colonial period, business leaders regularly were acknowledged by entry to the Queen's list, appointed by the governor to the executive council, or appointed to the legislative council before that body became elective. In Taiwan, symbolic incorporation acknowledged business leaders through membership in the Legislative Yuan or National Assembly before these became elective bodies. Also, prominent business leaders were selected to sit on the KMT's central committee and, in rarer cases, on the central standing committee.

As the strongest corporate states in East Asia, both Japan and Korea incorporated business leaders in policy deliberations but did so in institutionalized meetings with bureaucrats, party members, and cabinet officials.[33]

Purchase

Although illegal in each of the Confucian states, the obtaining of direct access through purchase (bribes, payoffs, kickbacks, etc.) is found in each of the six states, but to varying degrees. Table 12 provides information on the perceived impact of corruption on business activities in the six Confucian states:

Table 12. Corruption Ranking of Confucian States, 1995*

Country	Score	Number of Surveys
Singapore	9.26	7
Hong Kong	7.12	7
Japan	6.72	7
Taiwan	5.08	7
South Korea	4.29	7
China	2.16	4

*The index reflects the level at which corruption is perceived by business to affect commercial activities and is based on seven surveys. The score is the overall integrity ranking, with ten representing an extremely clean country, while zero indicates a country where business transactions routinely require kickbacks, extortion, etc. The second column indicates the number of surveys in which a particular country has been included. Variance was not significant for any of the East Asian countries.

Source: Adapted from "Transparency International Corruption Ranking 1995", in Hilton L. Root, *Small Countries, Big Lessons: Governance and the Rise of East Asia* (Hong Kong: Oxford University Press, 1996), xv.

Even though surveys of corruption are highly impressionistic, these findings jibe with conventional wisdom about the cost of doing business in the six states. Perceived as most corrupt is the rapidly developing PRC, with relaxing ideological controls and a poor enforcement system. Perceived as cleanest are Singapore and Hong Kong, the two former British colonies, with strong civil service traditions, good enforcement systems, and small territories to supervise. Japan, Taiwan, and South Korea cluster toward the center.

Very expensive elections create an environment of money politics in most of the states, and the expectation is that business interests will subsidize election costs in exchange for information, access, and influence. Because each of the countries has a strong state system, however, influence over legislators is regarded as insufficient to determine critical economic outcomes. The highly publicized cases have involved bribery of high cabinet officials (including presidents) and bureaucrats.

We referred above to the Recruit scandal in Japanese politics. It was not the first major scandal in post-war politics, credit for the creation of which goes to Lockheed Corporation. Eager to break into the Japanese market, Lockheed paid kickbacks of $50,000 on each airplane it sold to the president of All Nippon Airways. It also bribed prime minister Kakuei Tanaka, the secretary general of the LDP, the minister of the Ministry of Trade and Industry (MITI), the chief cabinet secretary, the Minister of Transportation, chairman of the LDP's Special Committee on Aviation, and both current and former parliamentary vice ministers of transportation.[34] Revealed initially in a US Congressional investigation, the scandal resulted in indictments and electoral changes in Japan. Tanaka himself, however, was re-elected (but resigned as prime minister).

An even larger scandal rocked the South Korean government in 1995. Former president Roh Tae Woo admitted publicly that during his five years in office he collected about US $650 million in contributions to his "governing fund" from businesses. Subsequent investigations revealed that most of South Korea's top *chaebols* had passed money to Roh regularly. The top four conglomerates were also the largest donors—Hyundai, Samsung, Daewoo, and Lucky Goldstar. Prosecutors established that the donations were in fact kickbacks or bribes in exchange for government contracts or favors.[35] Thereupon, Roh was indicted, tried, and found guilty.

Taiwan has not yet lost a premier or president to a major scandal, but the collapse of the Tenth Credit Corporation (noted above) brought down ministers and party leaders. The scandal was particularly embarrassing for the KMT leadership, then under Chiang Ching-kuo, because of the KMT's reputation for corruption on the Chinese mainland. Opposition politicians have charged President Lee Teng-hui with shady dealings, alleging that his family improperly procured land for a villa. This became Taiwan's "Whitewater" in the mid 1990s, but no official investigation followed the charges.

Sinologist Lucien Pye believes that "money politics in Japan and Korea, and to a lesser extent in Taiwan, has had the paradoxical effect of furthering democratic development".[36] He bases this judgment on the changed attitudes of the public to politicians and of politicians to themselves and generally to development of views more compatible with democracy. Also, revulsion to corruption when exposed has brought new people into politics.

This does not seem to accord well with popular reactions to corruption in Taiwan's politics. The public has become more inured to corruption and jaundiced about the political process. Respect for political institutions has declined under democratization. In only a few cases have political parties been able to use popular revulsion about money politics and corruption to institute laws, such as the Financial Disclosure Act, which would cleanse institutions and processes.

Representation

In all of the Confucian states except China, business leaders have run for political office at the national level, as legislators, and, in one noteworthy case, for the presidency. Chang Ju Yang of the United People's Party of South Korea (and founder of the Hyundai industrial conglomerate) ran for the presidency in 1992 and gained about 16 percent of the vote.

Although the Confucian states do not have party systems clearly differentiating ideological perspectives or pitting business interests against those of labor, several of the parties do speak for business interests and gain a large number of their votes and contributions. The LDP, because of its conservative outlook and advocacy of continued economic growth, wins the support of Japan's conglomerates and also the *Keidanren*, the federation of major industrial and trading organizations, such as those for automobiles, chemicals, banks, iron and steel, and petroleum.

The Democratic Justice Party in South Korea has a less strong business orientation and receives conglomerate support largely because it is the ruling party. We noted in chapter 5 that the KMT now has a relatively strong business orientation, but the DPP has attempted to cultivate support from Taiwan's SMEs.

A surer path to influence in the state may be through business associations, and they figure prominently in Japan and South Korea's political economy but have a somewhat lower profile in Taiwan. Reputedly the most powerful business association in Asia is *Keidanren* (Federation of Economic Organizations). It includes in its membership the chief executives of most of Japan's powerful corporations, and in its meetings, business leaders develop integrated policies toward political strategy and economic development.[37] *Keidanren* is a constituent element and primary funding source of the LDP. Observers credit the business association's decision not to fund the LDP exclusively in 1993 with that party's defeat at election time.[38]

Keidanren's success is attributable to the inclusion within its small membership (around 1,000 executives) of business interests that represent half of Japan's corporate assets and nearly half of its annual sales. Its large staff prepares position papers that are the basis for meetings between members, bureaucrats, and leading politicians. As one of the rare venues for meetings between the principals of Japan's political, business, and bureaucratic establishment, *Keidanren* leaders are able to influence the direction of national policy and even aspects of Japan's foreign policy.

This conventional view of *Keidanren* needs to be balanced against scholarship arguing that Japan's peak associations are losing influence to smaller groups, such as trade associations that are sector specific.[39] The latter are prominent in Korea, too.

In South Korea, state leaders have had regular personal contacts with major business leaders. While they often use formalized channels, much of the interchange occurs through consultation between state agencies and state-sponsored industrial associations. Such consultations and contacts were of signal importance during the launch of South Korea's export drive. Regular meetings, both formal and informal, occurred between big-business leaders and ministers and between middle managers in the private and public sectors (on both functional and sectoral issues). Even President Park Chung Hee held "deliberation council" meetings with participants chosen by business associations—in groups and as representatives of their industries (but not of their individual firms).[40] Such contacts assisted in information exchange, expanding the inclusiveness of policy-making, and creating a stable policy environment.

Taiwan's peak business associations are modeled on those in Japan and are commonly regarded as less powerful. As noted in chapter 5, business associations were established at the behest of the state; initially, they served as transmission belts, conveying government priorities and regulations to industry and commerce then compliantly carrying information and reactions back to the government. However, a few industrial associations, such as the Textile Association, had quasi-official roles and seemed to operate with as much authority as Japanese industrial associations.

Three peak associations—the National Federation of Industries, General Chamber of Commerce, and National Association of Industry and Commerce—today have the greatest authority. In theory, they represent all of business and commerce in Taiwan. With large staffs (but less than one-third, individually, the size of the *Keidanren* staff), they have the capability to collect information and prepare research reports and position papers. The industry and commerce association is regarded as the most influential in the 1990s because its chair has the closest relationship with President Lee Teng-hui. The personal connections of federation leaders determine their influence. All three organizations provide opportunities for regular meetings between business leaders, politicians, and cabinet ministers.

China presents an interesting case of change in the representation of business interests. During the 1980s, as the economy liberalized, the government created a large number of business associations. The structure of the non-governmental associations (or *minjian xiehui*) resembled the corporatist type found in Taiwan, for they were officially registered and only one organization represented each sector. The party-state still controlled structure and personnel of most associations in the 1990s, but some had demonstrated independence. This prompted a United Front Department official to opine that "the non-public economic sector . . . has started to seek the political means to protect its own interests".[41]

Most relevant to the differences in political economies of the Confucian states, however, are their perspectives and performance in the setting of industrial policy. Industrial policy refers to the use of state authority and power to guide the market. As Wade explains it, the state promotes high levels of productive investment and assists in the transfer of new technologies to production; the state guides investment into areas that would not be able to develop without government sponsorship; and the state pushes industries into international competition.[42] Industrial policy's objective is to help industries grow faster or decline less disruptively "by affecting production and investment decisions of decentralized producers".[43] States with strong industrial policies are also corporate states; those without industrial policies are *laissez-faire*.

There is no disagreement among those analyzing East Asian states that the PRC has followed an industrial policy. Until economic reforms of the late 1970s and 1980s, China's market was poorly developed. Most enterprises were state owned, and in a centrally planned command economy, the state made decisions on rules, rates, and direction of investment, industrial sectors to be emphasized, and targets for trade promotion. Coordination and implementation of policy decisions was problematical, but it was the state that allowed the development of the market and then directed it.

The other five Confucian states are capitalist, with varying ranges of freedom in their marketplaces. Experts agree that both the Japanese and Korean markets have been substantially guided by the state, notwithstanding a thriving private sector and few SOEs. In 1982, Chalmers Johnson developed the thesis that Japan was a "capitalist developmental state". Extremely powerful national ministries, the Ministry of International Trade and Industry (MITI) and the Ministry of Finance, worked directly with corporate conglomerates to devise economic development strategies and formulate national industrial policies.[44] MITI became the most powerful government agency by protecting domestic industries, developing strategic industries, and adjusting the economic structure to meet both internal and external changes.[45]

The state provided what has been called "administrative guidance" to the private sector. It issued directives or instructions that facilitated cooperation and compliance from business corporations. MITI nurtured new industries, such as electronics and computers, in which Japan soon developed superiority. It assisted in the formation of industrial cartels and, through foreign exchange licensing powers, was able to force declining companies to merge in order to increase their competitiveness.[46] MITI protected Japanese companies in their technological licensing agreements with foreign companies. The state even protected smaller enterprises from complete domination by the large conglomerates.

Korea's situation was different from Japan's as it began industrialization. It had undergone a devastating civil war, which left its population exhausted but highly unified. Extensive American military and economic assistance played a critical role in the rebuilding of infrastructure, as it had in Taiwan.[47] Then, for over 25 years, military-bureaucratic regimes dominated the state. At the start of its industrialization drive, Korea had a larger public sector than Japan.

Korea's Economic Planning Board (EPB), established in 1961 to prepare the government's budget and five-year plans, functioned in industrial policy analogously to Japan's MITI. EPB strategized about which industrial products to promote, which industries to assist in development and growth, and which industries should receive favorable tax treatment and credits.[48] Credit recommendations the EPB made to government banks were particularly important incentives in guiding the market because the developing conglomerates, unlike the Japanese, lacked banks and their own sources of finance. Chung-in Moon summarizes the pattern:

> (T)he state is pace-setter and guide, while business follows. State and business are interdependent, but in a vertical, asymmetric and, in some cases, hierarchical structure. Corporatist channels are state-controlled; the private sector is organized, subsidized and controlled by the state.[49]

Business in both Korea and Japan has been more assertive in the late 1980s and 1990s. Internationalization and liberalization of the Korean economy in particular have lessened the vulnerability of business leaders to government pressures.[50] As noted in several places, openness in East Asian economies and increasingly democratic political frameworks give business groups the opportunity to advance their interests directly to government.

Singapore is a contrasting case but still one that falls within the realm of corporatism, with the state playing a directing role in the economy. Its long period of single-party rule, mostly under the paternalistic leadership of Lee Kuan Yew, popularized the term "Confucian authoritarianism" for Singapore.[51] The state guided the market differently than in Japan and Korea. Although essentially a free enterprise economy, the state developed a public infrastructure, controlled labor prices, stimulated private savings for investment, deliberately sought out potential investors, and implemented export policies.

The Economic Development Board, which owned the remaining state enterprises after privatization, developed vast public housing estates. A National Wage Council controlled wages to keep Singapore's bargain with MNCs that its wage structure would makes its exports globally competitive. In fact, the state's policy of wage restraint was a critical factor in the success of Singapore's labor-intensive, export-oriented industrialization strategy.[52] The government developed a compulsory savings policy, through the Central Provident Fund, which required employers and employees to make contributions to savings and pensions (producing one of the world's highest savings rates), which became a major source for investment in industry. The Economic Development Board strategized on the future direction of the global economy and was able to sell Singapore to investors using a network of offices throughout the world.[53] And the Trade Development Board formulated and implemented export policies.

Both the Hong Kong and Taiwan experiences are anomalous and fit less well within the corporatist interpretation of economic development through state intervention in the market. Hong Kong is touted as the "world's closest approximation to a free-market, private enterprise, capitalistic economic system",[54] but Hong Kong's businesses have never operated on their own. The state provided basic law and order, an administrative system, and an economic infrastructure. These largely custodial functions were joined by increased social welfare functions, such as supplying public housing for half the population. The state also owned all land, which it leased to business corporations and individuals to raise revenue instead of relying on taxes.

Two additional characteristics of the Hong Kong state lead Wade and others to call it "a variant of a guided market economy". First, large banks and trading companies connected to those running the government (such as the Hong Kong and Shanghai Banking Corporation with assets valued at twice the colony's annual GDP) were in a position, collectively, to execute a development strategy.[55] Second, when the rate of Hong Kong's exports slowed compared to those of Taiwan and Korea in the 1980s, the state gave financial support to firms, largely through financing of research and development centers.

The state in Taiwan has been far more activist or interventionist than that in Hong Kong but less so than in Japan and Korea. This leads some critics to suggest that Taiwan has not been a corporate state, and it lacks an industrial policy. For example, Kuo Cheng-tian argues that the state lacked autonomy from influential business interests and associations; that it could not direct the economy because it was insufficiently centralized and had a weak bureaucracy and planning agencies; and that leaders were more committed to military and political than economic development.[56] Hamilton and Biggart acknowledge that Taiwan has a state planning system but believe the government lacks an implementation procedure.[57] Gary Gereffi points to the potential that Taiwan had for economic direction through SOEs but remarks that ethnic cleavage made it difficult for the state to rely on unqualified support from the subordinate capitalist class to compete with the large, vertically integrated Japanese and South Korean conglomerates and general trading companies.[58]

Wade disagrees with these formulations of the state's role in the economy and finds that the state has been activist (through its SOEs and also through state research organizations, especially in new, high-technology sectors). Because of ethnic cleavage between mainlander bureaucrats, SOE managers and the Taiwanese business community, and also because of the absence of huge conglomerates like those in Japan and Korea, the state pressured the private sector indirectly, through import controls, domestic content requirements, entry restrictions, and tax incentives.[59] Throughout, actions of the government met defining tests of market guidance by:

> 1) redistributing agricultural land in the early postwar period; 2) controlling the financial system and making private financial capital subordinate to industrial capital; 3) maintaining stability in some of the main economic parameters that affect the viability of long-term investment, especially the exchange rate, the interest rate, and the general price level; 4) modulating the impact of foreign competition in the domestic economy and prioritizing the use of scarce foreign exchange; 5) promoting exports; 6) promoting technology acquisition from multinational companies and building a national technology system; and 7) assisting particular industries.[60]

However, Wade's argument does not test well in certain sectors, such as the automobile industry. In his comparison of Korea and Taiwan, Chu finds that Korean economic officials created policy instruments and plans that affected the entire auto industry. In contrast, Taiwan's officials had much less influence on private firms because the state apparatus was poorly coordinated and lacked direct policy instruments and effective relationships with the private sector. He summarizes by noting that "the state's push for industrial upgrading has been incremental, intermittent, and reliant on state-controlled enterprises".[61] Yet in other sectors, such as petrochemicals or information technology, the state's role has been more prominent. To the present, scholars have not conducted comprehensive studies of Taiwan's major industrial sectors over the half-century of nationalist rule.

The case of Taiwan is essentially an argument over whether the glass is half empty or half full. Private entrepreneurs had greater freedom from direct government control, and the state did curb the formation of huge conglomerates for largely political reasons. In these respects, advocates of the neo-classical economics or *laissez-faire* approach are correct. However, as Karl Fields notes in his summary comparing Taiwan's economic development with South Korea's, the dominant intervening influence was the state. Although the Taiwan government had different reasons for its actions, nonetheless it imposed "institutional constraints, obligations, and incentives" on the economy.[62]

Our judgment varies slightly from Fields', in that the state has applied more incentives than constraints to industry. Describing his work with the chemical industry, a section chief of Taiwan's Industrial Development Bureau commented:

> We use no compulsory means. We have incentives and for high value products, we offer assistance—for example, tax exempt status. We help big business firms with special incentives and offer SMEs help in product development, usually a 50-50 split for new developments. But we can advise only. Our plans are very general and by no means so specialized as the Japanese. We have studied from the Japanese, but our relationship to businesses is much more distant.[63]

In summary, we can say that Taiwan has an industrial policy but it is relatively weak as compared to those of South Korea and Japan; its strength varies by sector and is highly reliant on incentives.

Conclusion

The objective of this comparison has been to highlight the similarities and differences between Taiwan's political economy and that of Asia's other Confucian states. Taiwan's political centralization has been greater than the other Confucian states except China. This high degree of centralization was essential in assisting economic growth and guiding industrial change when they became priorities of the government in the 1970s. Relaxation of political controls since the late 1980s and the growth of independence in the Legislative Yuan have reduced the ability of the state to direct economic changes or retarded the implementation of policies (as we noted with respect to privatization in chapter 6).

Taiwan's economy does not resemble that of any other Confucian state. The structure of the economy is more complex and rapidly changing than appears to be the case among the most comparable economies—South

Korea and Japan. Among free enterprise economies, Taiwan has a higher participation rate of SOEs, and they played a critical role in the economic transformation. Taiwan's SMEs have been more vibrant and influential in the export sector than SMEs in South Korea and Japan. Also, Taiwan has party enterprises whose influence is unparalleled in other capitalist economies.

Another structural dimension that distinguishes Taiwan's political economy is the linkage between business groups, SOEs, and KMT-enterprises. This provides state, party, and business opportunities for mutual interpenetration. The linkage potentially has strongly anti-competitive effects. Business conglomerates in Taiwan are growing very rapidly and now play a larger economic role than at any previous time; the same observation can be made of KMT enterprises. Only state enterprises have not kept pace, due largely to the privatization of China Steel in the early 1990s. But the privatization movement has stalled.

Once a highly authoritarian Confucian state, Taiwan has embarked on the transition to democracy. Taiwan's society in 1997 is as free as that of any other Confucian state. The society is open to new exogenous influences and is quickly changing. Business interests have used the guise of freedom to enter and in some cases dominate the political marketplace; in this respect, Taiwan's scandals and money politics are not greatly different from those of South Korea or Japan.

As Taiwan's polity became relatively less centralized, more opportunities became available for economic interests to influence the state. The KMT continues to co-opt business leaders and now has the largest number within the central standing committee in the recent history of the party as the party attempts to measure in its membership the changing dynamics of state and society. Systematic evidence is lacking on purchase of influence; impressions abound, and they suggest a large jump in corruption during Taiwan's democratization, but to a level no higher than that found in South Korea.

Business interests are better represented in Taiwan's political economy today than at any previous time. The transformation of the party-state gives business (large or conglomerate) a loud voice in national policy-making. But we cannot parrot Charles Wilson (commerce secretary during the US Eisenhower administration) and say that what is good for the Formosa Plastics Group is good for the country. Taiwan's international vulnerability makes the state sensitive to increased dependence on anyone, particularly its closest and most powerful rival, the PRC.

Throughout Taiwan's industrialization process, the state has led the market as often as it has been led by market forces. More interesting than control of market forces, in a comparative sense, are the indirect mechanisms used by the state to guide outcomes. The incentives favored by the state in urging economic change have been weaker than the policy instruments of states with full industrial policies. However, such mechanisms may have avoided some expensive mistakes, such as an attempt to develop an automobile export industry that would have been in the charge of either Japanese or American multinational corporations.

Notes

[1] Ezra F. Vogel, *The Four Little Dragons* (Cambridge, MA: Harvard University Press, 1991), 101.
[2] World Bank, *World Development Indicators 1993* (Washington, DC: Oxford University Press, 1993), 126.
[3] See Adam Przeworski and Henry Teune, *The Logic of Comparative Social Inquiry* (New York: John Wiley, 1970), 34.
[4] See Robert O. Tilman, 'The Political Leadership: Lee Kuan Yew and the PAP Team', in Kernial Singh Sandher and Paul Wheatley, *Management of Success: The Moulding of Modern Singapore* (Boulder, CO: Westview Press, 1990), 53-4.
[5] Quoted in Vogel, 1991, 77.
[6] James C. F. Wang, *Comparative Asian Politics* (Englewood Cliffs, NJ: Prentice-Hall, 1994), 122.
[7] For a recent, popular account, see Harold R. Kerbo and John A. McKinstry, *Who Rules Japan?* (Westport, CT: Praeger, 1995).
[8] Chalmers Johnson, *MITI and the Japanese Miracle: The Growth of Industrial Policy, 1925-1975* (Stanford, CA: Stanford University Press, 1982; also see Johnson's *Japan: Who Governs? The Rise of the Developmental State* (New York: W. W. Norton, 1995), 115-40.
[9] Karl von Wolferen, *The Enigma of Japanese Power: People and Politics in a Stateless Nation* (New York: Knopf, 1989), 33.
[10] Yingyi Qian and Barry R. Weingast, 'Institutions, State Activism, and Economic Development: A Comparison of State-owned and Township-Village Enterprises in China', in Mashiko Aoki, Hyung-ki Kim, and Masahiro Okuno-Fujiwara, *The Role of Government in East Asian Economic Development* (New York: Oxford University Press, 1996), 259.
[11] Chung Ming Wong, 'Trends and Patterns of Singapore's Trade in Manufactures', in Colin I. Bradford, Jr., and William H. Branson, *Trade and Structural Change in Pacific Asia* (Chicago: University of Chicago Press, 1987), 383.
[12] Quoted in Vogel, 1991, 79.
[13] Michael L. Gerlach, *Alliance Capitalism: The Social Organization of Japanese Business* (Berkeley, CA: University of California Press, 1982), 15-17.
[14] Meredith Woo-Cumings, 'The Political Economy of Growth in East Asia', in Aoki, Kim, and Okuno-Fukiwara, 1996, 332.
[15] Nicole Woolsey Biggart and Gary G. Hamiltion, 'Explaining Asian Business Success', in Marco Orru, Nicole Woolsey Biggart, and Gary G. Hamilton, *The Economic Organization of East Asian Capitalism* (Thousand Oaks, CA: Sage Publications, 1997), 106.

[16] Hamilton and Feenstra call the Korean conglomerates primarily vertically controlled in contrast to those in Taiwan, which are horizontally organized. See their 'Varieties of Hierarchies and Markets', in Orru, Biggart, and Hamilton, 1997, 73.
[17] Alice Amsden, *Asia's Next Giant: South Korea and Late Industrialization* (New York: Oxford University Press, 1989), 116.
[18] See Robert Wade, 'Industrial Policy in East Asia', in Gary Gereffi and Donald L. Wyman, *Manufacturing Miracles: Paths of Industrialization in Latin America and East Asia* (Princeton, NJ: Princeton University Press, 1990), 257.
[19] Yun-han Chu, 'The Realignment of Business-Government Relations and Regime Transition in Taiwan', in Andrew Macintyre, ed., *Business and Government in Industrializing Asia* (Ithaca, NY: Cornell University Press, 1994), 116.
[20] Chu, 1994, 116.
[21] China Credit Information Service, Ltd., *Top 500: The Largest Corporations in Taiwan 1996* (Taipei: 1996), 21.
[22] June T. Dreyer, *China's Political System*, 2nd ed. (Boston: Allyn and Bacon, 1996), 116.
[23] See R. S. Milne and Diane K. Mauzy, *Singapore: The Legacy of Lee Kuan Yew* (Boulder, CO: Westview Press, 1990).
[24] Bruce Bueno de Mesquita, David Newman, and Alvin Rabushka, *Red Flag over Hong Kong* (Chatham, NJ: Chatham House Publishers, 1996), 118-19.
[25] For Japanese campaigns, see Gerald L. Curtis, *The Japanese Way of Politics* (New York: Columbia University press, 1990, 163-77.
[26] See Yayama Taro, 'The Recruit Scandal: Learning from the Causes of Corruption', *The Journal of Japanese Studies*, vol. 16, no. 1 (Winter 1990), 93-114; see also Johnson, 1995, 217, 223.
[27] Wang, 1994, 78.
[28] Wang, 1994, 129.
[29] B. C. Koh, 'South Korea in 1995', *Asian Survey*, vol. XXXVI, no. 1 (January 1996), 55.
[30] *United Daily News*, December 18, 1996.
[31] *China News*, February 19, 1997.
[32] Richard Y. Chuang, 'The International Standing of the Republic of China', *American Journal of Chinese Studies*, vol. 3, no. 2 (October 1996), 121.
[33] See Johnson, 1995, 160.
[34] Johnson, 1995, 196-97.
[35] Koh, 1996, 54-55.
[36] Lucien W. Pye, 'Money Politics and Transitions to Democracy in East Asia', *Asian Survey*, vol. XXXVII, no. 3 (March 1997), 227-28.
[37] See Gary D. Allinson, 'Japan's Keidanren and Its New Leaders,' *Pacific Affairs*, vol. 60, no. 3 (Fall 1987); see also Mark Tilton, *Restrained Trade: Cartels in Japan's Basic Materials Industries* (Ithaca, NY: Cornell University Press, 1996), 22-49.
[38] Kerbo and McKinstry, 1995, 122.
[39] See Gregory W. Noble, 'The Japanese Industrial Policy Debate', in Stephan Haggard and Chung-in Moon, eds., *Pacific Dynamics: The International Politics of Industrial Change* (Boulder, CO: Westview Press, 1988), 35.

244 Wealth and Freedom: Taiwan's New Political Economy

[40] Jose Edgardo Campos and Hilton L. Root, *The Key to the Asian Miracle* (Washington, DC: The Brookings Institution, 1996), 89-90.

[41] Cited in Johathan Unger, ' `Bridges': Private Business, the Chinese Government and the Rise of New Associations', *China Quarterly*, 147 (September 1996), 818.

[42] Wade, 1990, 26; see also Stephan Haggard and Robert Kaufman, *The Political Economy of Democratic Transitions* (Princeton, NJ: Princeton University Press, 1995), 228.

[43] Wade, 1990, 233.

[44] Johnson, 1982, 18.

[45] Johnson, 1982, 16.

[46] See Ezra Vogel, *Japan as Number One* (Cambridge, MA: Harvard University Press, 1979, 70-79, and James C. Abegglen and George Stalk, Jr., *Kaisha: The Japanese Corporation* (New York: Basic Books, 1985), 260-88.

[47] Karl J. Fields, *Enterprise and the State in Korea and Taiwan* (Ithaca, NY: Cornell University Press, 1995), 5.

[48] Leroy Jones and Il Sakong, *Government, Business and Entrepreneurship in Economic Development: The Case of Korea* (Cambridge, MA: Harvard University Press, 1980), 150.

[49] Chung-in Moon, 'Changing Patterns of Business-Government Relations in South Korea', in MacIntyre, 1994, 143.

[50] Moon, 1994, 160.

[51] Wang, 1994, 190.

[52] Wong, 1987, 383.

[53] Manuel Castells, 'Four Asian Tigers with a Dragon Head', in Richard P. Appelbaum and Jeffrey Henderson, *States and Development in the Asian Pacific Rim* (Thousand Oaks, CA: Sage Publications, 1992), 35.

[54] Alvin Rabushka, *The New China: Comparative Economic Development in Mainland China, Taiwan, and Hong Kong* (Hong Kong: Westview Press, 1987), 145.

[55] Wade, 1990, 259.

[56] Cheng-tian Kuo, *Global Competitiveness and Industrial Growth in Taiwan and the Philippines* (Pittsburgh, PA: University of Pittsburgh Press, 1995), 59.

[57] Gary C. Hamilton and Nicole Woolsey Biggart, 'Market, Culture, and Authority', *American Journal of Sociology*, Vol. 94 (1988), 52-94.

[58] Gary Gereffi, 'Big Business and the State', in Gereffi and Wyman, 1990, 98. Suk-jun Lim adopts a different slant by analyzing the historically specific way that Korean leaders approached their problems of legitimacy as compared to Taiwan's. See his 'Politics of Industrialization: Formation of Divergent Industrial Orders in Korea and Taiwan', (Paper presented at the American Political Science Association Conference, San Francisco, CA, September 1, 1996).

[59] Wade, 1990, 156; also, see Laurence J. Lau, 'The Role of Government in Economic Development: Some Observations from the Experience of China, Hong Kong, and Taiwan', in Aoki, Kim, and Okuno-Fujiwara, 1996, 48.

[60] Wade, 1990, 27-28.

[61] Yun-han Chu, 'Industrial Change and Development State in Two East Asian NICs: A Case Study of the Automotive Industries in South Korea and Taiwan', *Proceedings of the National Science Council*, vol. 3, no.2 (July 1993), 218.
[62] Fields, 1995, 243.
[63] Personal interview with Ya-ger Wang, Section Chief, Third Division, Industrial Development Bureau, Ministry of Economic Affairs, May 11, 1996.

9 Conclusion

In this concluding chapter, we discuss the main themes of the book by summarizing the analyses of Taiwan's wealth and freedom: their dimensions and causes. The acceleration and interaction of wealth and freedom have spawned a range of social problems in Taiwan's new political economy that leave many citizens "doing better but feeling worse". The challenges Taiwan faces in the post-Cold War world foster uncertainty and apprehension about the future. Those future prospects now seem more limited.

Taiwan's Wealth

Dimensions

Taiwan emerged from World War II among a large number of low-income, developing countries. Fifty years later, its GDP amounted to US $261 billion, ranking Taiwan the 20th richest country in the world. Taiwan's wealth topped $13,000 per person in 1997, higher than that in any other Asian nation except Japan, Singapore, and Hong Kong, and about the 22nd highest globally. These figures are particularly noteworthy when one considers Taiwan's limited land area (the 132nd smallest in the world).[1]

These statistics were not a fluke. During the period from 1985 to 1995, when world economic growth increased only 2.9 percent, Taiwan averaged 7.9 percent in economic growth. Its GDP increase during this period was 15.4 percent, and the per capita GDP rate was 14.2 percent. The World Bank's 1996 report on the outlook for the global economy ranked Taiwan among the world's fastest integrating economies during the previous ten years.[2] Moreover, Taiwan's status among the world's trading nations—the 14th largest in the mid-1990s—was projected to jump to the 10th major global trading nation by the year 2010.

Gross indicators of economic instability were absent from Taiwan's economy. Its combined rates of inflation and unemployment—the "misery index"—stood below 5 percent in the mid-1990s.[3] While many European nations post double-digit composite figures of inflation and unemployment,

246

Taiwan along with Singapore and Japan have the lowest misery ratings in the world.

Taiwan has become a consumer society and in many areas compares favorably with the post-industrial nations of the West. Average caloric intake rose 50 percent during the post-war period. Ownership of material goods—homes, color TV sets, refrigerators, washing machines, telephones—exceeds 80 percent of the population. A good part of Taiwan's increased wealth has gone toward less materialistic purchases, notably education. For example, in fiscal year 1995, more than US $16.75 billion, or 17 percent of net government expenditures were allocated to education, science, and culture.[4] Attendance at lower schools was virtually universal, and the literacy rate, at 94 percent, ranks among the world's highest. Taiwan's youth routinely score at the top of the global charts in science and math skills.

Increased wealth is reflected consistently in Taiwan's high savings rate. Over the post-war period, national savings as a percentage of GDP ranged from a low of 14.6 in 1955 to a high of 38.5 percent in 1987 (falling to 25.8 percent in 1995, about 3 percent below the post-war average).[5] Increased wealth is also reflected in the time available for recreation: the number of hours in the work month fell from 228 in 1976 to 198 in 1995.[6] Taiwan's people increasingly use recreational time to travel abroad; in fact, the island's population is among the world's most well traveled.

In almost every facet of economic activity over the post-war period, Taiwan moved toward the top of the chart. These developments are so well known that the term "economic miracle" is now a cliché.

Causes

Taiwan did not independently create the economic development plan that brought it riches and wealth in the 1980s and 1990s. Instead, it followed a time-worn recipe for growth based on the experiences of the English and American industrial revolutions, modified by the late-industrializing powers such as Germany and Japan. The plan involved agricultural modernization, cultivation of nascent industries, and promotion of export industries. The plan also wrenched the production focus away from land and labor, toward technology and capital.

Chastened by its loss to the communists in the Chinese civil war, the KMT government retreated to Taiwan in 1949-50 with the aim of recovering the mainland. This goal required economic growth and development; land reform and agricultural modernization were its bases. Soon, agriculture was producing a surplus, and raw and processed food exports earned critically needed foreign exchange for the regime.

At the second stage, the government launched a program of import-substitution industrialization (ISI) during the 1950s to form the industrial foundation for later development.   State-owned enterprises (SOEs) played critical roles during this period and comprised at least half of industrial output.   But the benefits of ISI to the economy were short lived, and economic advisors urged a shift toward export-oriented industrialization, which occurred from the late 1950s to the 1960s—the third stage of Taiwan's economic development plan.

The policy of import substitution was not abandoned.   In fact, a second-stage import substitution policy helped cushion the state against exogenous shocks in the 1970s, and import controls and high tariff walls protected domestic industry up to the 1980s.   The policy also increased the role of SOEs in the economy.

Structural adjustments to the export promotion policy helped adapt Taiwan to changing conditions in the global economy in the 1970s and 1980s.   As Taiwan's wealth increased, it lost its comparative advantage in labor-intensive manufactures.   Following the Japanese example, enterprises ratcheted up, emphasizing technology and capital inputs; enterprises and capital also began to move offshore.

Several factors explain this economic progression and the dynamics of Taiwan's rapid growth.   Throughout Taiwan's industrialization campaign from the 1950s through the 1980s, it was ruled by a single-party authoritarian state.   Rulers shared consensus on the need for rapid economic development, and they were able to provide the infrastructure—economic, social, and political—that made it possible.   Labor was repressed, and capital was attracted to the economic development objectives of the state.   When diplomatic crises began to affect the regime, it was able to retain goodwill by initiating political reforms.

For several reasons, Taiwan had a weaker industrial policy during the period of industrialization than Japan or South Korea: elites' attitudes were more critical toward business; mainlander leaders were threatened by the rising economic power of Taiwanese capitalists; and an industrial policy was expendable early on because of the significant role played by SOEs operating mostly in upstream sectors of the economy.   Nevertheless, the state did guide the market during most of this period, and it caused progressive economic change.

We cannot discount the skills and abilities of the population in Taiwan's economic development.   Literacy rates were relatively high, and people worked hard.   A mostly free enterprise system allowed them to keep most of what they made, and industrialization turned their attention toward forming enterprises themselves in order to improve family circumstances.

The United States played a key role in Taiwan's economic development.   It gave more than US $4 billion in military and economic aid, which in some years in the 1950s covered 75 percent of Taiwan's budget.

American advice, encouragement, and assistance also influenced economic developments from land reform and agricultural modernization to export promotion. Finally, the United States provided the world's largest market to Taiwan's exports on preferred terms and conditions of access.

Taiwan also benefited from the timing of its industrialization. The Korean War enhanced its geographic importance for the United States, which redrew its defense perimeter in Asia to incorporate Taiwan. This war itself, followed shortly thereafter by the Vietnam War, benefited Taiwan directly as a recipient of military aid and indirectly by providing an expanded market for its manufactures and services (for example, as an R&R center for US forces during the Vietnam War).

Thus, the KMT party-state had a great deal to do with the creation of wealth in Taiwan, as did Taiwan's hard-working people. The United States' role cannot be ignored, nor can the fact that Taiwan began developing industrially during large-scale police actions in Korea and Vietnam.

Taiwan's Freedom

Dimensions

Taiwan has had a high level of economic freedom over the post-war period. Residents have been able to take and switch jobs without government permission; SOEs have not dominated the economy since the 1950s, and entry opportunities for entrepreneurs have been abundant (until the 1990s). Also, Taiwan has had a highly educated and attentive public, a fundamental requisite for a civil society, over much of the post-war period.

Other liberalizations of the society and polity occurred more slowly. For example, although citizens had constitutional rights of political speech and writing, they could not always exercise these because of the strictures of martial law (not lifted until 1987) and the temporary provisions. Even in the early 1990s, the right openly to advocate Taiwan's independence was not fully protected.

Too, although Taiwan had a freer press than most Asian countries, the government exercised explicit censorship and control over the media until the late 1980s. It was not until late 1996 that the KMT gave over its ownership rights to the Central News Agency. In 1997, the three major TV networks remained under government control, but the popularity of cable TV and authorization of public TV promised to break this monopoly on the news by the end of the century.

The end of martial law and lifting of the temporary provisions also unleashed public protests. Strikes, marches, demonstrations, and sit-ins all became legal means for citizens to petition government and seek redress of grievances and complaints. Most important, however, was the freedom of citizens to participate in elections and the competitive nature of these elections.

Local elections gave Taiwan's people a limited chance to take part in the political process from 1950, but opposition to the KMT was not permitted. Nor were the elections necessarily conducted fairly; in fact, the regime's ballot box stuffing in Chungli's 1977 local election helped stimulate the organization of *Tang-wai* opposition to the government. The formal inauguration of the opposition occurred in September 1986, when *Tang-wai* leaders established the Democratic Progressive Party (DPP). Chiang Ching-kuo tolerated this open dissent to his rule, which launched Taiwan's democratic era.

The DPP could compete in provincial assembly, county and town magistrate and council elections, but Taiwan's important offices were not open to party competition. The president was elected by the National Assembly, composed of octogenarian legislators elected on the Chinese mainland in the late 1940s. Less than one-fourth of the seats in the Legislative Yuan were elected in Taiwan's elections; another group of elderly legislators, also elected in the late 1940s on the Chinese mainland, held the vast majority of seats. The governor of Taiwan province and the mayors of Taipei and Kaohsiung were appointed by the president.

The first elections for all the seats in the Legislative Yuan did not take place until 1992; democratic elections of executives in provincial government and the cities of Taipei and Kaohsiung occurred in 1994; and finally, in March 1996, Taiwan's voters could freely vote for the presidency. These election were competitive: the DPP drew an average of more than 30 percent of the vote (except in the presidential election); the KMT split, and the New Party (NP) contested Legislative Yuan and presidential elections.

The KMT has democratized to function in Taiwan's democratic era, but it still operates with an unfair advantage in the political system. Rapidly growing KMT enterprises provide resources to the party's candidates in elections that cannot be rivaled by opponents. For this reason, as well as because of the lack of administrative neutrality in the executive,[7] in our judgment, Taiwan's democracy has not yet been consolidated.

Causes

Taiwan's wealth was a necessary condition for its democratization. Wealth ensured the regime could make expensive side payments to displaced elites, such as the aging parliamentarians. Of greater importance, Taiwan's wealth—and relatively egalitarian distribution of wealth—virtually guaranteed that a class of have-nots would not attempt revolution to capture power. Rapid economic development nurtured a growing middle class with a stake in the system and opposed to revolutionary change.

Economic development alone, however, was not a sufficient condition for democratic change. In our view, the primary and sufficient cause of democratization was authoritarian withdrawal: the decision of Chiang Ching-kuo to initiate political reforms in both the party and society. This decision was aided by four additional factors. First was the gradual development of a responsible opposition that continually pressured the regime and that staged precipitating events—for example, the Kaohsiung Incident and establishment of the DPP. Second was division within the elite over the best way to handle dissent. Overreaction—for example, the assassination of Henry Liu and death sentences to defendants in the Kaohsiung Incident—engaged the third factor, international reaction to Taiwan's authoritarian regime and strong pressures on it to reform. In this respect, the United States again intervened in Taiwan's development. Timing was the fourth factor, the development of Taiwan's political liberalization at the moment of the "Third Wave" of democratic transitions internationally, with abundant evidence for authoritarian elites of how quickly they could fall under democratic protest.

Several of these factors may be generalized to other societies. However, the nature of the KMT as a Leninist party, its history of competition with the Chinese communist party, its changing composition under Chiang Ching-kuo, and CCK's leadership itself: all are unique factors in the development of democratization in Taiwan.

A New Political Economy

Economic Concentration

Taiwan's political economy is new for several reasons. It is a mature industrial economy that is probably freer of government intervention and more liberal than at any previous time. The economic structure differs from that of the immediate post-war years or even of the 1970s. SOEs play a less important role in the economy comparatively, accounting for a lower relative share of industrial output. KMT enterprises are larger, but they still have a moderate economic importance. Conglomerates are considerably larger, and seem likely to become entities more closely resembling Korea's *chaebol* and Japan's *keiretsu*.

All three of these forces have new opportunities for expansion. They possess more capital and have greater access to technology than Taiwan's small- and medium-size enterprises (SMEs). They have aggressively expanded offshore to Southeast Asia and to mainland China (yes, even enterprises with KMT ownership of less than 50 percent have invested in Hong Kong and mainland China). With the increase in size of conglomerates and KMT enterprises come questions about the continued competitiveness of the Taiwan economy.

More troubling in the new political economy is the combination of SOEs, KMT enterprises, and business groups. We showed some evidence of this integration in the privatization case study. To the present, conclusive evidence is lacking of increased concentration of economic power in the hands of the three forms of enterprises. Nor can we assume that there is just one economic interest as businesses compete. For example, firms doing business in Taiwan compete for political influence with those doing business outside. However, suspicions feed journalistic inquiries and attacks by the DPP and NP opposition.

The increase in economic concentration contributes significantly to what some call Taiwan's new pluralist politics. Because business groups now invest and do business outside Taiwan, they are less subject to controls of the state and more able to influence it independently, as we saw in several episodes concerning Taiwan's plastics king, Y. C. Wang.

Political Deconcentration

The other side of Taiwan' new political economy is the changing characteristics of the government and new relationships between state and society. Power in the state has decentralized from the party and the Executive Yuan. We noted development of some autonomy in state agencies. Indeed, some observers of Taiwan's economic policy-making argue that it is under greater control of technocratic elites than of KMT partisans.

The Legislative Yuan now engages fully in the making of Taiwan's laws. It is often the butt of jokes, as legislators scuffle with opponents, hurl insults (and sometimes objects) at one another, and grandstand in front of TV cameras. But the legislature has become democratic to a fault, insisting on using all its constitutional powers. When presidential action abrades legislative prerogatives, the Legislative Yuan has demonstrated its ability to bring government to a virtual standstill, as it did in 1996 and 1997 by refusing to accept the president's nominee, vice president Lien Chan, as the legitimately appointed premier.

We also pointed out the increased freedom of groups and interests in Taiwan's society, as they now work through political parties, directly approach legislators or administrators, or collectively organize to apply the pressure of public opinion on decision-makers. Political change is, in fact, headed in the opposite direction from most recent economic changes—in the direction of greater pluralism in the society. This pluralism leads to some negative consequences.

"Doing Better, Feeling Worse"

Taiwan's public has never been wealthier or freer, but it is not necessarily happier in the 1990s. Some point with nostalgia to the ordered authoritarian society of the 1960s and 1970s, but most object to deteriorating social circumstances in the present.

High profile, unresolved crimes dominated newspaper headlines in 1997, and public opinion polls revealed an elevated degree of public concern with an apparent breakdown in law and order. People once accustomed to walking the byways alone became reluctant to do so; some parents sent bodyguards to escort their children to and from school. The index of crimes has not increased dramatically, but public perception of criminality has increased.

Pollution problems in Taiwan escalated during its industrialization drive, and in the 1980s the environment became a major public issue. Finally, under pressure from island-wide, grassroots environmental lobbies, the government adopted relatively stringent environmental protection laws. The enforcement of this legislation has not been uniform or strict. As Taiwan's first EPA administrator remarked: "When challenged by economic interests, environmental protection concerns were automatically compromised without exception".[8] Ten years after this observation, critics of the government's environmental protection record complain about inconsistent enforcement of the law. In 1997, the inconsistency was also a product of partisan struggle at the local level. In counties and cities still controlled by the KMT, traditional clientele systems resolved environmental conflicts by moderating demands of local communities. Where KMT control had loosened, environmental protesters could produce outcomes in their favor.[9]

Laxity in enforcement of the law is matched by the disproportionate influence of money in the political process since the onset of Taiwan's democratization. Money influenced local elections before the democratic era; money was the "mother's milk" of Taiwan's local factions, and vote-buying was common. Most of that money, however, came from the party-state to reinforce its control over society. Money influenced national level politics less because the KMT was not a very predatory party and because there were few important national races. When this situation changed in the 1990s, business interests saw value in election outcomes and influenced them by large campaign contributions. Laws against illegal contributions were not often enforced. Some see electoral rules as responsible for this high level of corruption; others see the root cause in the number of elections. Eliminating the five tiers of elections, the KMT proposal to revise constitutional provisions on elections, received support because many naively believed it would eliminate corruption.

Finally, relatively slower economic growth (but still averaging 6 percent increase in GDP annually in the 1990s) and increased economic concentration focused attention on growing inequality in Taiwan's society. Extravagances of the rich, such as $5,000 banquets, luxury homes, and jet-set trips to America and Europe, contrasted with the near poverty of the lower class. The ratio of the highest fifth's income to the lowest fifth's changed from 4.37 in 1974 to 5.42 in 1993),[10] one closely watched indicator of growing income inequality. These social phenomena caused more than one critic to charge that Taiwan's public was indeed "doing better but feeling worse".

Facing the Post-Cold War World

Taiwan now faces a transforming world order, and this presents both economic and political challenges. In 1997, Taiwan stood a hair's breadth away from acceptance into the World Trade Organization (WTO). Meeting the implementation requirements of WTO would further the liberalization of the domestic economy, but to implement agreements would require solving problems of the once heavily protected agricultural sector and some industries and services. The steady upward pressure of competition, however, will require more focused attention on government investments and R&D policies, as well as a strategy to enhance the productivity of Taiwan's labor force. This has remained stagnant during the 1990s, while Taiwan's trading competitors, such as Singapore, Hong Kong, and Japan have increased the competitiveness of their work forces. Thus, as Taiwan's trade dependence increases, it will need to respond to new niche opportunities and changes in the global economy; these responses, in turn, will motivate opposition from those adversely affected by change, who now have many more opportunities to protest, stall state action, and demand expensive compensatory payments.

The end of the Cold War has not reduced Taiwan's diplomatic isolation. A small number of countries recognize Taiwan diplomatically, but it is shut out of most of the world's governing councils—the UN, World Bank, and the IMF, to name a few. In many respects, this is the world's loss, as Taiwan is a wealthy, increasingly democratic state, and has repeatedly volunteered to assist peacekeeping operations. Taiwan is also among the world's most generous donors of economic and developmental assistance to Third World nations.[11] Continued denial of international status to Taiwan cannot help but increase frustration and discontent among the population.

China, of course, holds the cards on admission of Taiwan to a host of international governing councils. The end of the Cold War has not made China more eager to accommodate Taiwan's attempts to raise its international stature. In fact, the reverse seems to be the case. As China has liberalized its economy, expanded relations with other countries, and increased its rate of economic growth—becoming more like most of the capitalist nations which surround it—it has not liberalized politically. Talks to normalize the relations between China and Taiwan stalled for two years following the military exercises off Taiwan's shores in 1995 and 1996. While both sides prosper from increased cross-strait trade, neither side has softened its essentially non-negotiable positions. Yet the transfer of Hong Kong from British to Chinese jurisdiction did nudge the two sides toward a breakthrough in direct transportation. Shipping executives agreed to start direct cross-strait shipping between Xiamen and Fuzhou in China and Kaohsiung in Taiwan. This was an auspicious development for the establishment of direct trade and communication linkages.

Future Prospects

Taiwan has three alternative developmental paths: continuation of the status quo, unification with China, and independence. Each would affect its wealth and freedom, and each path depends on reciprocal interactions with mainland China, the United States, and, to a lesser extent, Japan. These three paths correspond roughly to policies of the KMT *mainstream* faction (Taiwan's government in 1997), the DPP, and the NP (similar to the *non-mainstream* faction of the KMT).[12]

Status Quo

A large majority of Taiwan's people like the *de facto* independence of their state in the international system. For example, a reliable 1995 poll showed that over 80 percent of respondents preferred different status quo situations, but only 6 percent favored immediate unification or independence.[13] Small states have more latitude in multi-polar global systems of power than during bipolar times. Perhaps accession to the WTO will give Taiwan's government sufficient cachet to deal with increasing domestic pleas for international status and recognition of Taiwan's varied achievements and contributions.

However, maintaining the status quo will become increasingly costly for Taiwan. China's new leaders are less patient than Deng Xiaoping, who was willing to wait for more than a generation for Taiwan's reunification with China. With the transfer of Macau to Chinese sovereignty in 1999, Taiwan will be the sole remaining obstacle to the extirpation of colonial and neo-colonial possessions of Chinese territory.

China now has vastly greater leverage over Taiwan's ability to continue as a *de facto* independent state. By 1997, China was well on the way to becoming Taiwan's major trading partner, and growth in Taiwan's economy has become ever more closely linked with cross-strait trade. Moreover, the trade expressed increased asymmetry. Without its surplus in mainland trade, Taiwan's international trade since 1993 would have registered a deficit instead of a surplus.[14] Disruptions to that trade, as occurred in 1995 and 1996 during the Chinese military exercises, sent a shock wave through the economy, caused capital flight, the highest rate of emigration in more than a decade (over 25,000), and a significant economic slowdown.

To continue the status quo requires economic stability and a moderately high rate of growth. There are domestic impediments to growth. One is the rising cost and decreasing availability of land; a second is the declining supply of water; third is stagnant productivity in the labor force; fourth is increased social costs of environmental protection;[15] and fifth are increasing costs of democratization, such as meliorating the effects of change on powerful constituent groups.

As a trade-dependent state, Taiwan is subject to global recessions and to any change on China's behalf in the mainland expansion of Taiwan's businesses.[16] These factors, along with the domestic impediments to economic growth, mean that Taiwan's leaders will have to work harder just to stay in place. Any decline in economic growth, however, will kindle the fires of support for either reunification or independence.

After the transfer of Hong Kong to the PRC, Taiwan's leaders lost no time in pointing out that Taiwan was not comparable. President Lee addressed the press with unequivocal remarks on Taiwan's distinctiveness:

> Regardless of whether it is viewed from a historical or political standpoint, Taiwan differs categorically from Hong Kong . . . . While (Beijing) may have applied its 'one country, two systems' formula to establish its rule in Hong Kong, its plan to take the same approach with Taiwan is mere wishful thinking . . . . The Republic of China . . . is a full-fledged democracy, and the vast majority of its people do not support this model of unification proposed by (Beijing).[17]

Reunification

While a continuation of the status quo is most likely for the next decade, Taiwan also now faces better prospects for unification with China than previously. The civil war leadership on both sides of the Taiwan strait has now passed from power. Economic systems on opposite sides of the Taiwan Strait are converging. Millions of Taiwan's residents have visited mainland China (a far smaller number of Chinese have visited Taiwan), and hundreds of exchanges take place annually. Investments pour from Taiwan into mainland China, and cross-strait trade increased an average of 20 percent annually before the late 1995 military exercises. These are auspicious signs for potential reunification.

We cannot assume, however, that increased economic interchanges will lead to political normalization, for that has not been the pattern of the last decade. The responses of China's leaders to student protest and to Taiwan's increased democratization have been stridently reactive and militaristic. Although China has moderated its rhetoric in international affairs, and since the end of the Cold War has pursued a less ideological foreign policy, it remains under the control of a Leninist communist party that is reluctant to withdraw from power. It also remains firmly in control of its population and keeps the world's largest military force to ensure that control. For China to renounce the use of force in its relations with Taiwan would be to undercut the pinions of support needed to govern its population.

Most specialists on the military balance between China and Taiwan believe that China will not be able successfully to project its force across the Taiwan Strait for another ten years. Paul Godwin finds Taiwan's systematic modernization of its military forces has made Beijing's decision to use military force "increasingly costly".[18] Lin Chong-pin argues that the superiority of China's quantitative military forces is countered by Taiwan's strategic advantage and suggests that Beijing is most likely to pursue unorthodox measures, such as psychological intimidation, by "staging large exercises near Taiwan, testing . . . missiles near or in Taiwanese waters, and flying fighters to skirt Taiwanese air space".[19]

Both the United States and Japan have at best ambivalent positions toward Taiwan's potential reunification with China. Reunification would make Asia a more peaceable region, as tension across the Taiwan Strait is one of two trouble spots in East Asia (the second, and in 1997 the far more serious, is North Korea), and both the United States and Japan would welcome greater peace. But neither power would see many long-term benefits in a unified, economically strong, and militarily powerful China, particularly if it were not democratic.[20] Both powers benefit more from the status quo than from unification.

In Taiwan, pressure for unification increases in a rhythm set by the Taiwan independence movement. The mainlander sections of the national elite, more and more likely to be displaced from power, look at unification differently than Taiwanese elites. Unification might reverse the downward mobility that mainlanders have experienced over the last two decades. It might give mainlander elites roles to play in other provinces or at the national level in China. Contrariwise, Taiwanese elites see little benefit to reunification with China.

Popular support for reunification has declined somewhat in the 1990s. Public opinion polls commissioned by the Mainland Affairs Council revealed a high point of 32 percent favoring unification in July 1991, dropping to less than 20 percent in 1995 and 1996.

Independence

Public support for the independence of Taiwan has grown slightly over the last half decade, from about 18 percent in national polls of 1991 to approximately 27 percent in 1996. Support for Taiwan independence has tended to track the votes given the DPP in competitive races. It is now larger than preference for unification with China, but the amount of support is labile, dependent on international circumstances and the way the question is asked of respondents. For example, a poll taken by the *United Daily News* on July 1 and 2, 1997, just after Hong Kong became a special administrative region of China, showed the greatest support for independence of recent polling results. Given only two choices—reunion with the mainland or full independence—a record 43 percent opted for independence, 34 percent supported union with China, and the remainder were undecided.[21]

The prospect for the independence of Taiwan usually is couched in terms of its feasibility, not its desirability. Most observers believe that it is not feasible under current international circumstances. Beijing authorities have demonstrated that they will use all means necessary to halt concrete steps along the path toward *de jure* independence. The United States sent two aircraft carrier groups to show its interest in peaceful outcomes and opposition to China's military exercises. Yet American military support to Taiwan in the event of Chinese aerial bombardment, missile attacks, or invasion of Taiwan proper provoked by independence actions is uncertain at best. The United States no longer has mutual security treaties with Taiwan, and the provisions of the Taiwan Relations Act are quite ambiguous as to the American commitment to Taiwan.

In fact, it probably is no longer necessary for China to use military means to influence Taiwan's movement toward independence. Economic pressures might be sufficient to deter such a change,[22] and there would not likely be a strong American or Japanese opposition to them. Fear of Chinese economic retribution is what made the Taiwan government tighten investment rules, a policy alteration made for political, not economic, reasons.

Although the United State and Japan would prefer an independent Taiwan to one unified with the mainland, neither power would support Taiwan's independence without the assent of Beijing, and such assent is highly unlikely. (The United States does support the normalization of Taiwan's relations with mainland China, short of reunification, and may use high level talks with China to resolve issues such as WTO accession.) Under no circumstances would an independent Taiwan be desirable to the PRC. Economic gains to the mainland would be no greater than opportunities of the status quo; political and diplomatic losses would never compensate for any small gains.

One might imagine that because most people in Taiwan are satisfied with *de facto* independence, they might equally support if not prefer a condition of *de jure* independence. Such thinking discounts the highly vocal and active minority who oppose Taiwan's formal independence, who would use all means—including, perhaps, active collaboration with the mainland—to prevent it. The *Tung-du* (unification v. independence) issue in Taiwan still engages deep passions and violent emotions, and one cannot exclude appeals to extra-legal means of action by participants.

Under President Lee Teng-hui, Taiwan has moved cautiously to fortify its *de facto* independence and has veered more closely to the goals and objectives of Taiwan independence advocates than toward those of advocates of reunification. Leaders and the public in general now, for the first time in Taiwan's history, have choices about which path to take. These choices too are products of Taiwan's wealth and freedom.

Notes

[1] John F. Copper, *Taiwan: Nation-State or Province?* (Boulder, CO: Westview Press, 1996), 2.

[2] *United Daily News*, May 27, 1996.

[3] *China Times*, June 9, 1997.

[4] *Republic of China Yearbook 1997* (Taipei: Government Information Office, 1997), 293.

[5] Council for Economic Planning and Development, *Taiwan Statistical Data Book 1996* (Taipei: Executive Yuan, 1996), 1.

[6] *Taiwan Statistical Data Book 1996*, 21.

[7] KMT partisans have filled most policy-making slots since retrocession. Party cells have yet to be abolished in the military, which opposes Taiwan independence. See Hung-mao Tien and Yun-han Chu, 'Building Democracy in Taiwan', *China Quarterly* 148 (December 1996), 1156.

[8] Cited in Jack Williams, 'Paying the Price of Economic Development in Taiwan: Environmental Degradation', in Murray A. Rubinstein, ed., *The Other Taiwan* (Armonk, NY: M. E. Sharpe, 1994), 253.

[9] See Shui-yang Tang and Ching-ping Tang, 'Democratization and Environmental Politics in Taiwan', *Asian Survey*, vol. XXXVII, no. 3 (March 1997), 292-93.

[10] *Taiwan Statistical Data Book 1996*, 61-62.

[11] In the eyes of opposition politicians, Taiwan has been too generous with its money in pursuit of international status. A report in *United Daily News* (January 16, 1997) said Taiwan was spending more than US $200 million to promote international contacts, chiefly in the underdeveloped states in Africa and Central America that continue to recognize Taiwan.

[12] See Jean-Pierre Cabestan, 'Taiwan's Mainland Policy: Normalization, Yes; Reunification, Later', *China Quarterly* 148 (December 1996), 1273.

[13] Richard Y. Chuang, 'The International Standing of the Republic of China: Achievements, Image, and Prospects', *American Journal of Chinese Studies*, vol. 3, no. 2 (October 1996), 138.

[14] See Tse-kang Leng, 'Economic Interdependence and Political Integration between Taiwan and Mainland China: A Critical Review', (Paper presented at the American Political Science Association Conference, San Francisco, CA, August 31, 1996).

[15] See Richard Louis Edmonds, 'Taiwan's Environment Today', *China Quarterly* 148 (December 1996), 1225.

[16] In early 1997, Chinese foreign minister Qian Qichen promised full protection for Taiwan businesses in China: "We will not affect or interrupt cross-strait economic cooperation with political differences". Qian urged Taiwan's authorities to relax restrictions preventing entrepreneurs from investing on the mainland (*People's Daily*, April 9, 1997).

[17] *United Daily News*, July 3, 1997.

[18] Paul H. B. Godwin, 'From Continent to Periphery: PLA Doctrine, Strategy and Capabilities Towards 2000', *China Quarterly* 146 (June 1996), 485.

[19] Chong-pin Lin, 'The Military Balance in the Taiwan Straits', *China Quarterly* 146 (June 1996), 593.

[20] Gary Klintworth, *New Taiwan, New China* (New York: St. Martin's Press, 1995), 245.

[21] *United Daily News*, July 4, 1997.

[22] A large group of analysts is convinced that all Beijing needs to do to endanger Taiwan's livelihood and security is bring substantial pressure on Taiwan's economy. See, for example, David Shambaugh, 'Taiwan's Security: Maintaining Deterrence amid Political Accountability', *China Quarterly* 148 (December 1996), 1304.

Bibliography

Books

Abegglen, James C. and Stalk, George, Jr. (1985), *Kaisha: The Japanese Corporation*, Basic Books, New York.
Aberbach, Joel D., Dollar, David and Sokoloff, Kenneth L. (eds) (1994), *The Role of the State in Taiwan's Development*, M. E. Sharpe, Armonk, NY.
Ahern, Emily Martin and Gates, Hill (eds) (1981), *The Anthropology of Taiwanese Society*, Stanford University, Stanford, CA.
Amsden, Alice (1989), *Asia's Next Giant: South Korea and Late Industrialization*, Oxford, New York.
Anderson, Terry L. and Hill, Peter J. (eds) (1996), *The Privatization Process: A Worldwide Perspective*, Rowman & Littlefield, Lanham, MD.
Aoki, Mashiko, Kim, Hyung-ki and Okuno-Fujiwara, Masahiro (1996), *The Role of Government in East Asian Economic Development*, Oxford, New York.
Appelbaum, Richard P. and Henderson, Jeffrey (1992), *States and Development in the Asian Pacific Rim*, Sage, Thousand Oaks, CA.
Baldwin, Robert E., Chen Tain-Jy and Nelson, Douglas (1995), *Political Economy of U.S.-Taiwan Trade*, University of Michigan, Ann Arbor, MI.
Bradford, Colin I., Jr. and Branson, William H. (1987), *Trade and Structural Change in Pacific Asia*, University of Chicago, Chicago.
Bueno de Mesquita, Bruce, Newman, David and Rabushka, Alvin (1996), *Red Flag over Hong Kong*, Chatham House, Chatham, NJ.
Campos, Jose Edgardo and Root, Hilton L. (1996), *The Key to the Asian Miracle: Making Shared Growth Credible*, The Brookings Institution, Washington, DC.
Central Bank of China (1996), *The Central Bank of China: Purposes and Functions (1961-1991)*, Taipei.
Chang Mau-kei (1989), *Social Movements and Political Transformation* (in Chinese), Institute for National Policy Research, Taipei.
Chen Chian-chung (1995), *Legislative Politics of the Financial Disclosure Law* (in Chinese), M. A. Thesis, Department of Political Science, National Taiwan University, Taipei.
Chen Ming-tong (1995), *Factional Politics and Political Change in Taiwan* (in Chinese), Yue-dan, Taipei.

262 *Wealth and Freedom: Taiwan's New Political Economy*

Chen, Shih-meng S., Lin Chung-cheng, Chu C.Y. Cyrus, Chang Ching-hsi, Shih Jan-ji and Liu Jin-tan (1991), *Disintegrating KMT-State Capitalism: A Closer Look at Privatizing Taiwan's State- and Party-Owned Enterprises* (in Chinese), Taipei Society, Taipei.
Cheng Tun-jen and Haggard, Stephan (eds) (1992), *Political Change in Taiwan*, Lynne Rienner, Boulder, CO.
China Credit Information Service (1996), *Top 500: The Largest Corporations in Taiwan 1996*, Taipei.
China News (1997), *1997 Directory of Taiwan*, Taipei.
Chiou, C. L. (1995), *Democratizing Oriental Despotism*, St. Martin's, New York.
Chiu Hungdah (ed) (1979), *China and the Taiwan Issue*, Praeger, New York.
Chiu Hungdah and Leng Shao-chuan (eds) (1984), *China: Seventy Years After the 1911 Hsin-Hai Revolution*, University of Virginia, Charlottesville, VA.
Chou Yu-jen (1993), *The Relationship between the Economy and the Polity* (in Chinese), Wu-nan, Taipei.
Chu Yun-han (1992), *Crafting Democracy in Taiwan*, Institute for National Policy Research, Taipei.
Clark, Cal (1988), *Taiwan's Development: Implications for Contending Political Economic Paradigms*, Greenwood, New York.
Clark, Cal and Chan, Steven (eds) (1992), *The Evolving Pacific Basin in the Global Political Economy: Domestic and International Linkages*, Westview, Boulder, CO.
Clough, Ralph N. (1978), *Island China*, Harvard, Cambridge, MA.
_____ (1993), *Reaching Across the Taiwan Strait*, Westview, Boulder, CO.
Copper, John F. (1996), *Taiwan: Nation-State or Province?* Westview, Boulder, CO.
Council for Economic Planning and Development (CEPD), ROC (1996), *Economic Development, Taiwan, Republic of China*, Taipei.
_____ (1996), *Taiwan Statistical Data Book 1996*, Taipei.
_____ (1996), *Plan for the Development of Taiwan as an Asia-Pacific Regional Operations Center* (in Chinese), Executive Yuan, Taipei.
Curtis, Gerald L. (1990), *The Japanese Way of Politics*, Columbia University, New York.
Davidson, James W. (1988), *The Island of Formosa: Past and Present*, Oxford, New York.
Deyo, Frederic C. (ed) (1987), *The Political Economy of the New Asian Industrialism,* Cornell, Ithaca, NY.
Dreyer, June T. (1996), *China's Political System*, 2 ed., Allyn and Bacon, Boston.
Evans, P. B., Rueschemeyer, D. and Skocpol, T. (eds) (1985), *Bringing the State Back In*, Cambridge University, Cambridge.
Fairbank, John K., Reischauer, Edwin O. and Craig, Albert M. (1965), *East Asia: The Modern Transformation*, Houghton Mifflin, Boston.
Fei, John, Ranis, Gustav and Kuo, Shirley W. Y. (1979), *Growth with Equity: The Taiwan Case*, Oxford, New York.
Feldman, Harvey J. (ed) (1991), *Constitutional Reform and the Future of the Republic of China*, M. E. Sharpe, Armonk, NY.
Fields, Karl J. (1995), *Enterprise and the State in Korea and Taiwan*, Cornell University, Ithaca, NY.

Friedman, Maurice (1958), *Lineage Organization in Southeastern China*, Athlone, London.

Galenson, W. (ed) (1979), *Economic Growth and Structural Change in Taiwan: The Postwar Experience of the Republic of China*, Cornell University, Ithaca, NY.

Garver, John W. (1997), *Face Off: China, the United States, and Taiwan's Democratization*, University of Washington, Seattle, WA.

Gereffi, Gary and Wyman, Donald L. (eds) (1990), *Manufacturing Miracles: Paths of Industrialization in Latin America and East Asia*, Princeton University, Princeton, NJ.

Gerlach, Michael L. (1982), *Alliance Capitalism: The Social Organization of Japanese Business*, University of California, Berkeley, CA.

Gilpin, Robert (1987), *The Political Economy of International Relations*, Princeton University, Princeton, NJ.

Gold, Thomas B. (1986), *State and Society in the Taiwan Miracle*, M. E. Sharpe, Armonk, NY.

Government Information Office, ROC (1996), *The Constitution, Republic of China*, 6 ed., Taipei.

_____ (1996), *Profiles of the Cabinet Members and Heads of the Executive Agencies*, Taipei.

_____ (1997), *The Republic of China Yearbook 1997*, Taipei.

Gordon, Leonard H. D. (1970), *Taiwan: Studies in Chinese Local History*, Columbia University, New York.

Haggard, Stephan (1990), *Pathways from the Periphery: The Politics of Growth in the Newly Industrializing Countries*, Cornell University, Ithaca, NY.

Haggard, Stephan and Moon, Chung-in (eds) (1988), *Pacific Dynamics: The International Politics of Industrial Change*, Westview, Boulder, CO.

Haggard, Stephan and Kaufman, Robert R. (1995), *The Political Economy of Democratic Transitions*, Princeton University, Princeton, NJ.

Hamilton, G. G. and Kao, C. S. (1987), *The Institutional Foundation of Chinese Business: The Family Firm in Taiwan*, Institute of Governmental Affairs, University of California, Davis.

Harding, Harry (1992), *A Fragile Relationship: The United States and China Since 1972*, Brookings Institution, Washington, DC.

Harrell, Steven and Huang Chun-chieh (eds) (1994), *Cultural Change in Postwar Taiwan*, Westview, Boulder, CO.

Hickey, Dennis VanVranken (1994), *United States-Taiwan Security Ties: From Cold War to Beyond Containment*, Praeger, Westport, CT.

Ho, Samuel P. S. (1978), *Economic Development of Taiwan, 1860-1970*, Yale University, New Haven.

Hood, Steven J. (1997), *The Kuomintang and the Democratization of Taiwan*, Westview, Boulder, CO.

Hsieh Chiao-min (1964), *Taiwan—ilha Formosa: A Geography in Perspective*, Butterworths, Washington, DC.

Hsing Mo-huan, Poser, John H. and Sicat, Gerardo P. (1970), *Taiwan and the Philippines: Industrialization and Trade Policies*, Oxford, London.

Huntington, Samuel P. (1968), *Political Order in Changing Societies*, Yale University, New Haven.

_____ (1991), *The Third Wave: Democratization in the Late Twentieth Century*, University of Oklahoma, Norman, OK.

Hwang Shiow-duan (1994), *Constituent Services* (in Chinese), Tang-shan, Taipei.

Hwang, Y. Dolly (1991), *The Rise of a New World Economic Power: Postwar Taiwan*, Greenwood, Westport, CT.

Jacoby, Neil H. (1966), *U.S. Aid to Taiwan: A Study of Foreign Aid, Self-Help and Development*, Praeger, New York.

Johnson, Chalmers (1982), *MITI and the Japanese Miracle: The Growth of Industrial Policy, 1925-1975*, Stanford University, Stanford, CA.

_____ (1995), *Japan: Who Governs? The Rise of the Developmental State*, W. W. Norton, New York.

Jones, Leroy and Sakong Il (1980), *Government, Business and Entrepreneurship in Economic Development: The Case of Korea*, Harvard University, Cambridge, MA.

Kerbo, Harold R. and McKinstry, John A. (1995), *Who Rules Japan?* Praeger, Westport, CT.

Kerr, George H. (1965), *Formosa Betrayed*, Houghton Mifflin, Boston.

_____ (1974), *Formosa: Licensed Revolution and the Home Rule Movement, 1895-1945*, University of Hawaii, Honolulu, HI.

Khanna, Jane (ed) (1995), *Southern China, Hong Kong, and Taiwan: Evolution of a Subregional Economy*, Center for Strategic and International Studies, Washington, DC.

Klintworth, Gary (1995), *New Taiwan, New China*, St. Martin's, New York.

Kuo Cheng-tian (1995), *Global Competitiveness and Industrial Growth in Taiwan and the Philippines*, University of Pittsburgh, Pittsburgh, PA.

Kuo, Shirley W.Y., Ranis, Gustav and Fei, John C.H. (1981), *The Taiwan Success Story: Rapid Growth with Improved Distribution in the Republic of China, 1952-1979*, Westview, Boulder, CO.

Lasater, Martin L. (1993), *U.S. Interests in the New Taiwan*, Westview, Boulder, CO.

Legislative Yuan (1994), *Legislative Yuan, Republic of China*, Taipei.

_____ (1996), *Roster of Legislators, Third Term, R.O.C.*, Taipei.

Leng Shao-chuan (ed) (1993), *Chiang Ching-kuo's Leadership in the Development of the Republic of China on Taiwan*, University Press of America, Lanham, MD.

Lerman, Arthur J. (1978), *Taiwan's Politics: The Provincial Assemblyman's World*, University Press of America, Washington, DC.

Li I-yuan (1982), *Society and Culture of Taiwan's Aboriginal Peoples*, Linking, Taipei.

Li, K. T. (1988), *The Evolution of Policy Behind Taiwan's Development Success*, Yale University, New Haven.

Lin, Ken Ching-yuan (1973), *Industrialization in Taiwan, 1946-1972*, Praeger, New York.

Lin Zhiling and Robinson, Thomas W. (1994), *The Chinese and Their Future: Beijing, Taipei, and Hong Kong*, American Enterprise Institute, Washington, DC.

Liu Chao-hsien (1993), *Research on the Republic of China's Law on Industrial Associations* (in Chinese), Ming-ho, Taipei.

Liu Fu-shan (1995), *Building a Farmers' Organization's System in a Developing Country: The Taiwan Experience*, Maw Chang, Taipei.

Long, Simon (1991), *Taiwan: China's Last Frontier*, St. Martin's, New York.

Luo Chang-fa, Liao An-ting, Chen Hsi-hung, Peng Tso-kuei, Chu Yun-han, Tsai Ying-wen, Chu Yi, Chen Wu-hsing, Hu Hung-yu, Kuan Chin-rong, Lin Kuo-ching, Tsai Hung-jin, Hsiao Kun-hsing and Chen Hsin-you (1994), *The Impact on Agriculture of Taiwan's Accession to GATT and Policy Responses* (in Chinese), Institute for National Policy Research, Taipei.

Luo Fu-hsun (1996), *Procedures and Techniques of Legislation* (in Chinese), Wu-nan, Taipei.

MacIntyre, Andrew (ed) (1994), *Business and Government in Industrializing East Asia*, Cornell University, Ithaca, NY.

Mendel, Douglas (1970), *The Politics of Formosan Nationalism*, University of California, Berkeley, CA.

Metzger, Thomas A. and Myers, Ramon H. (eds) (1996), *Greater China and U.S. Foreign Policy*, Hoover Institution, Stanford, CA.

Milne, R.S. and Mauzy, Diane K. (1990), *Singapore: The Legacy of Lee Kuan Yew*, Westview, Boulder, CO.

Ministry of Economic Affairs, ROC (1997), *Taiwan's Accession to the World Trade Organization: Reference Materials* (in Chinese), Board of Foreign Trade, Taipei.

_____ (1997), *A Report on the Conditions of ROC's Accession to the World Trade Organization* (in Chinese), Taipei.

Ministry of Finance, ROC (1995), *Government Finance of the Republic of China*, Taxation and Tariff Commission, Taipei.

_____ (1995), *Guide to ROC Taxes 1995*, Taipei.

_____ (1996), *The Financial Market Integration in Chinese Taipei*, Bureau of Monetary Affairs, Taipei.

_____ (1996), *The Financial System in the R.O.C.,* Bureau of Monetary Affairs, Taipei.

Moody, Peter R., Jr. (1992), *Political Change in Taiwan: A Study of Ruling Party Adaptability*, Praeger, New York.

O'Donnell, Guillermo and Schmitter, Philippe C. (1986), *Transitions from Authoritarian Rule: Tentative Conclusions about Uncertain Democracies*, Johns Hopkins, Baltimore, MD.

Orru, Marco, Biggart, Nicole Woolsey, and Hamilton, Gary C. (eds) (1997), *The Economic Organization of East Asian Capitalism*, Sage, Thousand Oaks, CA.

Patrick, Hugh T. and Park, Yung Chul (eds) (1994), *The Financial Development of Japan, Korea, and Taiwan*, Oxford, London.

Peng Huei-en (1995), *The Political Economy of Taiwan's Development* (in Chinese), Chia-hsin, Taipei.

Przeworski, Adam and Teune, Henry (1970), *The Logic of Comparative Social Inquiry*, John Wiley, New York.

Rabushka, Alvin (1987), *The New China: Comparative Economic Development in Mainland China, Taiwan, and Hong Kong*, Westview, Hong Kong.

Research, Development, and Evaluation Commission, ROC (1995), *Research on the Problems of Privatization of Public Enterprises and Their Resolutions* (in Chinese), Executive Yuan, Taipei.

David Robertson (ed) (1997), *East Asian Trade After the Uruguay Round*, Cambridge University, Cambridge.

Rozman, Gilbert (ed) (1991), *The East Asian Region: Confucian Heritage and Its Modern Adaptation*, Princeton University, Princeton, NJ.

Sandher, Kermial Singh and Wheatley, Paul (eds) (1990), *Management of Success: The Moulding of Modern Singapore*, Westview, Boulder, CO.

Schive Chi (1990), *The Foreign Factor: The Multinational Corporation's Contribution to the Economic Modernization of the Republic of China*, Hoover Institution, Stanford, CA.

_____ (1995), *Taiwan's Economic Role in East Asia*, Center for Strategic and International Studies, Washington, DC.

Shih Chao-hsien (1993), *Research on the Republic of China's Law on Industrial Associations* (in Chinese), Ming-ho, Taipei.

Sih, K. T. (ed) (1973), *Taiwan in Modern Times*, St. John's, Jamaica, NY.

Simon, Denis Fred and Kau, Michael Y. M. (eds) (1992), *Taiwan: Beyond the Economic Miracle*, M. E. Sharpe, Armonk, NY.

Skoggard, Ian A. (1996), *The Indigenous Dynamic in Taiwan's Postwar Development*, M. E. Sharpe, Armonk, NY.

Sutter, Robert G. and Robinson, William R. (eds) (1994), *Taiwan in World Affairs*, Westview, Boulder, CO.

Sutter, Robert G. (1996), *Shaping China's Future in World Affairs: The Role of the United States*, Westview, Boulder, CO.

Syu, Agnes (1995), *From Economic Miracle to Privatization Success*, University Press of America, Lanham, MD.

Tai Hung-chao (1974), *Land Reform and Politics: A Comparative Analysis*, University of California, Berkeley, CA.

Tilton, Mark (1996), *Restrained Trade: Cartels in Japan's Basic Materials Industries*, Cornell University, Ithaca, NY.

Tien Hung-mao (1989), *The Great Transition: Political and Social Change in the Republic of China*, Hoover Institution, Stanford, CA.

_____ (ed) (1996), *Taiwan's Electoral Politics and Democratic Transition*, M. E. Sharpe, Armonk, NY.

Tweeten, Luther and Hsu Hsia-hui (1994), *Changing Trade Environment after GATT: A Case Study of Taiwan*, Council of Agriculture, Taipei.

United States Relations with China (1949), Department of State Publications 3573, Washington, DC.

United States Trade Representative (1996), *1996 National Trade Estimate Report on Foreign Trade Barriers*, Washington, DC.

van Wolferen, Karl (1989), *The Enigma of Japanese Power: People and Politics in a Stateless Nation*, Knopf, New York.

Vogel, Ezra (1979), *Japan as Number One*, Harvard, Cambridge, MA.

_____ (1991), *The Four Little Dragons: The Spread of Industrialization in East Asia*, Harvard, Cambridge, MA:

Wachman, Alan M. (1994), *Taiwan: National Identity and Democratization*, M. E. Sharpe, Armonk, NY.

Wade, Robert (1990), *Governing the Market: Economic Theory and the Role of Government in East Asian Industrialization,* Princeton University, Princeton, NJ.

Wang, James C. F. (1994), *Comparative Asian Politics*, Prentice-Hall, Englewood Cliffs, NJ.
Wang, N. T. (ed) (1992), *Taiwan Enterprises in Global Perspective*, M. E. Sharpe, Armonk, NY.
Winckler, Edwin A. and Greenhalgh, Susan (eds) (1988), *Contending Approaches to the Political Economy of Taiwan*, M. E. Sharpe, Armonk, NY.
World Bank (1993), *World Development Indicators 1993*, Oxford, Washington, DC.
Wu Hsin-hsing (1994), *Bridging the Strait: Taiwan, China, and the Prospects for Reunification*, Oxford, New York.
Wu, Jaushieh Joseph (1995), *Taiwan's Democratization*, Oxford, Hong Kong.
Wu Wen-cheng (1987), *The Kuomintang and Political Development in Taiwan since 1968* (Ph.D. dissertation), Columbia University, New York.
Wu Yu-shan (1994), *Comparative Economic Transitions: Mainland China, Hungary, the Soviet Union, and Taiwan*, Stanford University, Stanford, CA.
Wu Yuan-li (1985), *Becoming an Industrialized Nation: ROC's Development on Taiwan*, Praeger, New York.
Yang Chih-heng (1991), *The Structure of Fiscal Policy* (in Chinese), Institute for National Policy Research, Taipei.
Zeigler, Harmon (1988), *Pluralism, Corporatism, and Confucianism: Political Association and Conflict Regulation in the United States, Europe, and Taiwan*, Temple University, Philadelphia.

Articles

Achen, Christopher H. (1996), 'The Timing of Political Liberalization: Taiwan as the Canonical Case', paper presented at the American Political Science Association Conference, San Francisco, CA.
Allinson, Gary D. (1987), 'Japan's Keidanren and Its New Leaders', *Pacific Affairs*, vol. 60, no. 3, pp. 385-407.
Amsden, Alice (1979), 'Taiwan's Economic History: A Case of Etatisme and Challenge to Dependency Theory', *Modern China* 3, pp. 341-80.
Barrett, Richard E. and Whyte, Martin K. (1982), 'Dependency Theory and Taiwan: Analysis of a Deviant Case', *American Journal of Sociology*, vol. 87, no. 5, pp. 1064-89.
Bosco, Joseph (1994), 'Faction versus Ideology: Mobilization Strategies in Taiwan's Elections', *China Quarterly* 137, pp. 28-62.
Cabestan, Jean-Pierre (1996), 'Taiwan's Mainland Policy: Normalization, Yes; Reunification, No', *China Quarterly* 148, pp. 1260-83.
Central Bank of China (1997), 'The Central Bank of China', *Central Banking*, vol. VII, no. 4 (forthcoming).
_____ (1996, 1997), *Financial Statistics Monthly*, various issues, Taipei.
Chang Ching-hsi (1995), 'Party Enterprises, Members' Ethics, and Party Corruption', (in Chinese) *Taiwan Economic Review*, vol. 24, no. 2, pp. 25-42.
Chao, Linda and Myers, Ramon H. (1994), 'The First Chinese Democracy: Political Development of the Republic of China on Taiwan, 1986-94', *Asian Survey*, vol. XXXIV, no. 3, pp. 213-30.

Chen Qimao (1996), 'The Taiwan Strait Crisis: Its Crux and Solutions', *Asian Survey*, vol. XXXVI, no. 11, pp. 1055-66.

Cheng Tun-jen (1989), 'Democratizing the Quasi-Leninist Regime in Taiwan', *World Politics* 42, pp. 471-99.

Chiu, Paul C. H. (1992), 'Money and Financial Markets: The Domestic Perspective', in G. Ranis (ed), *Taiwan: From Developing to Mature Economy*, Westview, Boulder, CO, pp. 121-193.

Chou Yangsun and Nathan, Andrew J. (1987), 'Democratizing Transition in Taiwan', *Asian Survey*, vol. XXVII, no.3, pp. 277-99.

Chu Yin-wah (1996), 'Democracy and Organized Labor in Taiwan: The 1986 Transition', *Asian Survey*, vol. XXXVI, no. 5, pp. 495-510.

Chu Yun-han (1989), 'State Structure and Economic Adjustment of the East Asian Newly Industrializing Countries', *International Organization* 43, pp. 647-72.

_____ (1993), 'Industrial Change and the Development State in Two East Asian NICs: A Case Study of the Automotive Industries in South Korea and Taiwan', *Proceedings of the National Science Council*, vol. 3, no. 2, pp. 203-23.

_____ (1995), 'The East Asian NICs: A State-led Path to the Developed World', in Barbara Stallings (ed), *Global Change, Regional Responses*, Cambridge University, Cambridge, pp. 199-237.

_____ (1997), 'Making Sense of Taiwan's Mainland Policy', paper presented at the Association for Asian Studies Conference, Chicago, IL.

Chuang, Richard Y. (1996), 'The International Standing of the Republic of China', *American Journal of Chinese Studies*, vol. 3, no. 2, pp. 109-47.

Clark, Cal (1994), 'Successful Structural Adjustment and Evolving State-Society Relations in Taiwan', *American Journal of Chinese Studies*, vol. 2, no. 2, pp. 181-94.

Copper, John F. (1994), 'The KMT's 14th Party Congress: Toward Unity or Disunity?' *The American Journal of Chinese Studies*, vol. II, no. 2, pp. 163-79.

Council of Labor Affairs, ROC (1996, 1997), *Monthly Bulletin of Labor Statistics, Taiwan Area, Republic of China,* various issues, Taipei.

Directorate General of Budget, Accounting and Statistics (1996, 1997), *National Income of the Republic of China*, various issues, Taipei.

Domes, Jurgen (1989), 'The 13th Party Congress of the Kuomintang: Towards Political Competition?' *China Quarterly* 118, pp. 345-59.

Edmonds, Richard Louis (1996), 'Taiwan's Environment Today', *China Quarterly* 148, pp. 1224-59.

Friedman, Edward (1997), 'Chinese Nationalism, Taiwan Autonomy and the Prospects of a Larger War', *Journal of Contemporary China*, vol. 6, no. 4, pp. 5-32.

Freund, Elizabeth M. (1996), 'States, Markets and Industry: State Enterprise Reform in Taiwan and China', paper presented at the Association for Asian Studies Conference, Honolulu, HI.

Godwin, Paul H.B. (1996), 'From Continent to Periphery: PLA Doctrine, Strategy and Capabilities Towards 2000', *China Quarterly* 146, pp. 464-87.

Gold, Thomas B. (1996), 'Consolidating Taiwan's Democracy', The Illinois-Taiwan Seminar Series, no. 1, Center for East Asian and Pacific Studies, University of Illinois at Urbana-Champaign.

Hamilton, Gary C. and Biggart, Nicole Woolsey (1988), 'Market, Culture, and Authority', *American Journal of Sociology*, vol. 94, pp. 52-94.

Ho, Samuel P. S. (1987), 'Economics, Economic Bureaucracy, and Taiwan's Economic Development', *Pacific Affairs*, vol. 60, no. 2, pp. 226-47.

Hood, Steven J. (1996), 'Political Change in Taiwan: The Rise of Kuomintang Factions', *Asian Survey*, vol. XXXVI, no. 5, pp. 468-82.

Howe, Christopher (1996), 'The Taiwan Economy', *China Quarterly* 148, pp. 1171-95.

Hsieh, John Fuh-sheng, Lacy, Dean and Niou, Emerson M. S. (1996), 'Retrospective and Prospective Voting in a One-Party Democracy: Taiwan's 1996 Presidential Election', paper presented at the American Political Science Association Conference, San Francisco, CA.

Huebner, Jon W. (1987), 'The Abortive Liberation of Taiwan', *China Quarterly* 110, pp. 256-75.

Hu Fu and Yu Ying-long (1983), 'Orientations of Voting: An Analysis of Structure and Patterns', (in Chinese) *The Annals* 11, pp. 225-79.

Hwang Shiow-duan (1996), 'Interest Groups and Legislative Politics', paper presented at the International Conference on Political Development in Taiwan and Hong Kong, Center of Asian Studies, the University of Hong Kong.

Jacobs, Bruce (1978), 'Paradoxes in the Politics of Taiwan: Lessons for Comparative Politics', *Politics*, vol. 16, no. 2, pp. 237-47.

Kau, Michael Ying-mao (1996), 'The Power Structure in Taiwan's Political Economy', *Asian Survey*, vol. XXXVI, no. 3, pp. 287-305.

Koh, B. C. (1996), 'South Korea in 1995', *Asian Survey*, vol. XXXVI, no. 1, pp. 53-60.

Kuo Cheng-tian (1996), 'Democratization and Economic Development in Taiwan', paper presented at the American Political Science Association Conference, San Francisco, CA.

Lee, Peter Ching-yung (1996), 'Social Welfare of Hong Kong, Singapore, and Taiwan', *American Journal of Chinese Studies*, vol. 3, no. 2, pp. 225-33.

Leng Shao-chuan and Lin Cheng-yi (1993), 'Political Change on Taiwan: Transition to Democracy?' *China Quarterly* 136, pp. 805-39.

Leng Tse-kang (1994), 'State-Business Relations and Taiwan's Mainland Economic Policy', *American Journal of Chinese Studies*, vol. 2, no. 2, pp. 43-64.

_____ (1997), 'Economic Interdependence and Political Integration between Taiwan and Mainland China', paper presented at the American Political Science Conference, San Francisco, CA.

Lerman, Arthur (1978), 'National Elites and Local Politicians in Taiwan', *American Political Science Review* 71, pp. 1406-22.

Li Chien-pin (1994), 'Trade Negotiations Between the United States and Taiwan', *Asian Survey*, vol. XXXIV, no. 8, pp. 692-705.

Li, K. T. (1994), 'Taiwan's Economic Development: Experiences and Strategies', *Industry of Free China*, vol. LXXXI, no. 2, pp. 13-27.

Lim, Suk-jun (1996), 'Politics of Industrialization: Formation of Divergent Industrial Orders in Korea and Taiwan', paper presented at the American Political Science Association Conference, San Francisco, CA.

Lin Chong-pin (1996), 'The Military Balance in the Taiwan Sraits', *China Quarterly* 146, pp. 577-95.

Lin Tse-min, Chu Yun-han and Hinich, Melvin J. (1996), 'Conflict Displacement and Regime Transition in Taiwan: A Spatial Analysis', *World Politics* 48, pp. 453-81.

Ling Ts'ai and Myers, Ramon H. (1992), 'Surviving the Rough-and-Tumble of Presidential Politics in an Emerging Democracy: The 1990 Elections in the Republic of China on Taiwan', *China Quarterly* 129, pp. 123-48.

Lo, Ven-hwei, King Pu-tsung, Chen Ching-ho and Huang Hwei-lin (1996), 'Political Bias in the News Coverage of Taiwan's First Presidential Election', (in Chinese) *Journal of Electoral Studies*, vol. 2, no. 2, pp. 63-77.

Long, Simon (1992), 'Taiwan's National Assembly Elections', *China Quarterly* 129, pp. 216-28.

McBeath, Gerald A. (1977), 'Taiwan in 1976: Chiang in the Saddle', *Asian Survey*, vol. XVII, no. 1, pp. 18-26.

Mihalca, Matei (1996), 'From Practice to Theory', *TOPICS*, vol. 26, no. 10, pp. 12-21.

Ministry of Finance (1996, 1997), *Monthly Statistics of Exports and Imports, Taiwan Area, R.O.C.*, various issues, Taipei.

Myers, Ramon H. (1984), 'The Economic Transformation of the Republic of China on Taiwan', *China Quarterly* 99, pp. 500-28.

Nathan, Andrew J. (1993), 'The Legislative Yuan Elections in Taiwan: Consequences of the Electoral System', *Asian Survey*, vol. XXXIII, no. 4, pp. 424-38.

Pye, Lucien W. (1997), 'Money Politics and Transitions to Democracy in East Asia', *Asian Survey*, vol. XXXVII, no. 3, pp. 213-28.

Rigger, Shelly (1994), 'The Risk of Reform: Factional Conflict in Taiwan's 1989 Local Elections', *American Journal of Chinese Studies*, vol. II, no. 2, pp. 131-61.

Robinson, James A. and Baum, Julian (1995), 'Party Primaries in Taiwan: Reappraisal', *Asian Affairs*, vol. 22, no 2, pp. 91-96.

Ruhr, Christopher (1995), 'Privatization: The Sun Sets on an Era of Government Ownership', *TOPICS*, vol. 15, no. 4, pp. 12-25.

Ryan, Michael P. (1994), 'East Asian Political Economies and the GATT Regime', *Asian Survey*, vol. XXXIV, no. 6, pp. 556-71.

Schive Chi (1994), 'How Did Taiwan Solve its Dutch Disease Problem?' *Asian Economic Studies*, vol. 5, pp. 183-202.

_____ (1995), 'Industrial Policies in a Maturing Taiwan Economy', *Journal of Industry Studies*, vol. 2, no. 1, pp. 5-25.

_____ (1995), 'Experiences and Issues of Privatization in Taiwan', *Industry of Free China*, vol. LXXXV, no. 1, pp. 19-34.

_____ (1996), 'Taiwan's Economic Policy Reforms in the 1990s: A Supply-Side Approach', *Joint U.S.-Korea Academic Studies*, vol. 6, pp. 209-26.

Schmitter, Philippe (1979), 'Still the Century of Corporatism?' in Philippe Schmitter and Gerhard Lehmbruck (eds), *Trends Toward Corporatist Intermediation*, Sage, Beverly Hills, CA, pp. 83-131.

Shambaugh, David (1996), 'Taiwan's Security', *China Quarterly* 148, pp. 1284-1318.

Tan Qingshan, Yu, Peter Kien-hong and Chen Wen-chun (1996), 'Local Politics in Taiwan: Democratic Consolidation', *Asian Survey*, vol. XXXVI, no. 5, pp. 483-94.

Tang Shui-yang and Tang Ching-ping (1997), 'Democratization and Environmental Politics in Taiwan', *Asian Survey*, vol. XXXVII, no. 3, pp. 281-94.

Taro, Yayama (1990), 'The Recruit Scandal: Learning from the Causes of Corruption', *The Journal of Japanese Studies*, vol. 16, no. 1, pp. 93-114.

Tien Hung-mao and Chu Yun-han (1996), 'Building Democracy in Taiwan', *China Quarterly* 148, pp. 1141-70.

Underwood, Laurie (1997), 'Inside the Ruling Party's Moneymaking Machine—KMT, Inc.', *TOPICS*, vol. 27, no. 4, pp. 12-32.

Unger, Jonathan (1996), ' 'Bridges': Private Business, the Chinese Government and the Rise of New Associations', *China Quarterly* 147, pp. 795-819.

Wang Jenn-hwan and Lee Zong-rong (1993), 'The State and Financial Capital: The Transformation of Taiwan's Banking Policy', paper presented at the American Sociological Association Conference, Miami Beach, FL.

Wang, Vincent Wei-cheng (1995), 'Developing the Information Industry in Taiwan', *Pacific Affairs*, vol. 68, no. 4, pp. 551-76.

Wang Zhi and Tuan, Francis C. (1996), 'The Impact of China's and Taiwan's WTO Membership on World Trade—A Computable General Equilibrium Analysis', *American Journal of Chinese Studies*, vol. 3, no. 2, pp. 177-204.

Wilson, James Q. (1980), 'The Politics of Regulation', in James Q. Wilson (ed), *The Politics of Regulation*, Basic Books, New York, pp. 357-94.

Winckler, Edwin A. (1984), 'Institutionalization and Participation on Taiwan: From Hard to Soft Authoritarianism?' *China Quarterly* 99, pp. 481-99.

Wu Yu-shan (1989), 'Marketization of Politics: The Taiwan Experience', *Asian Survey*, vol. XXIX, no. 4, pp. 382-400.

_____ (1995), 'Taiwan in 1994: Managing a Critical Relationship', *Asian Survey*, vol. XXXV, no. 1, pp. 61-69.

Yahuda, Michael (1996), 'The International Standing of the Republic of China on Taiwan', *China Quarterly* 148, pp. 1319-39.

Index

References from Notes indicated by 'n' after page number